Irena Sendler

Mother of the Children of the Holocaust

Anna Mieszkowska

Translated by Witold Zbirohowski-Koscia
Foreword to the American Edition by Alex Storozynski

PRAEGER

AN IMPRINT OF ABC-CLIO, LLC
Santa Barbara, California • Denver, Colorado • Oxford, England

Copyright © 2011 Witold Zbirohowski-Koscia (for the translation)

Copyright © Muza 2004 (for the text) All rights reserved. Originally published in Polish as "Matka dzieci Holocaustu. Historia Ireny Sendlerowej."

Copyright © Janina Zgrzembska family archives (for the photographs)

All rights reserved. No part of this publication may be reproduced, stored in a retrieval system, or transmitted, in any form or by any means, electronic, mechanical, photocopying, recording, or otherwise, except for the inclusion of brief quotations in a review, without prior permission in writing from the publisher.

Library of Congress Cataloging-in-Publication Data

Mieszkowska, Anna.
   [Matka dzieci holocaustu. English]
   Irena Sendler: mother of the children of the Holocaust / Anna Mieszkowska; translated by Witold Zbirohowski-Koscia.
   p. cm.
   Includes bibliographical references and index.
   ISBN 978-0-313-38593-3 (hard copy: alk. paper) 1. Sendlerowa, Irena, 1910–2008. 2. Righteous Gentiles in the Holocaust—Poland—Biography. 3. World War, 1939-1945—Jews—Rescue—Poland. 4. Holocaust, Jewish (1939–1945)—Poland. I. Title.
   D804.66.S46M3813   2011
   940.53'18092—dc22[B]   2010034861

ISBN: 978-0-313-38593-3

15 14 13 12 11   1 2 3 4 5

This book is also available on the World Wide Web as an eBook.
Visit www.abc-clio.com for details.

Praeger
An Imprint of ABC-CLIO, LLC

ABC-CLIO, LLC
130 Cremona Drive, P.O. Box 1911
Santa Barbara, California 93116-1911

This book is printed on acid-free paper ∞

Manufactured in the United States of America

This book I dedicate to the memory of all my collaborators who helped me rescue children from the ghetto.

—Irena Sendler, alias "Jolanta"
April 2004

Contents

Foreword to the American Edition by Alex Storozynski	ix
Foreword to the Polish Edition by Michał Głowiński	xiii
Preface to the American Edition	xvii
Preface to the Original Edition	xix
1. What Happened in Uniontown	1
2. Roots—Childhood—The Family Home	13
3. Studies in Warsaw in the Years 1927–1939	21
4. September 1939	25
5. Occupation	27
6. I Remember Them	33
7. The Great Action	55
8. I Saw It	61
9. Why Żegota Was Formed	67
10. How Sister Jolanta Rescued Children from the Warsaw Ghetto	73
11. Where the Children Were Taken	79
12. The Ghetto Uprising	85
13. The Arrest	95

14. Jesus, I Trust in You. A Hundred Days in Pawiak Prison	97
15. April–August 1944	107
16. What Sister Jolanta Did during the 63 Days of the Warsaw Uprising	109
17. Warsaw Free!	115
18. Fulfilled Vocation. The Postwar Fates of Rescued Jewish Children	121
19. The Director—Postwar Professional and Social Work	137
20. Grateful Memories	143
21. Do We Remember? We Will Remember!	149
22. Why Memories Were Revived So Late	151
23. Postwar Family Life	157
24. As Remembered by a Witness	163
25. Voices of the Saved Children	165
26. Conclusion	185
27. Life after the Book	191
Select Bibliography	211
Acknowledgments	217
Index	219

Foreword to the American Edition

After Germany invaded Poland in 1939 to carry out Adolf Hitler's Final Solution, the Nazis initiated the death penalty for any Pole, and their entire family, that helped Jews. Gambling against these odds of life or death was Irena Sendler, a tiny Polish woman who stood less than five feet tall, but whose temerity towered over those around her. Sendler instilled bravery into a secret network of Poles, convincing them to risk the lives of their loved ones to rescue the children of their Jewish neighbors.

The Germans ordered a wall to be built around the Warsaw Ghetto and corralled 400,000 Jews inside. The overcrowded, starving masses awaited deportation to concentration camps. After an outbreak of typhus, the Germans wanted no physical contact with Jews, so Sendler persuaded the Nazis to allow her to enter the ghetto to improve sanitary conditions to stop the spread of disease. Her real mission was to sneak out Jewish children under the noses of their German tormentors. One slip up for Sendler meant that she and the children would be shot on the spot. Yet Sendler and her couriers shuttled in and out of the ghetto trying to convince Jewish mothers and fathers to give their children a chance to escape. They offered no guarantees that they would make it out alive.

The children did not want to leave their parents, and they were often dragged away kicking and screaming in terror. Some of them were squeezed into boxes, or stuffed into burlap sacks to be smuggled out of the ghetto, while a barking dog was brought along to drown out the cries of the whimpering children. Others were hidden on empty tramcars, or dragged through basements and sewers, or through the back door of a court building that straddled the ghetto walls.

Anna Mieszkowska has done a great service documenting this important chapter of Holocaust history. Mieszkowska allows Sendler to tell the story in her own words, and explain how a clandestine network of Poles was set up to handle the children that escaped. It took at least ten Poles for every Jewish child that was saved. Once in Christian hands, the children were fed, clothed and given a new home. They were taught to pray in Polish in case they were stopped and questioned by Germans. They were given Christian names and forged birth certificates provided by priests. Yet their true identities were preserved on slips of paper, so that they could be returned to their parents after the war.

The commitment that these rescuers took was monumental in light of the danger that they faced. Compare this to the world's reaction to today's human tragedies. Many of us donate to charities. But how many of us have been willing to house a homeless person from hurricane Katrina, a refugee from the Haitian earthquake, or the genocide in Darfur? And there is no death penalty for that.

Irena Sendler and her cohorts were not angels, but their actions were divine. By 1942, they learned that they were not alone and that the Polish underground, along with the Polish government in exile in London had established the Council to Aid Jews, code named Zegota. Sendler was put in charge of Zegota's children section. At one point, she was captured and German Gestapo goons crunched her legs into a vice and smashed her bones with hammers, trying to get her to reveal the names of the children and helpers. She did not break, and after three months, the Polish underground helped her to escape.

I had the honor of interviewing Sendler in 2007, the year before she died. There was a grass roots movement to nominate her for the Nobel Peace Prize, but she brushed off her heroism as if it were nothing, saying: "If someone is drowning, you have to give them your hand. When the war started, all of Poland was drowning in a sea of blood, and those who were drowning the most were the Jews. And among the Jews, the worst off were the children. So I had to give them my hand."

Sendler was 97 years old when I spoke with her, and she was outraged by Holocaust deniers such as Iranian President Mahmoud Ahmadinejad. "Ridiculous," she said. "He should educate himself. Either he is not intelligent or has another intention. He must be saying this on purpose because there is no way an intelligent person could not know this."

As historian Feliks Tych pointed out, Nazi Germany began "the first war in history consciously waged against children. The mass murder of children became one of Hitler's war objectives."

And so it is fitting that Anna Mieszkowska's book is titled, *Irena Sendler: Mother of the Children of the Holocaust*. While the Jewish children were taught Christian prayers, none of Sendler's saviors wanted to convert them. There were 2,500 children in all. At one point Sendler stuffed the lists of children into a jar and buried it in the garden of a home at 9 Lerkarska Street.

But the horrors of German occupation were worse than anyone had imagined. Most of the Jewish parents were murdered. Sendler's story was not well known after the war, partly because of her own modesty, but also because the Soviet Union occupied Poland and installed an atheist Communist dictatorship where such issues were buried like that jar full of names. Sendler was harassed by the Communist regime and many of her Zegota colleagues were imprisoned. For Poland, World War II did not end in 1945. It did not end until Soviet tanks left Polish soil in the early 1990s. It has only been in the last two decades that Poles have been able to take an uncensored look at their own history. As a result, there has been a lot of digging.

Ironically, it was four Protestant girls from a high school in rural Kansas who unearthed Sendler's story for a new generation of Polish Catholics and Jews. When they read that Sendler had saved twice as many people as the industrialist Oscar Schindler, they wrote a play about Sendler called *Life in a Jar* for a class project. The play became a big story and a collection was taken to send the girls to Poland to meet their hero.

Sendler told these girls that Poland was "the only country not to succumb to Nazi aggression and instead put up armed resistance . . . the only occupied country in Europe where for any, even the smallest form of help toward Jews you could be punished by death." Sendler also told the girls, "I urge you not to make a hero out of me; that would upset me greatly." Sendler's humility notwithstanding, it's too late for that because her fortitude can only be called heroic. That is clear in Mieszkowska's book where Sendler finally receives the recognition she deserves.

–Alex Storozynski
President & Executive Director
The Kosciuszko Foundation

Foreword to the Polish Edition

"In the season of great dying
IRENA SENDLER
committed her entire life
to the rescuing of Jews"

—Michał Głowiński, *The Black Seasons*

This is the first book about Irena Sendler. Although it is not an extended interview, it is largely a book of Irena Sendler's own authorship. Anna Mieszkowska allows her protagonist to speak, using her actual words; she records her statements and her opinions and expresses them the way Irena Sendler does. This biography of Irena Sendler is beautiful and heroic, edifying and deeply moving. It is a life story that for decades has been awaiting its Plutarch.

For years her achievements were known to relatively few, to those whose lives she had saved, to a group of friends and acquaintances, and also to a few historians researching the history of World War II, and the Holocaust in particular. Events ran their course as if people had not only failed to realize but did not even want to be aware of a person living among them with such an extraordinary and extremely important life story—a figure so monumental, one could say as in Juliusz Słowacki's famous poem, she is fit to be sculpted by Phidias. Yet, in everyday life she is modest, affectionate, and kind, with a hand always ready to be held out to those in need, a person who it is simply a pleasure to be with.

There were various reasons why such a great woman was marginalized. Not least it was due to the general and specific falsification of many aspects of Poland's most recent history by the communists. On their list of national heroes there was simply no room for this social worker. Even if she was of the left, she was far from the ideological utopia of communism. She was of a left that in Poland had actually had a beautiful tradition. A number of issues came into play here. Since the start of the postwar period, matters connected with Jews were regarded as tricky, uncertain, and dangerous—matters that were better passed over in silence rather than discussed. This phenomenon became even more distinct in the second half of the 1960s with an eruption of official anti-Semitism, which combined the themes of the 20th century's two worst totalitarian systems: Nazism and Stalinism. In a world where such ideologies were imposed on people's minds, there was no place for Irena Sendler. After all, there is a reason why she became a generally appreciated and admired public figure only after the political changes of 1989. It is a democratic Poland that pays tribute to her in the form of such honors as the Order of the White Eagle,[1] or the Jan Karski Award,[2] which bears the name of another great figure in Poland's 20th-century history. And Irena Sendler's greatness has also been recognized abroad, above all in the United States, but also in Sweden, Germany, and other countries. The phrase "Sendler's list" has entered the language and has a chance of rivalling the phrase "Schindler's list," which was popularized by Steven Spielberg's film. Moreover, it should be stressed that the list of names of Jews saved by this Polish social worker is considerably longer than the list of those saved by the German entrepreneur.

Anna Mieszkowska's book is an accurate and detailed description of Irena Sendler's life. It shows her actions and achievements, her daily work and life, and it reveals her extraordinary moral stature. Only someone with the finest human qualities would be able to carry out a feat as remarkable as saving the lives of 2,500 Jewish children at the time of the Holocaust, and, what is more, also contribute to saving the lives of a large number of adults. Such an extraordinary achievement in a situation where the helping of just as single Jew was punishable by death required heroism, indeed, quite exceptional heroism. It was not enough to want to do good, to have the conviction that help should be provided to those who so desperately needed it, because whoever actually undertook this task needed great, in fact quite unimaginable, courage. Such people put their lives on the line not once, not in one heroic action, but all the time. Surely there is no better example of self-sacrifice.

FOREWORD TO THE POLISH EDITION

Throughout the Nazi occupation, Irena Sendler devoted her life to saving Jews. Yet in order to achieve as much as she did, even courage and commitment were not enough. These wonderful virtues were combined with the extraordinary energy she needed so as to lead children out of the ghetto and find hiding places for them where they at least had a chance of survival. Irena Sendler, aware that it was a matter of life and death for children whose only fault was having "non-Aryan blood," was able to find within herself that extraordinary energy and inventiveness to save them. And on top of that she also revealed exceptional organizational talent. An operation of such magnitude could not be carried out alone. Anna Mieszkowska's book is also a tribute to Irena Sendler's co-workers, most of whom were wonderful, outstandingly courageous, and selfless women.

To conclude, Irena Sendler has recently become a public figure, the subject of popular magazine articles and radio programs, a public figure who is the subject of documentary films. Irena Sendler is now a symbol of heroism and self-sacrifice—and she has all the attributes to also become a symbol of good, friendly relations that will help unite Polish and Jewish communities.

Michał Głowiński

Preface to the American Edition

Irena Sendler told me that when she was gone, I should often look to the sky. There, sitting on a cloud, she would accompany me through life. I do not know where Irena is today. But I do know she was watching at the world premiere of the film *The Courageous Heart of Irena Sendler*.

On April 19, 2009, almost 10 million Americans saw this teleplay based on the true story of a young Polish woman with a courageous and noble heart.

In Atlanta, Georgia, the broadcast was interrupted some 20 minutes before the end to issue severe weather warnings. Hundreds of outraged viewers in Georgia contacted CBS, demanding that the end of the film be rebroadcast.

The reactions of these disappointed viewers proved effective. After a few days, the last half hour of the movie was rebroadcast—quite contrary to normal Hallmark Hall of Fame practice, which is to air their movies only once before they are released on DVD.

For me this was good news! I understood that on that premiere night Irena was on a cloud above Atlanta. She had left a sign that she was with us. She had kept her word!

I am immensely pleased that the extraordinary story of my heroine has been recounted to the world.

John Kent Harrison, who directed the TV film, said that he had first heard of Irena Sendler in 2005. He couldn't stop thinking about her and very much wanted to meet her personally. Unfortunately, he arrived too late. Irena was already in hospital. He attended her funeral, and it was a very moving experience for him. When I asked him why he became interested in Irena Sendler, he replied: "I am a hunter of histories. I search for good stories that provoke emotions. Learning the story of Irena Sendler and the children she saved cannot leave anyone feeling indifferent."

For him, working on this film was like a taking a history course, in which he learned of the complexity of relations between Poles and Jews as well as of the enormity of human suffering.

Before she was offered the leading role in this film, Anna Paquin had known nothing about the existence of this extraordinary woman. When she read the script, she could not wait to play the part—despite all her other work. We talked after the showing of the Polish premiere in Gdansk, on August 31, 2009. We were both very moved. Together with Irena's daughter, Janka, the three of us held hands, and we had tears in our eyes. For Janka and me, Anna *was* Irena.

I am happy that, thanks to the TV film and this new translation of the book, Americans, both young and old, will learn about a woman who had the courage to stand up against a totalitarian state and save for herself and for others the dignity of existence.

Irena Sendler has already been commemorated in a special resolution by the U.S. House of Representatives. At Seton Hall University in New Jersey, she was posthumously conferred the Humanitarian of the Year award by the Sister Rose Thering Endowment, She was also recently granted the Audrey Hepburn Humanitarian Award. Handing his mother's award to the Polish ambassador, Sean Hepburn cited the maxim Irena Sendler so often repeated: "For the world to be a better place one needs to spread goodness; it is the duty of all decent people."

Anna Mieszkowska
Warsaw, February 15, 2010
[A. M.: I have deliberately given this date as it is the hundredth anniversary Irena Sendler's birth.]

Preface to the Original Edition

What I knew of Irena Sendler's story was from television and press reports. When in 2001 four American girls from a school in Uniontown (Kansas) travelled to Warsaw to meet the heroine of their Holocaust school play, *Life in a Jar*, the media reminded listeners and viewers of then 91-year-old Irena Sendler and her extraordinary wartime achievements. She is the mother of 2,500 children—the mother of 2,500 children rescued from the Warsaw Ghetto. I do not say "adopted" mother because she was their real mother, one who bore them life a second time.

In April 2003, Lili Pohlmann[3] arrived in Warsaw from London for the 60th anniversary of the Warsaw Ghetto Uprising. She visited Mrs. Sendler at the Brothers Hospitallers of St. John of God Care Home in Sapieżyńska Street. Pohlmann was deeply moved by this meeting. She could not understand why no one had yet thought of honoring this outstanding yet modest individual—even though Irena herself refused to be called a "heroine" and instead referred to the children she had saved as the heroes of mothers' hearts. Lili told me: "You must meet Irena and write about her." So I went. I encountered a cheerfully smiling elderly lady, dressed in black, seated in a comfy chair and speaking beautiful Polish, the language of literature. Hanging on the walls of her rather small room were neatly framed diplomas and distinctions. Arranged on a table within her arm's reach were photographs of her mother, her parents when they were still engaged, her children, and her grandchildren. There too, in a fine-looking frame, was a photograph of the four American students. It was thanks to them that the story of this brave Pole was recalled, and five years of wartime terror were recounted in 10 minutes!

My first encounter with Irena Sendler lasted one and a quarter hours. It was then that she told me, among other things:

"My father died when I was seven, but I'll always remember him saying that people are divided into good and bad. Nationality, religion or race mean nothing: what kind of a person you are is all that counts. The other principle I was taught since childhood is to offer a helping hand to anyone in need. I am 93 years old," continued Mrs Sendler, "30 spent in sickness and 60 in merciful health. For over 15 years now I've been confined to a wheelchair. I do not like journalists because they frequently distort what I say. In many of my interviews and in articles about me, it is erroneously repeated that the children I took out of the ghetto suffered from typhus. This demonstrates a complete lack of understanding of the realities of life in the ghetto. People with typhus, regardless of whether it was an adult or child, had practically no chance of being saved. Such distortions of the truth frequently proliferate. That is why I now wish to set the facts straight. Normally, as a rule I do not talk about the ghetto with people who were never there; I never talk about Pawiak Prison with people who had not been inside and I never talk about the Warsaw Uprising with those who had not experienced it.

Describing my experiences is very tiring for me. It brings back bad memories and nightmares. I then dream that I'm asking for permission to take a child and the parents want a guarantee for their child's safety. Back then I could never give such guarantees. Such thoughts are bad for my heart. I have not had an easy life. I have had to go through a lot, experienced so many personal tragedies . . . I have a daughter, daughter-in-law, a granddaughter, and many, many friends . . . I am visited by those I saved and by their children, and even grandchildren."

Irena Sendler agreed to coauthor this book about her extraordinary life. She granted access to all her documents—everything that was written about her as well as what she herself had put into writing over the years, not always with the intention of publishing but rather to leave her testimony to future generations. "Today younger generations do not realize that during the occupation even the closest relatives had no idea what other members of their family were doing," she tells almost all her guests.

"Much has been written about the war, the occupation and the Holocaust," she wrote for the Children of the Holocaust convention, "yet nowhere have I read a description of the great suffering endured by mothers being separated from their children, and the distress of children being handed over to strangers. Mothers, anticipating the imminence of their own death and the death of their entire family, hoped to at least save the child. And for a mother how can there be a greater tragedy than separation from her own child?! Those unfortunate women had to overcome their own feelings and the opposition of others in the family, for instance, the grandparents. Grandmothers, who remembered Germans from World War I and could not imagine them to be murderers, protested against their grandchild being handed over, but the mother's knew . . ."[4]

"One of the reasons I have decided to share my memories," she wrote back in 1981, "is my desire to explain to the younger generation of Jews now living all over the world that they are wrong to believe that Polish Jews, who were made to suffer in such an inhuman way, were passive, that they went to their deaths without putting up a fight, submissively. That's not true! You are wrong, my young friends. If you saw the youths living and working in those times, every day dicing with death, which was quite literally lurking round the corner and in every street—their dignified bearing, the self-denial and their everyday feats, the struggle for every piece of bread, to get hold of medicines for someone close who was dying, provide spiritual comfort through a good deed or just to read a book, then you would change your mind!

You would see wonderful girls and wonderful boys, bearing the torment, the terrible drama of every day in the Warsaw ghetto. It is not true that the ghetto martyrs died without putting up a fight! Their fight was every day, every hour, every minute, surviving in that hell year after year.

When they finally realized that there was no more hope for them, they heroically took up arms. That entire period of struggle, first nonmilitary, then military, was a series of collective acts of biological self-defense, and next they became acts of desperation and acts of honor. One has to remember and constantly repeat that of all the underground activities in Nazi-occupied Poland, helping Jews was among the most difficult and dangerous. From the autumn of 1939, every act of sympathy toward the persecuted [Jews] was punishable by death. That was the punishment not only for sheltering people of Jewish origin, not only for providing someone like that with 'Aryan' documents, but even for selling them something or giving anything out of pity, or showing them a safe way out."[5]

"For handing a Jew a glass of water or a piece of bread you could be killed," said Mrs. Sendler during our first talk. I then understood what Ruta Sakowska had in mind when she wrote that "everyone who knows Irena Sendler is enchanted by her extraordinary personality—intellect combined with fortitude, strength of character with a compassion for the sufferings of others and an unparalleled readiness for self-sacrifice."

When in the 1960s Irena Sendler's family was experiencing financial hardship, her daughter, Janina Zgrzembska, once asked: "Mummy, what did you do that we are suffering now?"

Twenty years later, when a foreign television crew came, her surprised granddaughter asked: "Grandma, what did you do that now you are going to be famous?"

Her daughter recalls how in 1988 she travelled to Israel and touched her mother's tree in the Avenue of the Righteous.[6] "For years mother told me nothing about her activities, but there I saw the surname Sendler and all doors opened before me. Only then did I understand what she had done."

Norman Conard, the history teacher in Uniontown, could not believe what his students had read in an American newspaper about an unknown Polish lady: "It must be a mistake, you'll have to check it. Oskar Schindler, immortalized in Spielberg's film, saved over 1,100 people.

How could this woman help save twice as many people, and children at that?"

This book is an attempt to answer this question, and to answer other questions that should also be asked. Who was Irena Sendler earlier, before in the tragic days, months, years of World War II, when she became sister Jolanta?

What had happened in her childhood and early youth to make her at the still young age of 30 so prepared for what was to follow? Was she not afraid? Were it not for the fact that everything she has written and talked about actually happened, her life could be taken for a brilliantly concocted movie plot. Her real-life experiences could be viewed as a gripping adventure in which she is pitted against an evil-minded and cruel foreign invader and some heartless compatriots. Because it indeed needs to be stressed: Irena Sendler's stance during the occupation was not only a symbol of willingness to fight, courage, fortitude, and compassion, it was also a symbol of how very much in making her decision she was alone.

How telling are her postwar fortunes? What did she do for over 50 years in her active professional life? Why does the past continually come back to her and refuses to be forgotten?

In July 2003, it was decided in Washington, D.C., that she should receive the Jan Karski Award.[7] The award ceremony took place at Georgetown University in Washington, D.C., on October 23, 2003. Among those present was Elżbieta Ficowska, the youngest of the children saved by Sendler and chairperson of the Association of "Children of the Holocaust" in Poland.[8] She accepted the award on Irena Sendler's behalf and was accompanied by the Polish president's wife, Jolanta Kwaśniewska.

**

This book could never have been written without Irena Sendler's active help, because there are facts and events historians and archivists are unable to uncover even after many years of research. Such facts and events can only be retrieved from the memories of witnesses.

I made use of Mrs. Sendler's rich archive as well as her personal knowledge and experience. The chapter "Voices of the Saved Children" was her suggestion. It was on her request that her life, so full of eventful and often difficult experiences, should start with the adventure involving the American students, for they were the ones who brought back faith in the meaning of her long and arduous life, and provided her with the strength to continue. They were the ones who made her name and wartime achievements known throughout the world.

Irena Sendler in the spring of 2003. (Courtesy of the Janina Zgrzembska family archives)

I regard it as my responsibility to let this book's protagonist, a modest person, with great humility remembering the past and everyone who during the occupation helped her to save the lives of Jews, speak using her own words. Thus the numerous, extensive quotations from her articles as well as the interviews she gave to national and foreign journalists. Some have been updated and corrected many years after they were originally made.

In saving the lives of Jewish children during World War II, Irena Sendler won her own personal struggle against evil, against the heartless cruelty of the outside world. She became a symbol of goodness, love, and tolerance.

Notes

1. November 10, 2003.
2. October 23, 2003.
3. Lili Pohlmann is a distinguished promoter of Polish culture in Britain.
4. An unpublished statement made by Irena Sendler in 2003.
5. Irena Sendlerowa, "O działalności kół młodzieży przy komitetach domowych w getcie warszawskim.," *Biuletyn Żydowskiego Instytutu Historycznego*, 1981, nr 2 (118), p. 98.
6. Irena Sendler was awarded the Yad Vashem Righteous Medal in 1965, but her tree was not planted until 1983. The phrase *Yad Vashem* (in Hebrew meaning "memorial and name") is symbolic. It originates from the Book of Isaiah (56: 5). It is the Lord's promise to people who are foreign but hold fast the covenant: "*To them I will give in my house and within my walls a memorial and a name better than that of sons and daughters; I will give them an everlasting name which shall not be cut off.*" From M. Grynberg, *Księga Sprawiedliwych*, Warszawa, 1993, p.11.
7. The Jan Karski Award has been conferred since 2001 by the American Center of Polish Culture and the Jan Karski Foundation chapter.
8. The Association of "Children of the Holocaust" (SDH) in Poland was founded in 1991. It is an association of those who as Jewish children had been saved from the Holocaust. At first there were just 45 members, but today it has approximately 800 members, with regional branches in Krakow, Wrocław, and Gdansk. This association is a member of the Federation of Jewish Communities in Poland and the World Federation of Jewish Child Survivors of the Holocaust. Its mission is to build a community of Holocaust survivors for the purposes of: mutual support, preserving the memory of Holocaust experiences, preserving memories of life in the Jewish community before the war, and helping members overcome the sense of loneliness and isolation. The association's first chairperson (for two terms in office) was Professor Jakub Gutembaum, who was succeeded by Zofia Zaks, while Elżbieta Ficowska is the current chairperson for her second term in office.

1

What Happened in Uniontown

In September 1999, four students who would later be called the "Sendler quartet"—Megan Stewart (14), Elizabeth Chambers (14), Sabrina Coons (16), and Gabrielle Bradbury (13)[1]—from a school in Uniontown, 93 miles from Kansas City and with just 300 inhabitants—thought up a project for a school competition. They were inspired by a 1994 article in *U.S. News & World Report*, which was published after the premiere of Steven Spielberg's famous film *Schindler's List* and was about people who during the war had rescued the lives of Jews but never acquired Oskar Schindler's fame.[2] Among the many people mentioned was the name of a Polish woman, Irena Sendler, and information about how she had saved 2,500 children. The girls' teacher, Norman Conard, was skeptical: "Haven't they added a zero too many?" He told his students to find evidence to corroborate this sensational press report. They devoted all their free time for over half a year. They read books about World War II and the Holocaust. One of the first questions they asked their teacher was: "What was the ghetto?" "Keep searching," he told them. They telephoned American World War II veterans. They scoured microfilms. They watched specially purchased film documentaries. Many people, total strangers inspired by their passion, helped them.

During a history lesson in February 2000, they appeared for the first time in their play: *Holocaust. Life in a Jar*. Elizabeth, who played "Sister Jolanta," later told a Polish journalist: "Other students had plenty of comments. They said I had to show more emotion. They didn't feel like I really wanted to save those children."[3] At the time, the girls did not know that Irena Sendler was still alive in Warsaw. They received her address from the Jewish Foundation for the Righteous in New York. On February 10, 2000, they wrote, apprehensively, their first letter: "Your experiences are a great inspiration to our group. And a motivation to work. We admire your courage. You are one of the greatest heroines of the last century. Are you in touch with the children you saved? We would like to contact them." The reply came a few weeks later.

On March 24, the 91-year-old Irena Sendler wrote:

"My dear, beloved girls, so close my heart! I was deeply moved to read your letter. I am above all interested to know what made you take up this subject. I am curious whether you are exceptions or whether many young people in your country are interested in the Holocaust. I believe your work to be outstanding and worthy of propagation. Although in the history of the world there were cases of Jews being persecuted, up until then there had never been a state that aimed to liquidate the entire nation. I have spoken to several people who survived the Holocaust because they were saved by Żegota. Very few of them still live in Poland. Most have moved to other parts of the world. Generally, they do not like to talk about those terrible times, they do not want to think about it, they want to forget. . . . For over 10 years now I have been unwell. I can hardly walk. Many of my diseases result from my experiences during the occupation and in a Gestapo prison. I am a war invalid."

Many important letters followed, and the correspondence lasts to this day.

On April 6, the girls sent their second letter, with questions regarding Irena Sendler's actions to save Jewish children. They also sent a copy of their play. After she had read the Polish translation, Irena Sendler wrote a long letter with explanations and corrections, putting straight certain facts that the American students could not have known. She was nevertheless amazed by their intuition. She wrote: "Your sensitive hearts subconsciously anticipated that what is continually said about the Holocaust is not entirely satisfactory. You decided to look for something more, to search for the truth about those cruel times. . . . The title, *Life in a Jar*, is very close to the truth. Lists of children rescued by Żegota had to be made so that after the war they could be returned to their kinfolk. The lists were also necessary for the sake of those who need constant financial support. . . . Your wisdom and intuition correctly suggested what it was like when the children were handed over to me by distraught parents and grandparents. Although so many years have passed since those tragic events, there are nights when in my troubled dreams I still hear the weeping, the cries of despair, the terrifying sobs. The fact that you ask about my illegal release from prison, thanks to a bribe given to a Gestapo officer, shows that in preparing to write your letter to me you have reached for the correct information."

Despite the need to attend school, the girls travelled increasingly further from home to perform their play. The audiences were moved—the young, but even more so the old. They played in parishes of various denominations, schools, old people's homes, culture and community centers, as well as many other places they were invited to. And the number of invitations just grew. Everyone was stirred by a play about the five-year, wartime nightmare presented in only 10 minutes! The stage scenery was simple, an iron gate with the sign "Warsaw Ghetto," and the actors portraying this tragedy were basically children. Perhaps that is why audiences found it so poignant? Because the fact that the play is heartrending is known by all those who have seen it. Jews were particularly moved,[4] but there were also others who felt touched. After seeing the play, John Shuchart, a history teacher, invited the cast to a restaurant. They told him how their work on the project had changed their lives. They felt it themselves, and those closest to them, family and friends, knew it. "Do you have any dreams?" he asked. "We'd like to meet Irena Sendler," replied Megan. "You will," he promised. It was thanks to John Shuchart that the dream was fulfilled. His Jewish friends provided the necessary financial support so that he could send the girls a large cheque to cover the costs of their trip to Poland.

This was a major success, but it was preceded by a failure. They had won the interschool history contest in Kansas and had qualified for the finals in Washington, D.C. However, they did not get to the final stage where three groups out of the several hundred that had qualified competed with one another. A disappointed Megan complained that it was all the fault of an interfering journalist who kept "poking a microphone under the noses of jury members and asking what they thought of us. That must have annoyed them, I reckon."

In another letter, Irena Sendler wrote: "I am pleased that you decided to search for the truth. That is how you found that tiny, faint trail which led you to me."

In July 2003, Irena Sendler told me with joy about her American adventure: "I basically don't like interviews and meetings with journalists because in the past all too often, even though I had taken the trouble to prepare for them the relevant materials and precise information, they went and changed it and wrote whatever they wanted; they alter facts. In the winter of 2000, in February, I think, an American journalist telephoned and asked me for an interview. Having had those unfortunate past experiences with journalists, I refused. A few hours later the secretary of one of the professors at the Medical Academy informed me over the telephone that her boss had been in America a couple of weeks earlier and had heard from a colleague who works in one of the hospitals over there an interesting story. In a village school, four girls, aged 13–14, had written a play about me and how during the German occupation I had helped to rescue Jewish children from the Warsaw ghetto. They very much wanted to write to me, but they didn't know my address. This got me interested, so I agreed to give them my address. Shortly afterward I received their first poignant letter and the play in which I was the protagonist. In a subsequent letter I learned that someone who had been deeply moved by their play had offered them help ($6,500) to travel to Poland. When they asked John Shuchart what he would like from their Polish trip, he said: 'Give Irena Sendler a big kiss and visit Auschwitz (that's where my entire family died).'"

Even today Irena Sendler admits that she greatly feared the meeting, both the emotions and the responsibility. "I have had an ill-fated, sad life. For 15 years now I have been confined to a wheelchair, and suddenly this important meeting for which one has somehow to prepare. I had to plan a program for their visit. I wanted the girls to see in Warsaw the places I had described in my letters. I devised a plan so that they would be able to see the garden at No. 9 Lekarska Street, where I had buried the jar with the lists of children saved from the ghetto, Pawiak Prison, the plaque and house where the Żegota organization had had its headquarters (24 Żurawia Street), the Gestapo headquarters in Aleja Szucha (Szucha Avenue) and the so-called 'trams' where newly arrested Poles were made to sit, the Young Insurgent monument in the Old Town, Umschlagplatz and the Heroes of the Warsaw Ghetto Monument as well as the tablet commemorating Żegota. I also wanted them to go and listen to a Chopin concert in Żelazowa Wola. The whole program was agreed with my friend Zofia Wierzbicka,[5] and I asked her to oversee their stay, to select a different person to accompany them each day. The girls saw all of this. They visited Auschwitz, which shocked them greatly. They only failed to go to Żelazowa Wola, because there wasn't enough time. I also arranged for them meetings with two of the children I had saved: Elżbieta Ficowska and Professor Michał Głowiński.

"The girls arrived on May 23, 2001, together with their history and form teacher, Norman Conard, his wife, Karen, Elizabeth's grandparents, Megan's mother and another of the girls' schoolteachers, Ms. Bonnie. The trip began when they met the 'children' of the Holocaust and showed them their play. The entire house was in tears . . .

Sabrina Coons, Janis Underwood, Megan Stewart and Elizabeth Cambers at the Żegota tablet. (Photo by Michał Dudziewicz)

"The next day I met them in Zofia Wierzbicka's house. It is difficult to describe in words. I was taken aback and deeply moved by the fact that someone had written a play about me, about what I did, something I regard to be quite normal for those times. And so far away from Poland! I was interested, fascinated by the fact that in America, in the state of Kansas, in tiny Uniontown there were 13-, 14-year-old girls who took up such a difficult subject, one that was not popular in that country. For a long while none of us could say anything. After all, a legend had become reality. I greeted them with the following words:

"'I welcome you with all my heartfelt warmth and sincerity. You come to Poland, the only country not to succumb to Nazi aggression and instead put up armed resistance. You come to Poland, the only occupied country in Europe where for any, even the smallest form of help toward Jews you could be punished by death. You come to Warsaw, which after 63 days [of the Warsaw Uprising], drowning in a sea of blood and fire, unfortunately, surrendered!'

"Despite a year's correspondence, it was only when the girls and I personally met that within ourselves we all experienced a deep spiritual and psychological change," Irena Sendler later recalled. "Not only they, but also Elizabeth's grandparents, Megan's mother and their teacher Norman Conard many times stressed that I had altered their lives, both individually and as a group." "Irena's story gave them strength," said Megan's mother in an interview. "They matured faster in the last year," confirmed Norman Conard. "I did all I could to make them feel well in Poland. All my friends who accompanied the girls during their stay became very fond of them," added Irena Sendler. In the letters they wrote after their return from the trip to Poland, the girls did not hide the emotional impact it had had on them and emphasized how wonderfully well organized it was.[6]

"When we parted in 2001, we had no certainty that we would ever meet again," recalls Mrs. Sendler. "Yet their passion together with enormous determination meant that a year later, in July 2002, they returned. By then I was at the Brothers Hospitallers of St. John of God Care Home, where the prior not only gave us the most beautiful room to greet the guests, but was also present there throughout and at the end gave each of them gifts. This time, apart from the four girls and their teacher, there were two new girls who had joined the group, as was John Shuchart, who had funded both trips. Above all they wanted to meet my wartime co-workers or people who in some other way had been associated with me during the war. But this was summer, the time of vacations, and so they managed to meet only one of my colleagues, Anna Marzec, who during the war had worked in Social Welfare Center IV. There was also a meeting with Professor Tomasz Szarota, a distinguished scholar of Poland's most recent history. They were astonished when, referring to archive documents, he told them that, on account of her underground activities to save Jews, Irena Sendler's name was featured among others on 'a blacklist drawn up on April 28, 1944, most probably by Department IV (concerning Jews and Communists) of National Armed Forces intelligence."[7]

They also visited Elżbieta Ficowska's family, whom they had already met during their first visit. Moreover, Elżbieta Ficowska, together with her daughter, had been in the United States in March 2002 for the institution of Irena Sendler Day in the states of Kansas and Missouri.

"This second meeting moved me deeply. We maintain a regular correspondence.[8] The girls write about their lives, their plans for the future. Today they are 17 or 18, they have changed schools and entered new circles. Their teacher, Norman Conard, says the play has a new cast.

My girls inspired younger classmates," says Mrs. Sendler, ending her account. "Kathleen Meara is 17 and has taken over Liz's role to play me," she stresses, with pride showing me Kathleen's first letter to her. The girl also informs her of a new, expanded script.

A very warm letter, including his photograph and own poem, was also sent by Nicholas Thomas, a 12 year old who also joined the cast:

Remember the Children

Remember the children
thrown out of school.
Remember the children
killed, not cool.
Remember the children
trapped in barbed wire.
Remember the children
lost from desire.
Remember the children
lost and all gone.
Remember the children
in that Holocaust.[9]

***

Extract from a letter Irena Sendler wrote to the girls on September 14, 2000:

We, my couriers and I, got the children out of the ghetto in four ways.

The first method. A lorry would go to the ghetto with various sanitary items. The driver was Antoni Dąbrowski, who also worked with me in the resistance. Inside the ghetto, at a prearranged spot he would collect a child accompanied by me or one of my couriers. The child had to be very well hidden in a large box among the detergents or, if it was unlucky, in a sack. Such an unfortunate child, frequently taken from its parents by force, would scream out of sheer terror. No one has ever described in words what at such moments went through such a tiny, frightened individual's mind. We had to get that child past the gate, which was always guarded by the Germans, and it would just take an instant for the guards to hear the child. Once Mr. Dąbrowski said to me: "Jolanta, I can no longer run this dangerous operation with you because one day the guards will hear the cries and the Germans will shoot the lot of us." I urged him to think something up and not desist from further cooperation. After a few days, looking very pleased with himself, he declared: "I've come up with a good idea. I'll take a bad dog into the driver's cabin. When we approach the gate, I'll tread on the dog's paw so that its yelping drowns out the child's cries."

The second method was to take the children to the ghetto tram depot. The husband of one of my couriers was a tram driver.[10] On the days he was on duty we would bring a child. He would put the infant into the empty tram car and drive it to an agreed stop on the so-called Aryan side. There I or one of my couriers would be waiting to receive it. The child always had to be taken to one of four (later 10) nursing points, which were organized at the homes of the most upstanding and courageous of our co-workers. At such a place the child was surrounded with the most tender of care to at least in a small way soothe the tragedy of being separated from its family.

The third method: Some of the houses in the ghetto were next to the basements of houses inhabited by Poles. [Once the children got through,] the rest of the procedure was the same.

The fourth method: The law court in Leszno Street was within the ghetto. Some of the entrances in the building were open. You could also get into the building from "the Aryan side." (It is with great pain that I use these words.) Through our underground organization, we were able to contact two of the courtroom ushers. When given an agreed signal, these decent and exceptionally courageous men would open the door for us on the ghetto side. You would then enter the building with a child, and next the child, accompanied by one of the ushers, would leave the building on the Polish side.

All these "ways of getting out" concerned small children (there were also a few babies). Older children, 12 to 13 year olds, as well as youths from 14 to 18, got out by completely different means.

On the basis of an agreement reached with the Jewish police (a terrifying majority of whom treated their compatriots in an appalling fashion),[11] the Germans organized special work brigades from among Jewish skilled workers and youths. Every day these brigades left the ghetto, under tight security, to go to various work sites, from which they returned very tired after 10–12 hours of toil. Every day the Jewish community nominated a leader who was responsible not only for the members' work but also for their return. The group members were counted on the way out and the same number of people had to return. We managed to find a Jewish community worker who wanted to leave the ghetto. So we got several of the boys and girls under our care to join the brigade. The whole group were to gather at a collecting point in Grójecka Street on the Aryan side.

One of us would report to this point, collect those under our charge and take them to the home of a Żegota organization member. After two or three days, members of the People's Army would take these youths to join the partisans.

I urge you not to make a hero out of me; that would upset me greatly.

***

Norman Conard's letter to Irena Sendler:

July 26, 2002

Dear Irena,

You are such a marvellous woman. We send our love from America. You have so much warmth, and your inspiring words still resound in our ears. The girls and John [Shuchart] continually talk about the wonderful trip to Poland and the friends, of whom over there we now have so many. But the most important thing for us was the time spent with you. You are the light in the darkness, the warm voice the world needs. We shall continue to show *Life in a Jar* and say what the world could be like if people cared for one another.

We send you our love and thank you for your goodness. Together with Karen, my wife, you remain in our prayers and hearts.

***

Irena Sendler's letter to Norman Conard:

Dear Professor Norman Conard!

All your letters are such a joy to me. I would be delighted to receive the names and character descriptions of the new cast members now performing the play written by my dear girls.

I am still so impressed by your tireless energy and dedication with which every day you realize your ideals, those that produced the play *Life in a Jar*. Your constant and extensive efforts to make those values more profound and widespread, among hundreds and thousands of people, is to your credit. Dear Professor, your efforts to improve the world, to extinguish the causes of hatred and war so that goodness may finally prevail, are a reason for deep satisfaction.

***

At the end of March 2003 the first *Life in a Jar* cast gave their hundredth and last performance.

***

On March 7, 2003 Irena Sendler wrote to the girls:

> It is not true that the period of your unique work to spread love, goodness, all that is most valuable in life and the broad concept of tolerance is now drawing to a close. Neither is this the end of our relationship, our mutual and strongest feelings of love. Despite your very young age, with such high values and natural acting ability, you have carried out great work for the world, your country, for Poland and also for me.
>
> I strongly believe that you will always pursue the same path to finally extinguish the flashpoints of war and evil and let goodness prevail!
>
> Remember that my thoughts will always be with you.

***

In June 2003, the hundred and first performance of *Life in a Jar* (and for the very first with a new cast) was played in New York. It would happen that people who had seen this play travelled to Poland. They would then try to find Irena Sendler. They would say how thanks to the play Irena Sendler has become the subject of numerous press articles as well as television and radio programs in the United States—and not only there. The details of her story can now be found on the Internet. On the initiative of Norman Conard, the Irena Sendler Project (www.irenasendler.com) was created, which now has a great influence on many people, especially America's young people. Those who have seen them perform say that the girls' acting is evocative and moving.

And what about the play itself? It is astonishing for its simplicity and brevity, and yet it contains such a deep moral truth.

***

When in May 2003, together with Mrs. Sendler we started working on the book, she handed me the *Life in a Jar* play script and said:

"Please don't be put off, just read it carefully. This is written by children. There are some mistakes, but they wrote it without my help, exclusively on what information they themselves had managed to gather. No one other than I could have corrected them."

"What mistakes?" I asked.

"For a start, I could not officially take children out of the ghetto—all the more so if they were suffering from typhus! The Germans would have shot them at once. Yet the idea that I saved children on the pretext that they were suffering from a serious disease is repeated several times. Secondly, the German guard could not have forbidden me to go to the ghetto after my escape, because by then the ghetto no longer existed! Thirdly, although I was in hiding, I looked after my mother to the end. She died in my arms. And another thing, none of my couriers knew that I was working for Żegota. But my dear girls had no way of knowing this when they wrote the script to their play. I explained all this in our correspondence and when we met. And as far as I know, they now play a new, corrected version."

"The short play they wrote is of great credit to them," Mrs. Sendler adds with pride. "Despite their very young age, they were able to show their country two issues: the tragedy of the Jewish nation during World War II and—what is particularly important to me—that there are ways of avoiding such cruelties by spreading love and tolerance to all people, regardless of race, nationality, background, or religion. The tragic truth about the Holocaust expressed by these American girls is not directed against the German nation. It is only a need to express caution, so that such heinous crimes are never repeated in the world again. Their great efforts to realize this goal has borne beautiful fruit. After every performance of the play, the number of people moved by their ideals increases. They inspire those closest to them, but also much wider circles of people. By changing themselves they change the world. They bring goodness! They show that for the world to be a better place it is essential to love all people and be tolerant. Our acquaintance and friendship has changed us all. As they themselves say, they and their families have changed for the better, and I, after hard personal experiences and despite much sickness, have now a new lease of life."

Notes

1. Shortly afterward Gabrielle left the group. In the play she was replaced by Janice Underwood.
2. 'The Other Schindlers.', *U.S. News & World Report,* 21st March 1994.
3. Marcin Fabjański, "'Życie w słoiku' trwa dziesięć minut." *Gazeta Wyborcza–Świąteczna,* nr 116, May 19-20, 2001.

4. Rabbi Joshua Taub told a Polish journalist: "Those girls had the courage to come to a Jewish house of prayer and tell Jews about a part of their history. If I had tried to tell it, no one would have been moved. They would have said: a rabbi is yet again telling us about the Holocaust because he has to. But they showed that part of our history is not only important to Jews." Marcin Fabjański , "'Życie w słoiku' trwa dziesięć minut." *Gazeta Wyborcza–Świąteczna*, nr 116, May 19-20, 2001.

5. Zofia Wierzbicka (1916–2001), a pedagogue.

6. During their visit the girls also met the then U.S. ambassador in Poland, Christopher Hill.

7. Tomasz Szarota. "Cisi bohaterowie." *Tygodnik Powszechny*, nr 51–52, December 22-29, 2002. More on this subject in an article by the same author entitled, "Listy nienawiści." *Polityka*, nr 44, November 1, 2003, and in Elżbieta Ficowska's rectification, "Nagroda dla Ireny Sendlerowej." *Polityka*, nr 47, November 22, 2003.

8. In February 2004, Mrs. Sendler received from Kansas the joyful news that the girls and their teacher would visit Poland for a third time.

9. "Pamiętaj o dzieciach wyrzuconych ze szkół./Pamiętaj o dzieciach zamordowanych, to nie była zabawa./Pamiętaj o dzieciach osadzonych za kolczastym drutem./Pamiętaj o dzieciach bez marzeń./Pamiętaj o dzieciach straconychna zawsze./Pamiętaj o dzieciach Holocaustu."

10. The tram driver, Leon Szeszko, was executed by shooting on November 13, 1943.

11. This fact is confirmed in many memoirs from the war. Antoni Marianowicz writes in his book entitled *Życie surowo wzbronione* (Warszawa, 1995, p. 67): "An entire elite of young lawyers joined the Jewish ghetto police. The students of Berenson, Brokman, Neufeld, Schönbach—people of high moral principles. At first this was justified; after all law and order had to somehow be maintained within the ghetto. A concentration of many thousands of people could not survive without law enforcement and some form of internal organization. The people who were in the police force could not foresee that imminently its role would change—that soon they would be used to send out the transports as the chief helpers of the Germans in the liquidation of the ghetto, that their role would be extremely shameful."

2

Roots–Childhood–The Family Home

Irena Sendler believes she owes a great deal to traditions taken from the family home. She was born in Warsaw on February 15, 1910. For participating in the January Uprising of 1863, her great grandfather (from her mother's side), Karol Grzybowski, was sent to Siberia, where, after a year (spent manacled to barrows together with some Georgian prince), he died. His small estate near Kalisz had served as the headquarters for Polish insurgents in that area.

"His wife, that is my great grandmother," recalled Mrs. Sendler, "and her son Ksawery (then aged three) had to find shelter with local peasants because the tsarist police were still looking for them. After several months of hiding, they moved to Warsaw. To support herself and her son, my great grandmother embroidered and knitted sweaters."[1]

Irena's grandfather, Ksawery Grzybowski, graduated from a horticulture and farming college, and throughout his adult life managed large landed estates. He never regained the confiscated estate of his parents. Ksawery married young, at the age of 19, to a widow who already had three sons. Together they had a further three children, two more sons and a daughter, my mother. Toward the end of the 19th century, he administered the estate of Drozdy near Tarczyn, where, after his retirement, he built himself a small house. During World War I, he was forced to move to a place near Uman in Ukraine, where his son was the director of a sugar refinery.

Irena's father, Stanisław Krzyżanowski,[2] was a physician. He was also socially active and very much engaged in the independence movement, helping those who were persecuted for participating in the 1905 Revolution (during the school strikes, he defended the rights of Polish students) and for belonging to the Polish Socialist Party. On account of his patriotism and political activities, he had problems completing his studies in medicine at the Imperial University of Warsaw. He moved to Krakow, but there too he was sent down. He finally completed his studies in the small town of Kharkiv, Ukraine, in 1908.

Whilst staying with his parents in Tarczyn, he became acquainted with Ksawery Grzybowski's daughter. The young doctor married Janina Grzybowska in the Ukrainian town of Pohrebyshche near Kiev in 1908.

"For that was where one of my mother's brothers, Mieczysław, a chemical engineer, was the director of a sugar refinery," recounted Mrs. Sendler. "Another of her brothers, Edmund, was also a chemical engineer and the director of a sugar refinery in nearby Ryżawka. Mother's youngest brother, Ksawery, still went to school. So the objective was for the whole family to be able to attend the event."

The following year, in 1909, the young couple returned to Poland. Stanisław Krzyżanowski worked as a doctor and the assistant of Professor Alfred Sokołowski[3] at the Holy Spirit Hospital in Warsaw. One day, two-year-old Irena contracted whooping cough. She was choking so much that there were fears for her life. And this was their only beloved child.

Dr. Erbrich, who was a friend of the family, said that a change in the climate would help cure the child. They decided that it was essential for them to move out of Warsaw. Two days later they were already settled in a new place, a small spa town near Warsaw called Otwock. They moved into the house of Dr. Władysław Wroński, who had died several months earlier and so all the rooms were vacant. Little Irena recuperated quickly, but her parents now had financial problems. In those days there was no social insurance or even any health insurance funds. In those days physicians could only earn money as so-called free practitioners, and in Otwock there were already four physicians. At first, as a new and unknown doctor, Irena's father had very few patients and was rarely called out to treat the sick at home. Virtually his only patients were the poor inhabitants of nearby rural areas who could not really afford to pay for treatment. He actually felt obliged to leave them some money to purchase the necessary medicines.

That period of her family life was recalled by Irena Sendler many years later as follows:

"In the first winter, Mother had to sell her winter clothes to buy food. Father could not do this because he needed to keep warm when travelling in a horse cart to tend to the sick. Mother only left the house in the

Irena Sendler's family. From the left: Kazimiera Krzyżanowska (aunt), Konstancja Grzybowska (grandmother), Janina Grzybowska (mother), Stanisław Krzyżanowski (father) and Wiktoria Krzyżanowska (cousin). (Courtesy of the Janina Zgrzembska family archives)

evenings when Father returned from treating his patients. In this difficult situation, Father's sister and brother-in-law, Maria and Jan Karbowski, came to our assistance. Jan Karbowski was a transport engineer, a very talented and business-oriented man. Over several years he made a considerable fortune building railways in Russia. They returned to Poland when we were suffering such hardship, and so they decided to help us. They bought a large building (a former hotel that had been owned by the Wiśniewskis) in Chopin Street, not far from Dr. Józef Geisler's Health Center.[4] The plan was to convert the hotel into a sanatorium. My uncle did not grant this large estate, which was inside an extensive park, to my father, but he rented it to him so that my father could put it to good use.

With all his passion and energy, Father set up an exemplary sanatorium for patients suffering from lung diseases. His professionalism, diligence, and great love for his vocation brought him success.

"The result of all this was the constant arrival of new patients. The innovation in his method of treatment comprised not only specialist and surgical operations, but above all, use of the local climate, whose attributes were quite unique in the country. It mainly involved patients relaxing on a veranda at all seasons and even when temperatures fell below freezing. Apart from performing the profession he loved, Father was also active doing social work. He was the chairman of the Polish Motherland Circle in Otwock, deputy chairman of the Friends of Otwock Society, and deputy chairman of the local Social Welfare Council. My family home was always open to all those in need. Anyone could come with their problems and receive help. Father would treat the poor inhabitants, both Polish and Jewish, for free. Despite his numerous tasks, every day he would read foreign professional journals. He felt it very important to expand his knowledge of medicine. I remember my family to be very loving and open to all those in need.

"I was a very pampered child. When they visited us and saw just how extraordinarily mollycoddled I was, both my aunts, who were teachers, would say to my father: 'What are you doing, Stanisław? What will become of this child?' My father would then answer: 'We cannot know what life holds in store for my daughter. She may not have fonder memories than when she was mollycoddled.' As I often remember how difficult my life has been, I also reflect on how prophetic those words were.

"When World War I broke out, living conditions soon deteriorated. The Germans introduced ration cards for everything. There was a shortage of food and sanitary items. Materially it was even worse than in World War II, because by then we had learned how to 'dodge' the orders and regulations of the occupation authorities. Illegal trade flourished. We owed a lot to the Warsaw street traders who at great risk travelled to distant places and brought food. But it was quite different in 1914.

"The lack of disinfectants resulted in a typhoid epidemic. There were many sick in Otwock. Apart from my father, none of the other four physicians visited those suffering from spotted typhus—so scared were they of getting infected! But Father would always help those in need. That is how he contracted the disease. On February 10, 1917, following several days of grave illness and a very high fever, he died. He was barely 40. Shortly after Father's funeral, all the patients returned home or moved to local hotels as the sanatorium had to be closed for overall disinfection. In that time, Mother and I had to live with strangers. I do not write about our despair because words cannot describe what we were feeling then in our hearts. When the sanatorium reopened, Mother took over its administration.

"I vividly recall a beautiful gesture from the Jewish community in Otwock. After Father's death, two of their representatives came to Mother, offering to provide financial support for my education. Mother was deeply moved, but turned down their offer. She said she was young (32 at the time) and able to work; therefore, she felt she could cope. Even in Father's lifetime the Jews showed us great sympathy and gratitude for the fact that he treated so many of them free of charge. Their children were invited to our house and I'd play with them. Thanks to these contacts they'd learn Polish and I would learn their language.

"In 1918, an extremely virulent influenza pandemic broke out, commonly known as the Spanish Flu. The disease killed many people, while others consequently suffered serious complications. I also became infected, with inflammation in both lungs and my ears. After proper treatment, the pneumonia passed, as did the infection in one of my ears. But pus in my other ear started getting through to my brain: I had to be operated on immediately. In this time, my grandfather had returned from Russia, and so he took me to Warsaw, to Dr. Solman's private surgery in Szucha Avenue, where I underwent a trepanation of the skull. The operation was successful, but as a result I started suffering terrible headaches. It was so bad that I couldn't go to school. After I returned with grandfather to Otwock, I had to have lessons at home with a private teacher. The physicians comforted Mother, telling her that over the years my migraines would eventually ease. They did, but even now, every day I suffer from headaches.

"In 1920, Aunt and Uncle Karbowski returned from Russia. They decided that trying to run the sanatorium without my father was pointless, so it was closed. The building and grounds were purchased by the local authorities, who converted them into a correctional center for children.

That same year, Mother and I left Otwock. To this day I remember many things from that time, as it was the happiest period of my childhood. It is a memory I have been preserving over many years, for Mother recorded our family history. Many times, as an adult, I returned to read this family history. Unfortunately, it is now all gone: destroyed in the flames of the Warsaw Uprising.

I remember that in that happy period Mother actively participated in cultural life. She frequently performed with the Spójna Society theatrical troupe, an organization comprising members of the intelligentsia, devotees of Otwock, caring for the cultural development of the local community. As a young girl I was proud that my mother was an 'actress.' I remember being in a religious procession with other children, dressed in a Krakow costume and sprinkling flower petals. Jurek, the son of Dr. Władysław Czaplicki, taught me to sing. He was around 15 at the time. Jerzy Czaplicki[5] had a natural-born talent and liked singing best when he was perched high up on one of Otwock's beautiful pine trees. This appealed to me greatly. I, too, wanted to climb up one of those trees, but was unable to. Jurek would then put me on his shoulders, and together we'd sing. Jurek's singing made him famous the world over. Later he became a celebrated baritone singer, and travelled a lot.

"My grandfather, Ksawery Grzybowski, undertook every effort to make up for my father. One day, together with Mother, Grandfather, and my darling kitten, we took the last narrow-gauge train out of Otwock. This was during the Polish-Bolshevik War, and the very next day the Bolsheviks entered Otwock. Over the subsequent two days they also took Anin and Wawer, on the outskirts of Warsaw, and it was there that in a famous and hard-fought battle the Polish Army, under Józef Piłsudski's command, drove them back, thus saving Europe by staunching the Bolshevik floodtide.

"After leaving Otwock, we moved to Grandfather's house in Tarczyn. There we were shocked to discover that his beautiful garden was full of the graves of German soldiers who had perished in World War I. (The cemetery was not closed until the late 1990s, when the bodies were exhumed.)

Meanwhile, Mother's youngest brother, Uncle Ksawery, returned, after fighting in Józef Piłsudski's Legions. By profession he was an agricultural engineer and before the war Grandfather had sent him to an agricultural college in Tabor, southern Bohemia. His fate was interesting in that he found himself on Piłsudski's list of all the Poles studying abroad; thus he was enrolled to fight in the Polish Legions. This was when the Polish state was just emerging. And one of the first actions of this new state's authorities was to parcel out landed estates. Large estates had to be divided into smaller allotments, which were then sold to peasants at very low prices. Uncle Ksawery was appointed to supervise this process in the powiat of Piotrków. Although he himself had a wife and daughter to support, in his Piotrków Trybunalski home he also provided accommodation for my mother, grandfather, and me. We lived separately, getting by thanks to Grandpa's pension, his savings and Mother's occasional earnings (from handicrafts).

After passing appropriate exams, I started attending the third form at the Helena Trzcińska Gymnasium (middle school). Up until then, I had been taught privately, and this was my first contact with an ordinary school. I always got very good marks for humanistic subjects, but trailed with maths."[6]

***

On February 15, 1997, Irena Sendler returned to writing her memoir, which she entitled "Pages from the Calendar." On the first page she wrote:

"I feel my departure is near. Today I am 87. I do not intend to write chronologically, but I wish to describe various matters concerning my interesting profession. I feel I should start by explaining how I became publicly and professionally involved in social care. In secondary school I joined the scouting movement. This was my passion. From my father I also inherited an interest in politics. When in May 1926 during the long break I heard that a [newspaper] supplement had been issued concerning [Piłsudski's] May coup, I rushed out into the street to purchase it. Then at school I organized a press meeting. This did not please the headmistress, and I was suspended from school for a couple of days.

"Having passed my *matura*-end-of-school exam, in 1927, I decided I wanted to study something concerning social care. It turned out that nothing like this was available in Poland at the time, but such studies were possible in Paris. At a family meeting, my uncle and aunt declared that they would be able to finance such studies, but . . . Paris in those days was considered too dangerous and alluring for a lonely, young girl. After all, I was only 17!"

Notes

1. Here I make use of extensive fragments from Irena Sendler's manuscript memoir, which she had been writing since 1987. Toward the end she dictated what she wanted to write to Jolanta Migdalska-Barańska. At my request, she verbally added information to what had been written during our many meetings from May 2003 to March 2004.

2. Stanisław Krzyżanowski's (1877–1917) contributions in propagating the use of climate to treat pulmonary tuberculosis are extensively discussed in Witold Stefan Trybowski's doctoral thesis, published as a monograph, *Dzieje Otwocka uzdrowiska*, Otwock, 1996, pp. 18 and 54.

3. Alfred Marcin Sokołowski (1850–1924), a doctor of pulmonology, propagator of using sanatoria to treat tuberculosis and the founder of sanatoria.

4. Józef Marian Gesiler (1859–1920), physician. In 1890, he built baths in his Otwock villa, which, once extended, became the first permanent lowland sanatorium in Poland.

5. Jerzy Czaplicki (1902–1992) was a famous singer and pedagogue.

6. Irena Sendler's handwritten recollections, which she began in 1987.

3

Studies in Warsaw in the Years 1927–1939

Seventeen-year-old Irena Krzyżanowska decided to study law at the University of Warsaw. She thought this would provide her the basis to undertake social work. "I was disappointed," she sighed many years later. In her memoir she wrote:

"The head of the department, Professor Ignacy Koschembahr-Łyskowski, was a great erudite, but also a great bore, and, as it turned out, an enemy of female students. After two years (in keeping with the curriculum) of studying Roman Law, I understood that this was not the way to learn what interested me most and therefore I changed my course at the Humanities Faculty to Polish Studies.

"These studies appealed to me because they involved a compulsory two-year course in pedagogy.

I was an undergraduate in the 1930s. It was a time when people were struggling to reduce university tuition fees so that youths from working class and peasant families could also study, as well as a time of terrible anti-Semitic brawls. The university authorities tolerated this situation, and the eventual result was the introduction of the so-called 'ghetto bench' system. On the last pages of student indexes Polish Aryan students had instructions to sit on the right side, whereas Jewish students had to sit on the left side. The objective was to segregate the Jews at lectures. To show my solidarity, I always sat together with them on their side. After every lecture, youths from the extreme rightwing ONR (National Radical Camp) would beat the Jewish students as well as any Poles who sat with them on the benches on the left side. The leader of the ONR at the university was a law student called Jan Mosdorf.[1] Once a female Jewish student friend of mine was beaten so severely that I attacked one of the assailants with my fists and spat at his feet, exclaiming: 'You bandit!' Another time the same culprits pulled Jewish female students by the hair from the second floor all the way down to the ground floor. This put me into a state of shock, something came over me, and I crossed out the 'Aryan right side' entry in my index booklet. For this I was punished very harshly. When in June I submitted the index to have my lesson and exams results signed, it turned out my rights as a student were suspended. In subsequent years, I applied to have my suspension cancelled, as I was close to finishing all my courses and starting to write my master's thesis. And yet each time my application was turned down. This happened three years in a row. Each year I would go to the dean's office and ask to be allowed to attend classes again, and I'd always get a negative response. I would have probably never completed my studies if not for what happened in 1938. It was then that the presiding rector of the university went abroad for several months. In my desperation I went to Professor Tadeusz Kotarbiński (a renowned philosopher of logic, and a very good person), who was standing in for the rector at the time. I told him about my problems. The professor patted my shoulder and said I had done well to cross out that shameful entry. 'Go now, attend lectures today,' he added as we parted.

"Thus I set about finishing my master's thesis, which I wrote under the guidance of Professor Wacław Borowy. In June 1939, I took my final examinations and defended my diploma thesis."

***

Irena Sendler's first professional job was in the Mother and Child Aid Section of the Citizens' Committee for Social Help. The chairperson of the section committee was Professor Helena Radlińska,[2] and Maria Uziembło[3] was the manager. Apart from helping the unemployed (at the time many people were out of work in Poland), this was also a kind of training ground for the Free Polish University School of Social and Educational Work. Irena Sendler started working at the Mother and Child Aid Section on August 1, 1932. Before that she had tried to find employment as a Polish teacher, something she was fully qualified to do, but failed to get a post because her university was passing on the opinion that she was too "red" to work in schools.

"My monthly salary was 250 zlotys," she recounts, "which wasn't bad in those times. I paid 60 zlotys for the flat and 40 zlotys for the electricity, heating, and telephone. That left me 150 zlotys for food. My husband, Mieczysław Sendler, whom I married in 1931, was a junior assistant at the University of Warsaw Faculty of Classical Philology. We lived modestly, but this wasn't poverty."

The Mother and Child Aid Section had three offices: the head office was at 1 Opaczewska Street (Ochota District), while the other two were at 15 Targowa Street (Praga District) and 86 Wolska Street (Wola District).

Years later, Irena Sendler recalled with satisfaction: "From the very first days in this job, I was delighted by the wonderful atmosphere of kindness, tolerance, and love for every individual and the spreading of the ideals of goodness and social justice to the entire world. I became quite imbued with this atmosphere.

"I was quite absorbed. It was as if I had found myself in another world—a world that was so close to my heart, because it was the one in which I had been raised by my parents. At the very start, I was told that my basic job was to interview those applying for help in the community. Yet, to my great surprise, I learned that no instructions would be provided as to how these interviews should be conducted. It was only later that I realized the underlying wisdom and appropriateness of this approach. The objective was to give the social worker freedom and independence. After one or two months, each one of us was tested. At a general meeting we had to present our individually developed methods of work. Help—medical, legal, material, or all three—was provided according to what was actually needed. Nevertheless, the authorities of those days were not pleased with our work for two basic reasons: our newspaper, *Człowiek w Polsce*, was revealing the tragic consequences of unemployment, and our social mission was proving to be very expensive to realize.

"Legal aid was one of the major divisions in our organization. One of its subdivisions was devoted to helping evictees, people who for failing to pay their rent over several months were, in accordance with the law of the day, evicted, regardless of the time of year or the number of affected children. There were four lawyers employed in this subdivision. Another legal aid subdivision concerned unwed single mothers and their children, who could only obtain the financial support they deserved from the natural father through a court of law. A third subdivision, that of health care, concerned the protection of unemployed single mothers who had no health insurance and thus no right to health care. This subdivision included a gynecologist, a pediatrician, and a nurse.

"Apart from conducting interviews and testifying in law courts, our work as social workers (or guardians) involved cooperating with solicitors to defend unemployed single mothers.

With time, I was put in charge of the subsection caring specifically for unemployed single mothers, whose number was continually rising with the influx of girls from the countryside who moved to Warsaw in search of work. After a year in this job, I wrote an article in *Człowiek w Polsce* to raise awareness of the desperate need for laws to alleviate the plight of these unfortunate young women.

"In this wonderful and beautiful institution, everyone worked with great enthusiasm and dedication. Yet, unfortunately, there was a constant shortage of money to address the needs of those under our charge. Moreover, rightwing politicians in the government and parliament did not like us because some of our staff belonged to leftist political groups.

"In the spring of 1935, the Mother and Child Aid Section was closed. Our entire team was promised employment at the Social Welfare Department of the City of Warsaw. But that's not how it happened. Individual team members were indeed given new jobs, but in different places.

The head office was in the Free Polish University building in Opaczewska Street, but there were also three other centers, in Ochota, Wola, and Praga.

"I was given a post in Social and Health Care Center VI at 25 Siedzibna Street, which was responsible for poor (and usually unemployed) people living in the barracks of so-called Annopol. Next, I worked various sections of the Social Welfare Department at 74 Złota Street, where I also instructed new members of staff."

Notes

1. For the sake of historical truth, it should be explained that during World War II, Mosdorf became a prisoner of Auschwitz concentration camp (where he died) and completely changed his attitude toward Jews. I was told this by Adam Wendel, himself a former concentration camp prisoner and prewar communist. Jan Dobraczyński also writes about it in his recollections: *Tylko w jednym zyciu*, Warsaw, 1970, p. 214.

2. Helena Radlińska (1879–1954), political and educational activist, pedagogue, historian of education, and librarian.

3. Maria Uziembło (1894–1976). Her daughter, Aniela Uziembło, who also befriended Mrs. Sendler, published recollections about her mother in *Gazeta Wyborcza* on August 30, 2001.

4

September 1939

"On August 30th," recollects Irena Sendler, "I escorted my husband[1] to the station. He was leaving for the front. We stood on the platform among a crowd of others who were also leaving or seeing their loved ones off. To this day I still see that train before my eyes. At the time the atmosphere reminded me of World War I. I had premonitions; I feared war. Once my husband left, I was so upset that I got on the wrong tram, which took me to Praga instead of Wola. I got off in some deserted place. When, after a long trek, I finally got home; it was very late, I was extremely tired, and my mind was filled with foreboding. The next day I had agreed to meet my friend Ewa Rechtman. We decided to have some ice cream, and it turned out that in that café we were to have our last meeting. I was very concerned about her because the persecution of Jews in Nazi Germany was common knowledge. The following morning, Mother turned on the radio at around six and we heard that at dawn German army units had crossed the Polish border, and there were reports of people being wounded and killed. It was hard for me to eat breakfast, and I set off for work earlier than usual."

In her memoir, Irena Sendler describes that time as follows:

"When at dawn, in the early morning of September 1, 1939, the first bombs fell on Warsaw, all the staff of City of Warsaw Social Welfare Department, in the head office at 74 Zlota Street, as well as in all its agencies, turned up for work as usual. The president of Warsaw, Stefan Starzyński, issued three key instructions to the Social Welfare Department.

"Some of the head office staff were to organize special social care points throughout Warsaw. These were to provide essential aid to refugees from the regions of Poznań, Pomerania, and elsewhere—refugees fleeing from the barbarity of the German invaders. (I, myself, had to organize such points in three different places, for one area would be bombed and then the point had to be moved elsewhere.) The remaining staff of the head office and all the other centers were to work as usual in these most abnormal conditions. Another important instruction was to organize pay for the wives of soldiers and officers. And, finally, President Starzyński also decreed that all the city administration departments and enterprises were to remain continually operational (day and night). He was adamant with regard to this resolution and himself never left his post. He never went home and instead remained in the City Hall, from where he frequently travelled to the most threatened areas to provide essential help and engage his entire team to tackle the most difficult yet also very important tasks. His magnificently heroic, courageous, and patriotic stance inspired the capital's entire population. People felt encouraged to stand up and fight; the terrible wounds inflicted upon this beloved city were somehow alleviated. The effects of constant bombing were tragic—thousands of people wounded or killed, hundreds of houses burned to the ground. Improvised graves in plazas, squares, and courtyards added even more tragedy to the situation. The fires and constant air raid alerts made everyday life for the city's inhabitants difficult to bear. The president's voice, as he made his radio broadcasts, was comforting. It raised hopes.

"When on September 6 I saw members of the government pack their suitcases into luxurious limousines and leave the capital, I was deeply shocked.

"On September 23, after the bombing of Warsaw power station, Polish Radio, which broadcast its programs live, including the President Starzyński talks that had such a strong morale-boosting effect on the embattled people of Warsaw, was silenced."

Notes

1. Mieczysław Sendler (1910–2005), historian, spent 1939–1945 war in Woldenberg POW camp for officers. Mieczysław and Irena Sendler divorced in 1947.

5

Occupation

The city's capitulation was signed on September 28, 1939, and in the days that followed, German army units proceeded to take control of the capital. People started clearing the rubble. Life in the city was returning to normal as her inhabitants went back to work.

Irena Sendler almost immediately became involved in conspiratorial activities of the Polish Socialist Party (PPS). She carried out many tasks, including the delivery of money to University of Warsaw professors, who now found themselves in a very difficult financial situation. She went to the families of those who were imprisoned or had been executed. She also supplied medicines and essential sanitary items to people hiding in the forests.

Irena Sendler recalls: "Already in the autumn of 1939 the Germans ordered the city administration to sack all Jewish employees and also cease providing aid to the Jewish poor.[1] [So] first five of us—Jadwiga Piotrowska, Jadwiga Daneka, Irena Schultz, Jan Dobraczyński (our manager), and I—and later 10[2] of the most trusted people in the social welfare head office and other centers, organized cells to help the Jews."

The Childcare Section was part of the old Social Welfare Department. Its task was to bring Polish homeless children to care centers. Unofficially, the Childcare Section also looked after the homeless children of the future Jewish district.[3]

"It should be stressed," says Mrs. Sendler, "that we were not acting in the name of any political organization (though in other aspects of our work each one of us was politically engaged) but as vocational social workers who, guided by a sheer sense of humanity and the elemental principles of social welfare (principles we loyally adhered to), felt the need to help the most unfortunate and wronged Jews."

In his foreword to the second volume of *Archiwum Ringelbauma*, Feliks Tych writes: "Hitler's war waged against most of the countries of Europe to impose a new Nazi *order* on the continent, to make Europe subordinate to Nazi Germany and to create *living space* for the German race of *super-humans* by no later than the summer of 1941 became **the first war in history also consciously waged against children**. The mass murder of children became **one of Hitler's war objectives**. In this case, it did not concern all the children of occupied countries, but those representing a specific group: **Jewish children**. And, in this particular case, it concerned **all the children**.

"In accordance with the will of Hitler, his closest political associates, the tacit consent or pretended lack of knowledge of most of German society and also the passivity of most societies in occupied Europe, those Jewish children, including babies (just like all other Jews who had found themselves under the direct or indirect control of the Third Reich) were sentenced to death. They died murdered in the cruellest ways one could possibly imagine: in gas chambers, through starvation, in front of firing squads (alongside their murdered mothers), or burned alive in houses, synagogues or barns. The sentence was executed in the eyes of a world that was quite oblivious to the crime, its only alibi being disbelief."[4]

In Warsaw there were 20 social aid centers. Day after day the inhabitants of all the districts became increasingly pauperized. What (illegal) help the social welfare department was able to provide was hopelessly inadequate in face of the most urgent needs.

Irena Sendler recalls: "After consulting the matter with colleagues and Warsaw local community guardians, a neighborhood self-help program was devised. In every larger house we tried to find a family that was better off and able to provide a hot meal to one of their poorer neighbors. This neighborly help action proved to be successful and all centers started implementing this idea.

Transports from Germany of Polish POWs suffering from typhus were arriving in Warsaw already in 1940. They were put in the former military Ujazdowski Hospital in Piękna Street. The food in this hospital was quite insufficient for the malnourished patients who had languished in the terrible conditions of the German stalags.

"It became a matter of urgency to supply extra food for our soldiers. Various institutions took care of individual wards. One of our colleagues, Róża Zawadzka, had relations and friends among the local landed gentry whom she recruited to help us. From many places outside Warsaw precious donations were coming in, namely, food.

"Apart from delivering provisions, we also established contacts between the soldiers and their families, many of whom lived in other parts of the country. We therefore helped out in the writing of letters. Moreover, we brought them books and even gramophones and records with songs. Among the several hundred ordinary conscripts there were two officers, whom we helped to escape. This was a very risky operation as the hospital was under constant German supervision and observation. After a year of work in this subdivision, I moved to another center nearer home (6 Ludwiki Street), where my ailing mother lived. There my job was to decide which families were the poorest and in the greatest need of aid. It was from this working class district (Wola) that the Germans deported large numbers of youths to work in the Third Reich. In order to save these young people, we established the Wola Cooperative, where they could be officially employed in shoemaking, carpentry, and tailors' workshops. With time the Germans realized what we were doing and demanded that our employees should have medical certificates. We helped youths in the greatest danger of deportation acquire medical certificates, falsely stating that they were suffering from pulmonary diseases. Later, after being accused of helping ghetto Jews, I was transferred to another center in distant Grochów, very far from my home and sick mother."

***

Those who knew German culture for a long time could not believe in Hitler's criminal intentions. They believed Germany was a part of Western culture and civilization. People deluded themselves that what was written and said about the tragic fate of German Jews was merely propaganda. Yet the fears of the few who treated Adolf Hitler's threats seriously were the ones that turned out to be true.

On December 1, 1939, a regulation was introduced on the basis of which all Jews were obliged to wear armbands with the Star of David. Likewise, their shops were to be marked with the Star of David, and gradually Jews' freedom of movement was restricted. Houses and flats were confiscated, bank accounts blocked, and Jewish employees were sacked from Polish institutions. Finally, Warsaw was divided into three districts: German, Polish, and Jewish. The city's inhabitants were now forced to move. Even Jews from other parts of the country were transported into the Warsaw Jewish district. When on November 16, 1940, the Warsaw ghetto was finally closed, it contained over 400,000 people (over 130,000 of whom had been forcibly moved there).

An order issued by Hans Frank on October 15, 1941, prohibited all Jews from leaving the ghetto and all Poles from helping Jews. For Jews and Poles alike, the punishment for breaking this rule was death.

"When the Nazis decided to murder the Jewish nation, I could not look on with indifference," stresses Sendler. "I had many people who were close to me in the Jewish district. Among others, there was my friend Ewa Rechtman and Józef Zysman. Ewa worked in the Centos at nr 2 Leszno Street. Centos was a charity [Society for the Care of Orphans and Abandoned Children, founded in 1924 for children orphaned or abandoned as a result of World War I] that had about a hundred care centers and dayrooms as well as fourteen orphanages.

"What was the purpose of our work? In order to help the Jews, we had to gather information so that we knew which Jews were in the greatest need, and we also had to forge hundreds of documents. The surnames of the Jews we helped had to be changed into Polish ones. For myself and my friend Irena Schultz, I managed to acquire the work passes of a sanitary unit responsible for fighting infectious diseases. Later, I was also able to obtain such passes for my other couriers. Thus, up to the spring of 1943, we were able to enter the ghetto quite legally.

"We were helped in this matter by the invaluable Dr. Juliusz Majkowski, who was the director of the Sanitation Center. The Germans were terrified of typhus, and in those atrocious sanitary conditions together with the overpopulation and hunger an epidemic was bound break out. Not wishing to have physical contact with any potential carriers of this disease, they left it to the Poles to try and control the situation. Sometimes we would enter the ghetto several times a day. We had money from the social welfare department fund, food and medicines (including precious typhus vaccines), and disinfectants. We also smuggled in clothes by wearing several layers every time we came, which was not a problem for me as I was very slim.

"On entering the ghetto, I would put on a Star of David armband as a gesture of solidarity with the Jewish population. The other reasons were that it would not draw the attention of any Germans I encountered there and also not arouse the suspicion of Jews who didn't know me. Once I was so shocked by the tragic scenes I had witnessed in the ghetto that on leaving it I forgot to take the wretched armband off. This happened in July 1942, when German repression had already increased. A German gendarme reacted immediately and started hitting me, while a Polish policeman struggled to take my pass; the situation suddenly became very dangerous. What saved me was a stroke of luck. In my desperation I pleaded for the Polish policeman to phone Dr. Majkowski for him to confirm who I really was. The telephone call was made; not by the Polish policeman, but, to my amazement, by the German gendarme! And again I was lucky in that Dr. Majkowski realized the German was referring to me. Thus he confirmed that the pass was absolutely genuine and that I had been sent to the ghetto on his instructions. On another occasion, I was again attacked for wearing the armband, except this time the assailant was a Jewish policeman."

Notes

1. Polish citizens of Jewish origin had been officially entitled to social aid from the state since 1923.
2. Irena Sendler's couriers were: Jadwiga Piotrowska, Iren Schultz, Izabela Kuczkowska, Janina Grabowska, Wanda Drozdowska-Rogowiczowa, Zofia Patecka, Lucyna Franciszkiewicz, Jadwiga Daneka, Maria Roszkowska, and Wincenty Ferster.
3. "What was the ghetto?" was the question history teacher Norman Conard heard asked by his teenage students at the Uniontown school. An accurate answer may be found, for instance, in the Polish-English book *Getto Warszawskie – Warsaw Ghetto* (Parma-Press, Warszawa, 2002), where Anka Grupińska writes: "The first effort to create a ghetto in the capital was already undertaken on November 4, 1939. After a few days, the order was suspended, probably on account of differences between the Gestapo and the Wehrmacht . . . In March 1940, a district traditionally inhabited by Jews was officially declared an 'epidemic infected area' (*Seuchensperrgebiet*). Notices prohibiting entry were installed along the border of this area. On March 27, 1940, the Judenrat was instructed to build a wall enclosing the Jewish district, which covered 4 percent of the city's area, and on May 10th Adam Czerniaków was given a plan of this closed district. At the start of June the first borders of the ghetto were marked out and twenty sections of the wall were raised. The construction of the wall was still being completed when the ghetto was finally closed . . . On October 12, 1940, the Germans issued an order for the Judenrat to officially institute the ghetto . . . Several hundred thousand Jews were crammed into an area of barely 400 ha (2.4 percent of the city's total area). Enclosed within the 18 km long, 3 m high wall were 73 of Warsaw's 1,800 streets, some 27,000 homes, a cemetery and a sports pitch. There was not a single park or garden. The area was subjected to permanent changes. After a new delimitation in October 1941, the ghetto was split into the so-called large ghetto and small ghetto, the two ghettos being linked via a footbridge over the Aryan Chłodna Street. . . . The outside of the ghetto wall was guarded by German and Polish police, whereas Jewish police guarded the wall from the inside. . . . Smuggling and

the work of self-help groups failed to meet the needs of this closed district. In the ghetto, hunger was ubiquitous."

4. *Archiwum Ringelbluma. Dzieci – tajne nauczanie w getcie warszawskim*, vol. 2. ed. Ruta Sakowska, foreword by Feliks Tych, Warszawa, 200, p. v. [Words were emphasized in italic and in bold by the author.]

6

I Remember Them

"I recall the people I visited in the ghetto with respect, admiration and affection. I remember their great commitment in working for the benefit of others," says Irena Sendler, and then, deeply moved, adds, "I remember them all, the old and the young."

Who were the young house committee activists so ardently and affectionately recalled by Irena Sendler in her extensive description of five Warsaw ghetto youth circles?[1]

"House committees were first founded at the start of the war as air raid defense units for the purpose of creating air raid shelters, putting out fires, et cetera. All houses had such committees (in the so-called Aryan districts as well as in the old Jewish district). Nevertheless, events soon transformed these house committees into special care units, as help was spontaneously organized to save people from annihilation. That is why at first the work of these committees was not clearly defined. They operated on an ad hoc basis, resulting from the initiatives of individuals, circumstances in particular houses, and the most urgent needs as they arose. It was only later that they came under the control of Jewish Social Self-Help, or rather the so-called Coordination Commission, which the invader next forced to be transformed into the Jewish Social Welfare Society. With time the systematic and deliberate destruction of the Jewish community severely limited the effectiveness of the last of these institutions, which consequently had to be restructured. Nevertheless, it continued to be called the Jewish Social Welfare Society. Despite the numerous reorganizations at 'the top,' the house committees, which were at the very bottom of this institutional hierarchy and working with the very poorest Jews, did everything they possibly could to prevent adults and children from starving to death. Their actions were in many respects a desperate struggle for biological survival, yet they were also a sudden, wonderful, heartfelt, spiritual surge to alleviate the suffering of fellow human beings. At first the house committees were spontaneous and disorganized. But once the Jewish district was tragically cut off from the city, resulting in a daily worsening of conditions for the inhabitants, the work of these committees was taken over by the most outstanding social activists of the underground movement. People such as Dr. Emmanuel Ringelblum, Szachno Zagan, Chaim Kapłan, or Jonasz Turkow.

"Therefore it is not surprising that, despite all the German invaders' efforts and the pressure they put on the Judenrat (who in turn forced house committee members to limit their actions, not infrequently resorting to terror, persecution, maltreatment, and various other forms of repression), these committees served as examples of the most beautiful and selfless social activity among the broad masses. They became places where strong will and character, spirit, and fortitude were forged. They helped create an unprecedented social stance arising from the noblest humanitarian motives. For hundreds of thousands of people they served as a refuge where people genuinely helped each other. Apart from the greatest achievements of social work, I also often witnessed small, mundane incidents. Where there is a struggle for life and death, where the acquisition of a single potato, beetroot, or onion rises to become an insoluble problem, one cannot expect only positive stances. Anyone making such claims would simply be lying or proving that they had never been, never experienced together with those inhabitants that hell.

"Acting within the house committees were the youth circles, which played a great role not only in social aid but also in the fields of education and culture. Their invaluable contribution was in the struggle against hopelessness, the struggle for personal and national dignity. Their far-reaching work, in my opinion, contributed to deepening political awareness and mobilized people to oppose the enemy authorities, the police, and the Judenrat. Each circle would have a guardian from the house committee who took interest in the circle and helped it by selecting as leaders youths with organizational skills. Thus the circles began, with the initial help of the guardian, and it was on the performance of the first youth activists that the circle's later development and effectiveness depended.

"One of the reasons for founding youth circles was to find a way for youths to cope with the constant threat of death. Another important motive was to help young people experience higher values, to take up a proactive stance with regard to those living around them and the very complex problems they faced. It was also a search to find their own place, define their own role in the tragically demoralized ghetto community. Their place was in the youth circles.

Young people, led wisely and with commitment by their guardians, were to lay the foundations of their own refuge, their own safe haven.

"Circles were supposed to arouse enthusiasm and the will to act. They usually developed rapidly, though this also depended on the particular area or even particular house. They appeared in places where the need arose, wherever there were appropriate local conditions and possibilities. Their work not infrequently, though often only subconsciously, inspired youths to revolt; it helped prepare cadres of boy, even child fighters. Youth circles underwent many changes, just like the house committees out of which they emerged.

"While in the first period, that is before the ghetto was closed, the youth circles only played a minor role, after that date, once conditions for many thousands of people in the enclosed area began to rapidly deteriorate, with a continual sense of danger, despair and fear every minute, day and night, these circles became a haven, a place of respite, of human dignity, faith in a better future, a place where a young girl and a young boy could be together, feel how they wanted to feel, think, ask questions and receive answers. In the starving, dying Warsaw ghetto these youth circles gave its young inhabitants the most valuable things possible: a smile, a sense of joy, and faith in humanity.

"In those terrible times, those terrible conditions—when many people died each and every day, when it was enough to go out into the street to encounter the corpses of children—to evoke a smile on someone's face or be moved by something beautiful was neither simple nor easy."

***

"I do not remember how many circles there were in all. Fate put me into closer contact with five.

The Youth Circle at (16?) Sienna Street was run by **Ewa Rechtman**, the assistant of Professor Stanisław Słoński[2] at the humanities faculty of the Free Polish University. She was not only an outstanding Slavicist with very promising academic potential, but also a graduate of the School of Social and Educational Work with the rare talent of being able to combine academic insight with a passion for social work. Her deep knowledge, as well as exceptional qualities of spirit and character, garnered for her general respect, love, and sympathy. And on top of that, her simplicity, openness, and great personal charm all promised her a wonderful future. Unfortunately, like that of many others, her future ended in the ghetto. And although all her Aryan friends pleaded that she should remain on our side, that we would do everything to 'keep' her—as it was then termed—to find a safe place for her, she always responded in the same way: 'Don't insist, dears, I won't stay with you because I can't put you at risk.' That sentence contained the essence of her personality, her beautiful, generous soul.

"When the ghetto gate closed behind her, when she disappeared from her beloved Free Polish University and was unable to work with the children of the Polish and Jewish proletariat and unemployed in the district of Ochota, Ewa Rechtman did not give in! Oh no! She immediately became involved in social work (officially in Child Welfare) in a house committee, setting up her own youth circle.

"And when I visited her, which I did very frequently to show that we were still with her all the time, just as before, to show that the evil walls of shame had changed nothing, her sensitive and caring eyes would notice that hidden behind my mask of cheeriness was a profound sadness, and she'd comfort me: 'Don't worry about me, I have the same work as before. Look! My Rachaels and Nuchims are no different from the Marys and Felixes of Opaczewska Street. Both need a bit of affection and a lot of bread.'

"She started acquainting me with her boys and girls. I frequently attended their meetings, where they prepared plans for the nearest future, reported on current problems, and discussed all sorts of matters.

"I remember one meeting in peculiar. It was the winter of 1941/1942, the most tragic ghetto winter on account of the greatest hunger and cold. It was mainly for these reasons and the appalling overpopulation that a spotted typhus epidemic broke out. The situation was made even worse by a cruel instruction of the German authorities by which residents were forced to bathe in disinfectant. The German authorities organized this in a grossly inadequate way, which not only failed to stop the disease from spreading but actually got even more people infected.

"In such conditions the only defense against contracting the terrible disease was Weigl's vaccine. But to purchase it in the ghetto required vast sums of money. It therefore became essential to obtain the vaccine from beyond the ghetto walls.

"On account of the fact that my underground movement colleague Irena Schultz and I were employed at the Health and Social Welfare Department, and thanks to my couriers, who were employed in various parts of the health service, we were able to provide ghetto youth circles with the necessary vaccines. Nevertheless, due to the extremely restrictive circumstances, the amounts we obtained were quite inadequate in relation to the needs.

"It was on the day of the aforementioned youth circle meeting that I brought several doses of the vaccine. And it was during the meeting that among other things discussed was the issue of who should receive the vaccine. The problem was as follows: receiving the vaccine gave 99 percent protection against contracting the disease, and I stress, in that time, typhus was decimating the ghetto inhabitants! How would the youths resolve this extremely difficult dilemma?

"It seems to me that the decisions they made bear them the best possible testimony as to their considerable social sophistication and exceptionally high moral standards. The vaccines were given to: two boys who were the only guardians of younger siblings, as both parents had died; and a girl who was the most active member of the circle and the most engaged in social work.

The remaining dozen or so circle members raised no objections; they showed no regrets or hard feelings. Quite the opposite, they displayed great dignity and respect for a just decision, even if it could cost them their lives.

"Circle members devoted a lot of work to the care of children. In particular, they looked after sick children who in many cases had been left unattended for days. They organized collections of clothes, and of food for those who were suffering the most from hunger. They took particular care of orphans living on the verge of death. The enthusiasm, dedication, and the honest and conscientious approach to every matter made them not only liked but also respected and admired by others. The youths in turn loved their guardian, Ewa. Her every action, her every comment was treated as a battle order for the whole group. And for her they became the greatest source of comfort. She gave them all she had to give. She was their mother, father, sister, friend. She was with them through the very worst to the bitter end. She would give them her last earned cents, herself on the verge of starvation. They kept up the good work to the end of July 1942. It was then that they were taken in one of the first mass transports from the so-called small ghetto to Treblinka.

"It was a beautiful day when a horde of armed Hitlerites formed a tight cordon to seal off the streets of the small ghetto. Thus the youths' fate was sealed.

"On hearing the news, we tried everything we could to save them. We tried to get through in ambulances under the pretence of continuing our disinfection work, but to no avail. Our most determined efforts were dashed by the intransigent hatred of the enemy, who physically sealed the inhabitants in a ring of death.

"Life was very difficult for us without Ewa. She was a decent, noble person of exceedingly rare goodness and subtlety, someone who loved all people. Her humanitarian approach to others, regardless of race, nationality, background, amazed us and made her not only loved but also regarded with the greatest respect. We just could not come to terms with the fact that of all people it was she who got into the murderous clutches of those butchers. Ewa's heroic death was one of the most dramatic episodes in our group's history. Even now in my nightmares about those terrible times I hear her voice, always soft, gentle, and soothing, the voice of the greatest goodness. Young generations should cherish her because this was a quiet yet great hero!"

***

"The youth circle at 9 Smocza Street was overseen by **Ala Gołąb-Grynberg**, a nurse by profession and graduate of the Social and Educational Work School at the Free Polish University. In the ghetto she was a supervisor of nurses. Her work had many aspects, but her greatest passion was to deal with children and youths. As this was what also interested me the most, thus we frequently met. Her daily work involved contact with physicians, which she used for the benefit of her youth circle. With Professor Ludwik Hirszfeld's[3] prior consent, she organized a secret medical nursing course for boys and girls. The circle was extremely important on account of the terrible sanitary conditions that prevailed inside the ghetto. The youths acquired theoretical knowledge thanks to lectures provided by physicians whom Ala had engaged in this social action. In particular, I remember doctors Henryk Landau and Rozenkranc, who despite their age, poor health, and traumatic experiences from the occupation, devoted all their energy to work with those youths.

"I attended one such lecture. The house committee building was cold, a small candle served as the only illumination, and in the corner was a blackboard on which Dr. Landau noted the most important points of his lecture. From his pockets he would produce all sorts of teaching aids to better illustrate what he was trying to explain.

"The youths were listening carefully and, despite the very poor light, taking notes. Then the deep, studious silence was brutally interrupted from just outside the building by the characteristic sound of German army boots, terrifying yells, and the startling cries of a child. The youths and I were overcome with fear. Our thoughts were suddenly far removed from academic comments about epidemic diseases.

"Only the lecturer, externally at least, showed no signs of fear. He was calm and collected. Without even pausing, he continued to explain the complex medical subject of his talk. It was only when one of the female listeners started spasmodically weeping, tears streaming down her face, did he interrupt the lecture and say, 'Haven't you realized yet that we are on the frontline day and night? This is a continuous battle. We are frontline soldiers. Soldiers have to be tough. Here, crying is out of the question.' Then he returned to his lecture. We, the young ones, felt ashamed. His incredible composure rubbed off on us.

"Such was the secret school. Our youths also received practical training in various units of the ghetto health service, according to a chart prepared by Ala Grynberg. What were the practical benefits of such courses? There were two.

"First, by being engaged in active work, youths escaped the pervasive sense of hopelessness. Second, having acquired a great deal of practical knowledge, our youths became invaluable to the ghetto health service in the combating of diseases, in knowing how to avoid them, and generally helping people to stay alive. Ala, always an excellent administrator and social worker, did everything she could to surround her youths with the best possible care and assistance. She was proud of her young friends.

"Often she would emotionally tell me how her children had on many occasions acted to stop the spreading of diseases or worked in health care units, standing in for the professional staff who had been deported.

"Even though she was continually exposed to danger on account of her very responsible jobs (being in charge of team of nurses and undertaking diverse social tasks), she also spent a lot of time contacting the so-called Aryan side. The chief reason for this, apart from her emotional ties with many dear friends, was her keen desire to save the young people under her charge. She searched for help everywhere. She approached people, pleaded, argued, demanded. In many cases she was successful, thanks to her exceptional intelligence, boundless energy, and social passion.

"In many other cases, like the rest of us, she was quite helpless against the enemy's might.

She had her own house, a husband and a child—a beloved daughter, then aged five or six.

When I saw her for the last time in August 1942, already after many tragic deportations, she was very composed, but also very sad. By then her husband was already fighting with the partisans, and her daughter had for a long time been in a relatively safe place on the Aryan side. I asked Ala to immediately leave the ghetto.

"She had good contacts with our underground units, which made it relatively easy for her to leave the ghetto whenever she wanted. On the other side we had prepared a safe hideout for her. But she refused. Staring at the blazing sun-heated tenement-house rooftops in Smocza Street (she lived in a garret), she was engaged in a bitter internal struggle. I understood her! Her child was on the other side, her husband was fighting in the forest, but here too were things she loved—her work, her responsibilities, the sick, the young, the old—and tragic Umschlagplatz.[4]

"It was a difficult choice, a tragic one. By then I was not so well oriented in what was happening in the ghetto, but I knew that not everyone could be saved. One had to try to save only those that could be saved. It was in this spirit that I spoke with Ala—not knowing that this would be our last conversation. She stayed and died a few days later on the infamous Umschlagplatz-Treblinka route. She died together with her beloved youths. Her husband was killed fighting as a partisan. Two years after the war, a new family collected her daughter from an orphanage and left the country."

***

"As far as I remember, the guardian of the youth circle in Ogrodowa Street was **Józef Zysman**—an outstanding lawyer, excellent solicitor, a thoroughly upright person and a great patriot—a Pole. He had an intelligentsia background. His family had been fully assimilated. It had a great tradition in the struggles for Polish independence and very progressive views. Being exceptionally talented, already as a University of Warsaw student and later as a legal apprentice he always stood out from his peers. Not only did he stand out intellectually, but also in terms of character, indomitable spirit, and exceptional morality. All these qualities made him respected and admired by those who knew him.

"For several years he held relatively high positions in society—bearing in mind that these were the 1930s. For a long time he was the chairman of the Union of Court and Defense Counsel Apprentices. He belonged to a leftwing group of defense lawyers, called Tusculum, where together with other distinguished members he tried to change the attitudes among more bourgeois and rightwing legal fraternities. As a zealous fighter for social justice, he eventually developed a passion for legal advice, which he provided along with other leftwing lawyers at the Mother and Child Aid Section of the Civic Social Welfare Committee.

"It was with these lawyers as well as the indefatigable communist activist and defense lawyer Bronisława Luidorówna that he defended Polish unemployed workers from eviction. Another problem he devoted a great deal of time and energy to were the rights of children born out of wedlock. Józef Zysman was a great erudite and brilliant speaker, sensitive to every type of human suffering, who was a well-known figure among the Polish proletariat. He had particular recognition among the unemployed in the suburbs of Wola and Ochota, as well as the outskirts of Praga, wherever legal consultancies operated.

"In 1939, as an officer of the reserve, he is mobilized. With great pride, but as a leftwing activist also with considerable concern, he dons his Polish officer's uniform and leaves for the front. With total dedication he fights throughout the Polish September Campaign and ends up in Lwów. There he remains until the German Army takes over the city. He manages to safely return to his family in Warsaw, but by then it is the tragic time of the ghetto.

"His sensitive nature cannot accept what is happening around him. It is exceptionally difficult for him to be imprisoned and isolated from the world. He not only felt he was a Pole, his whole life confirmed it, [but he was also a Jew] and this Nazi division of Polish society hurt him most. Yet despite feeling quite shattered himself, he fully understood the need to protect youths from a psychological breakdown. Thus he involved himself in social work within the ghetto, while at the same time maintaining constant contact with the Aryan side.

"His work with youths concentrated mainly on social issues. He taught youths how to love fellow human beings and not be egoistical. His boys and girls were employed in actions such as the collection of clothes and food as part of the so-called winter aid. However, this was not enough for him. He was eager to extend his range of activities.

"Together with a group of Polish Socialists (headed by the defense lawyer Antoni Oppenheim and engineer Jerzy Neuding) he gathered materials for an underground newspaper that was circulated both within and beyond the ghetto, on the Aryan side. In this newspaper, he wrote about the situation as it was, and about how it ought to be. Some of his youths were drawn into this political activity as underground newspaper carriers.

"As an ardent patriot, in his work with youths he attached great importance to maintain a strong faith in the Polish fatherland. The youths loved him, they valued and trusted his words. I used to meet Józef Zysman, Antoni Oppenheim, and Jerzy Neuding in the presbytery of a Roman Catholic church in Leszno Street. The parish priest, Prelate Popławski, was known for his exceptional stance in complex issues concerning the ghetto.

In long, sincere conversations, the three Jewish activists envisaged, despite everything, quite optimistic plans for the future. Alas!

Engineer Neuding was killed in one of the first executions of April 1942. The lawyer Oppenheim was shot dead on the Aryan side. Józef Zysman decided to remain in the ghetto, even though his friends begged him to leave what was clearly a hopeless situation. He did, nevertheless, contact friends on the Aryan side to organize the escape, via underground sewers, of his three youngest children, including his son. He himself, his wife, and other older members of his family decided to stay. He felt his place was to be among the least fortunate. He entrusted his son to me and also wrote me a letter containing many philosophical reflections; it was a precious document of those times that was unfortunately destroyed during the Warsaw Uprising. Apart from a description of what the ghetto really meant, the main thought in this letter was as follows: The only way in which humanity may be reborn is through the omnipotence of love. Hatred generates evil and only love has the lasting power to give humanity hope. It is only through love that the world may be reborn.

"To this day, after so many years, I still see the look in his kind, warm, wise eyes as he entrusted his son to me, saying: 'Raise him up to be a good Pole and a noble person.' His last will and testament was written down by his wife.

"His friends could not accept the thought of him remaining in the ghetto. They used all possible arguments to make him leave. When in the autumn of 1942 the situation deteriorated ever more rapidly, literally day after day, when even some of the surviving youth circle members decided to leave, our friend finally crossed over to the Aryan side. Yet on the other side he also had terrible experiences: blackmail and no certainty of finding shelter for the next night.

"When meeting friends he was so subtle and careful not to upset anyone that, preoccupied with our underground activities, we failed to realize that he had new problems. In general, it was increasingly more difficult to find a safe place. And although all those around him tried hard not show it, someone like Józef Zysman could not bear to see his friends exposing themselves to the mortal danger of continually breaking criminal Nazi law.

"His noble spirit, love of humankind, and morality started putting desperate thoughts into his head. In the end, solely on account of his good and noble nature, he decided to spare his friends the danger of hiding a Jew. He went to the Hotel Polski and reported for what the Germans 'promised' to be a journey abroad.³ He died a martyr's death, a wonderful person, barely 37, perfidiously tricked and murdered by criminals."

***

"The guardian of the youth circle in Pawia (Peacock) Street was **Rachela Rozenthal**, a professional teacher and graduate of the University of Warsaw. She was talented, intelligent, sensitive and subtle. She did Polish studies in the years 1929–1934. This was a time when a major wave of anti-Semitism passed through the university. She experienced painful incidents of discrimination, and was herself frequently exposed to persecution by other students from the Camp of Great Poland.[6] These experiences had a profound effect on her world outlook. Although she belonged to the Democratic Youth Movement (which incorporated both Polish and Jewish youths with views then considered progressive) and participated in many useful actions, the pain of witnessing continued discrimination, including ghetto benches and beatings, made her feel increasingly isolated in society.

"She graduated with a master's diploma and a deep conviction that the only place for her would be in a school, instructing Jewish children. She started her teaching career with great energy and dedication. Her first pupils were the children of poor Jews. Teaching these children, and also the need for social work, engrossed her completely and gave her a great deal of satisfaction. When the war broke out, Rachela already had a few years' experience working with the poorest children from Dzika, Wałowa, and Nalewki streets.

"After the creation of the ghetto, she became involved in organizing secret lessons. But for someone with such a lively and at the same time sensitive character as hers, mere teaching was not enough. Already knowing how the poorest children lived, she immediately realized that once the ghetto was closed, they would have an exceptionally difficult time. With all her heart and will power she wished to provide maximum help to those most unfortunate ones.

'A youth circle was the best place to realize her noble designs. Rachela gathered together a large group of youths (15–25). She set them the tasks of providing material aid of all possible forms, organizing recreation for children and keeping up faith in their nation, people subjected to such great suffering who still had a right to their own place in this world. For this purpose, she showed them aspects of their ancient culture, she selected appropriate Jewish literature, and recited the greatest Jewish poetry. She also paid a lot of attention to the children's right to smile and play.

Although in those conditions it might have seemed virtually impossible, methods using appropriate toys, dolls, and puppet theatres were widely known to bring smiles to children's tired faces.

'Rachela, already well practiced in all sorts of work with children in the Jewish school and spurred on by the pain and despair of the tragic fate of the ghetto inhabitants, desired with all her young heart to show that, contrary to everything, her children had a right to smile, to experience joy and to play.

"Hence she constantly had new ideas and initiated actions designed to help children live in relatively normal conditions. Was she successful? Yes, and only thanks to the energetic and devoted work of the boys and girls from her youth circle. She was able to inspire, organize, and engage them in appropriate work. Youth circle members actively helped run so-called children's corners, which were organized through the house committees by Centos, as well as in other diverse cultural and educational actions.

"The youths adored Rachela, as did the children. When she appeared, they'd immediately form a circle around her and there'd be no end to explosions of laughter and joy. I would visit children's corners with Rachela, and, on seeing the happy faces, on the one hand we felt immense joy and on the other hand our hearts were pained at the thought of what would happen with these children tomorrow? The day after tomorrow? What would be their fate? It was at such moments that Rachela proved to be an invaluable companion. Calm, very composed, with her own specific philosophy of just living for today, she was able to instill courage in everyone and, as we used to say in those days, show spirit.

"Frequently she'd remark: 'I don't know what will happen tomorrow, but I know what is happening today, my children are laughing, they're clapping their little hands, forming circles and stamping their feet.' Only someone who knew living conditions in the ghetto can understand this. Only such a person can appreciate how much work, toil, and effort and incredible self-denial was required to create for unfortunate, impoverished, distressed, and exhausted children conditions in which they could laugh and play—at least for a day, because the next day was always so uncertain. All of us knew this, as did exceptionally intelligent and wise Rachela.

All her kinfolk died during the great deportation of July 1942. She survived only because that day she happened to be working in the small ghetto. She loved her family, and simply cherished her parents. This was such a terrible blow that she was close to losing her mind. What probably saved her happened just by chance.

"We advised her that it would be best if she started leaving the ghetto with work brigades employed on the Aryan side. We thought that the change of scenery (not constantly having to look at the tragic sites that made the blood run cold), that this 'difference' would prevent her from taking any desperate measures.

"At first, Rachela wouldn't hear of it, insisting that she could not leave her children and youths.

We adults would in all certainty not have been able to persuade her, had help not come from the youths themselves. The boys and girls rose to the occasion. Like us, they realized that after the killing of her entire family something inside her had snapped, she was on the verge. They understood that their beloved guardian could only be saved if she was somehow shocked out of it. This shock could be work on the other side of the wall. While all our arguments failed to convince her, they found a new argument: 'Miss, you cannot be with the children now because you are sad, and this would have a very bad effect on the infants. Looking at you, Miss, they would no longer be calm.' This convinced her! She started going out to work with the so-called rag-and-bone men.

"This lasted for some 10–15 days. One day they were sorting the rags at a house in Grojecka Street when some terrible news reached them: 'They are raping the ghetto again. New mass deportations.'

"Someone else then shouted out: 'We're not going back to the ghetto!' Before Rachela realized what was going on, her work companions had dispersed. The overseers responsible for the entire brigade on pain of death (the number of group members was recorded on its way out and exactly the same number had to return to the ghetto) had also left their posts. Rachela could not even think of returning to the ghetto as that would have been madness—returning to the ghetto wall now meant certain death.

"And again we do not know what would have happened to brave Rachela were it not for another chance incident—luck was a great ally of all those who survived the occupation. It so happened that the rag sorting point in Grojecka Street was also our secret organization's rendezvous point, above all for people from the ghetto.

'On that very day, I had some underground business to settle there. Seeing Rachela helplessly alone and realizing that she would have almost certainly been shot at the ghetto gate if she returned without the other workers, I offered her my help. Emotionally battered, poor Rachela basically had no choice. She went with me, someone she knew well and now had to trust. I found a fairly safe place for her. It was then that her life turned a new chapter.

"Later, as often happened for those forced to hide during the occupation, she frequently had to move from one flat to another, depending on a multitude of factors. After changing locations several times, the new hosts no longer knew where Rachela was originally from. And it was then that she met a young engineer, also a member of the PPS, who fell in love with this very pretty, kind, and pleasant girl, now of course bearing a totally different name. On account of the need for great caution, no one from those around her knew the whole truth. Naturally, she was also forced not to say anything.

"And so amid the conspiratorial struggles, the suffering and tears, a ray of light illuminated her doorstep. All the appalling experiences and the ongoing terrible war did not create a good situation for young people, yet the will to live, so frequently even in such hard times, proved stronger, and amid the most tragic events beautiful feelings were born.

"So it happened in this case. Rachela, now called Karolina, found in Stanisław a true friend and guardian. He knew nothing about her real background. Yet with his kindness and love, he very gradually restored the image of a caring young Polish male, so badly distorted by young members of the ONR in her student days who had treated Jewish girls far from gallantly.

Once Stanisław started caring for her, the psychological wounds very gradually began to heal. After her most recent experiences, she needed kindness and warmth.

"Then for a long time I lost contact with Rachela/Karolina, as together with Stanisław she joined the partisan movement. Fate brought us together again quite unexpectedly during the Warsaw Uprising. I then saw her in a new role. This was no longer the calm, composed Rachela I knew of old, the one who organized fun and games for children in the ghetto pandemonium.

"Now I saw a soldier, armed and determined to fight the enemy with bullets. Her old courage, which she had expressed in the ghetto by heroically staying to look after the starving children, was now transformed into the need to shoot dead the Nazi enemy. She was a fighter! In her unit, she was known for her extraordinary valor. If it was just too difficult, too dangerous for anyone else, then it would certainly be a job for Karolina. Such was her reputation.

"After liberation, together with Stanisław they created a normal family, with a well-brought-up daughter. But neither the husband nor the daughter knew of Karolina's previous history.

Soon after the war, we ran into each other in the street. After the first outburst of mutual joy at having both survived that hell, she told me: 'Remember that Rachela perished with her entire family on the other side of the wall, now she is a completely different person.' And then for the first time I saw her cry. She wept for a long time, as if with her tears she wished to drown her tragic past, all those bad days. With her tears she was saying farewell to her original family home, to her life story, to her past.

"She never returns to those subjects. When she meets people she knows from those old days, she pretends to be someone else. Between her and me, the only person who knows her earlier past, there is a specific intimacy.

"There are times when she avoids me. We may not see each other for two or three years. There are times when she manages for a while to forget about her past. Then she is happy and enjoys the present. At other times, however, she is overcome by a boundless longing for the close ones she lost, her siblings, parents, and the community where she grew up. At such times she visits me, she wants to be in touch with me. I am the person who links her with her original family home, who reminds her of her kinfolk and is associated with those memories, so difficult to erase, with those times. I understand her well! I understand and respect this split personality.

"I never impose my company on her because I know that when she avoids me, it means that she is happy living in the lives of her husband and daughter, with her current circle of friends."

**

"The guardian of the youth circle at No. 24 Elektoralna (Electoral) Street was the professional teacher **Jan Izaak Kiernicel**, a graduate of Warsaw University with a master's degree in Polish studies—an exceptionally talented erudite and with very good academic prospects. A year before the war he started work on a doctoral thesis under the guidance of Professor Wacław Borowy. He had considerable literary skills. His broad range of interests also made him a very interesting person.

"He came from a wealthy intelligentsia family, with whose world views, since adolescence, he could not agree. While still studying, he was given a large family inheritance. "I didn't get it through my own work, so how can I accept it?" he'd tell his friends. And then, to the horror of his relatives, he gave the entire fortune away to a charity.

"With a tendency to philosophize, he was what some people would term a duffer. Always modest, he was incapable of asserting his will on others. All his energy was devoted to acquiring knowledge. He linked his academic interests with social work. Youths adored him (he taught the older classes in lyceums—secondary schools), but he was also respected and appreciated by fellow teachers. This was a great personality. Any sign of anti-Semitism pained him, all the more so as he considered himself to be fully Polish. The war broke out when he was doing military exercises. The fighting took him all the way to the defense of Warsaw, yet even then he was often abused and persecuted on account of his background. Incarceration in the ghetto was for him a particularly tragic experience.

"For long weeks after being forced along with other Jews into the ghetto, he seemed to have lost contact with reality. For days he absorbed philosophical and historical books in search of a solution to the political upheavals.

"Perhaps he would have had a nervous breakdown or done something extreme at the very start of his stay within the ghetto walls were it not for the youth circle. Acquaintances, seeing the desperate state he was in, encouraged him to start working for a house committee. This teacher who loved young people, this natural pedagogue, seeing so many boys and girls in his house living without purpose, in those terrible circumstances, driven day to day nearer to desperation and breakdown, overcame his own crisis. His soul opened up to everything that was the best, the most beautiful, and valuable. He set about forming a youth circle. No one could inspire young people to work and act the way he did.

"Thus, his circle became one of the best.

"Members were engaged in teaching children who were too sick to attend other organized classes. He scrupulously researched the situation of families in his area to find the most forsaken urchins. Initially, although it took a lot of searching, he was generally able to secure places for them in orphanages. Later this became practically impossible as all the care homes were filled way beyond capacity.

"But the great social activist Jan Izaak and his brave youths could not pass a child in such a tragic situation with indifference. Soon they found the right contacts on the so-called Aryan side and the urchins were sent on their own to care institutions beyond the ghetto wall.

"Apart from saving individual children, this youth circle also carried out beautiful work of a more spiritual nature for the community. It certainly stood out as far as the organization of cultural, educational, and intellectual life was concerned. There was a permanent discussion club where every Tuesday and Thursday talks were given on diverse subjects, ranging from philosophy to literature, history, and other disciplines.

"On account of their guardian and teacher, there were also very interesting literary evenings, usually to mark a specific anniversary. I'll never forget one such evening dedicated to the anniversary of the October Revolution.

The very idea of organizing such an event in the wretched, closed ghetto, where every gathering of people was severely punished, made it a highly memorable occasion. After an exhaustive introduction, followed by an excellently argued lecture by the guardian himself, came an impressive artistic programme. Both the selection of poetry, by authors such as Tuwim, and its delivery were just spellbinding. To this day, I can see and hear a beautiful girl of 15 or so reciting the revolutionary poetry of Broniewski with such feeling, earnestness, and understanding that in our secret venue we began to think our intensely desired liberation was waiting for us just beyond the door. Then very quietly but so wonderfully, played with such great talent and virtuosity, we heard Chopin's *Revolutionary Etude*.

"Perhaps no writer is capable of reproducing the atmosphere, the sheer experience that was awakening in people at that moment in time—an evening that thanks to poetry and art was liberating in people all the finest emotions. But, unfortunately, these feelings were only to be stifled the moment they left the building and saw the most hideous wall of hatred and murder.

After a few months of intensively getting to know his youths and learning their individual aptitudes, Jan Izaak made a very prudent decision. He divided the circle into small groups, according to particular interests and abilities.

"Henceforth, some members organized care of abandoned children, others taught sick children, and yet other youths organized the discussion and literary evenings. Those who were the most militant, who showed the greatest interest in politics, now formed the circle's covert action group. And what did they do?

"They became carriers of the underground press. The house caretaker, being fully aware of the dangers involved, let them use his small office for storing and distributing these illegal newspapers. With time, in this office, they also started duplicating some of the more interesting articles to be distributed both inside and outside the ghetto. The need to maintain the utmost caution and practical limitations as to the number of copies that could actually be printed made this group's work a significant contribution to the upholding of political awareness. It was with considerable difficulty that they could carry at most a few underground newspapers at any one time.

"These few youths formed a highly secret conspiratorial cell. The youth circle had an invaluable contact called Wanda Zieleńczyk (Dziula).[7] This wonderful activist and communist took a lively interest in the ideological work of the ghetto youths. I would bring all sorts of material on the life and activities of youth circles within the Jewish Residential District to her parent's flat in Koszykowa Street. On one occasion, I was very lucky to avoid arrest; I left just 15 minutes before the police arrived.

"Most of the youth circle members died in the tragic July of 1942. The remainder, together with their guardian, joined work brigades sent to work on the Aryan side and thus managed to escape from the ghetto. Some went to the forests, while three of the boys and a girl remained with Jan in Warsaw. They were all very actively engaged in the underground movement. Their guardian quickly arranged places for them in secret secondary school classes. The girl also started attending a course for nurses. With great enthusiasm, Jan worked in the underground press, while at the same time he also gave lectures at secret classes in Warsaw, Otwock, and Świder.

"There were also some very difficult moments when they desperately had to find a place to stay, and they were not infrequently hounded by blackmailers and informers. Finally came the tragic Warsaw Uprising. The girl, having appropriate training, joined the Medical Service. I never managed to find out from her what she actually did. The three boys and Jan were in the Old Town when it all started. It is said they fought bravely almost to the very end. Just before the insurgent Old Town was bloodily crushed, one of the boys, the youngest, was sent out with a message and never returned to base. Another of the boys was killed on the very last day of fighting. The third boy got out through the sewers with one of the last insurgent groups. Later, he joined detachments of the Polish Army bound for Berlin. As well as being involved in the armed fighting, he also wrote interesting frontline reportages for the military press. I met him one more time after the war in the Jewish Committee, where he was looking for kinfolk. Unfortunately, he found no one in Poland. Soon afterward, he moved to France, where he had some distant relatives. There he married, has two children and is happy. Jan Izaak died in Warsaw a few years after the war."

***

"While in terms of organization all the youth circles were fairly similar, there were differences between them in other respects. Though in the main they concentrated on upbringing, ideology, education, and culture, each circle had its individual character.

"The many thousands of people enclosed within the ghetto did not constitute a homogenous group (some considered themselves to be Jews, but there were others who knew nothing of the Jewish language and felt they were Poles raised for centuries in Polish culture), so too the ideological and educational program in individual circles varied. And everything they did had profound educational and ideological meaning. The importance of their work increased as month after month the situation became more tragic. The teaching program became richer because life was posing increasingly more urgent problems.

"For example, during the terrible winter of 1942, which was the worst on account of the hunger and freezing temperatures, ghetto youths used all their energy and initiative to save the youngest children. How did they do it? They would find the wealthiest communities to put on cultural events. There they were able to charge double the normal price for a ticket and raise as much money as possible.[8]

"How much fortitude, self-denial, and social conscientiousness verging on heroism must have been required when they, themselves, frequently hungry and mistreated, recited poetry or sang, with the thought: 'I'm doing it for children who are even more hungry than me.' [It is worth noting here that education and culture was promoted in the youth circles and house committees by some outstanding Jewish artists, such as Jonasz Turkow,[9] who, incidentally, 20 years later nominated Irena Sendler's candidature for the Righteous Among the Nations award. – A.M.]

Moreover, the youth circles contributed greatly to propagating a sense of social responsibility among young people and combating the selfish attitudes of some who in the bitter struggle for survival frequently forgot about the basic rules of living in a community. They stimulated youths intellectually and culturally. They inspired youths ideologically to help them overcome the pervasive sense of hopelessness. The example set by thriving youth circles encouraged the more passive circles to try harder.

"These youths, not always understood by the generally maltreated and quite distraught adult community, frequently persecuted by the ghetto police and continually hiding from the invader, were exceptionally receptive to every kind word or gesture; they were extremely appreciative if people showed just a bit of consideration and warmth—these were wonderful young people.

They constantly searched for new ways to prepare for the armed struggle. They struggled together for survival, every day. There everyone tried to make sure no one else from their "large family" felt lonely. The war had separated those many boys and girls from their workshops or studies. Some were now willing to take up any work in order to survive, while others engaged themselves in underground activities, ready to stand on all fronts in the struggle for freedom. Others still undertook the dangerous task of secret teaching, but many more became quite apathetic and totally despondent. These were the ones who required special attention. They needed to be surrounded with care and helped to endure that period of hell. The fate of their families was usually tragic. In the circles, the youths were helped to overcome their inhibitions, shyness, and awkwardness. Here they summoned up the civilian courage to express their own opinions, views, and judgements. Not infrequently they became so enraged that it required a great deal of tact, composure, and persuasiveness to stop them from taking any rash and untimely actions. In their work, the youth circles searched for methods and advice on how to shake the sad, hopeless ghetto out of its despair-driven stupor, to revive the community and restore faith in the future. The young waited with hope for a better tomorrow. Despite the murders, slaughter, and cruelty around them, they believed they'd be able to build a better, more wonderful world—that the time for them would come. Thus they became increasingly involved in the ghetto's growing political underground.

"They observed the preparations in the ghetto for an ultimate, armed showdown with the Nazi oppressor. Some belonged to paramilitary units readying themselves expressly for armed conflict. At the same time, they saw what was happening around them and felt increasingly isolated. Their work steadily became harder without the benefits of teaching them anything useful. It was becoming increasingly more difficult to find a common language and understanding with the older generations. Some were keen, while others approached work with ever greater reluctance. It was now more difficult to find consistency and solidarity among the youths themselves.

Looming over the ghetto were the dark clouds of its terrible end."[10]

Notes

1. An important supplement to Irena Sendler's description can be found in Robert Szuchta and Piotr Trojański's book *Holokaust, zromumieć dlaczego*, Warsaw, 2003, p. 172: "In Warsaw by the end of April 1940 there were 788 house committees in 878 houses, in May 1940 there were 1,518 in 2,014 houses and by September 1940 there were some twenty thousand committees. Later their number fell, to 1,108 in January 1942 . . . The committees appointed social welfare commissions for: finance, events, claims for benefits, child care, clothes collection, etc. Circles were also formed for: youths, women, the care of old people's homes, orphanages, deportee shelters or soup kitchens. An extended house committee could have 30–40 members. The committees organized scores of meetings to collect money for ongoing activities as well as collections of food (bread, bowls of soup), coal, medicines, etc. House committee members tried to compel the wealthy inhabitants of the ghetto to contribute generously, they wrote petitions . . . Pickets were

organized to ask housewives to donate some of their potatoes, carrots or beetroots when they returned from the market. There were also so-called spoon actions in which the tenants of a house would each donate a spoon (teaspoon) of flour, sugar, kasha and such like. Moral sanctions were imposed on those who refused to contribute: blacklists were posted in the entrances to houses stating which residents had avoided helping the community and as a result other people would not shake hands with them.

2. Stanisław Słoński (1879–1959), a linguist, the organizer and director of the University of Warsaw Slavic Studies School.

3. Ludwik Hirszfeld (1884–1954), microbiologist, immunologist, serologist, one of the founders of the science of blood types. In 1941, he was the head of the Health Council and a professor of the secret Medical Faculty of the University of Warsaw inside the Warsaw ghetto.

4. *Umschlagplatz* (German): a reloading yard and railway siding by Stawki Street, where Warsaw ghetto inhabitants were gathered for deportation to death camps.

5. In 1943, the Gestapo used the Hotel Polski to hold Jews with foreign citizenship papers (usually forged) under the pretence that they would be exchanged for German citizens held by the Allies. In fact, most of the Jews were murdered in concentration camps or Pawiak Prison.

6. Camp of Great Poland was a National Democracy organization in the years 1926–1933. Later, it was renamed the National Radical Camp.

7. Wanda Zieleńczyk, pseudonym Dziula (1920–1943), a youth activist and poet who was arrested by the Gestapo on July 21, 1943, and shot in Pawiak Prison on August 27, 1943.

8. Antoni Marianowicz writes about this in his book *Życie surowo wzbronione*, pp. 59–60: "In his orphanage [Doctor Janusz Korczak] organised concerts. I once went to one of those concerts—I got the tickets from my father, who had undertaken to help distribute them. This help basically meant that Korczak gave father some carnets of tickets and father later gave Korczak the money for the tickets he had managed to sell, but father, not wishing to waste time, would simply pay for the tickets himself. Thus I always had plenty of tickets for myself and my friends."

9. Jonasz Turkow (1898–1988), actor, director, and theatre manager who after the war settled in Israel.

10. These are extensive fragments (corrected and supplemented) from Irena Sendler's recollections that were published in 1981 in *Biuletyn Żydowskiego Instytutu Historycznego*, nr 2, pp. 89–118. ("O działalności kół młodzieży w getcie warszawskim.") In the last fragment (which was left out for editorial purposes), Irena Sendler wrote: "The later histories of the youth circles, after the first liquidation, lasting from July 1942 to the autumn of that year, are closely tied with the overall tragic history of the ghetto. After the various terrible, bloody transports and the great action, both the house committees and the youth circles virtually

ceased to exist. The survivors of the decimated ghetto were put to work in so-called barns [workshops producing items for the Germans on ghetto territory], a few months later to rise as the first center of resistance in Warsaw, take up arms and engage in bloody battle against the enemy. The ranks of those heroic insurgents included many boys and girls from the youth circles." Elsewhere in her memoir, Irena Sendler describes the play corners for the youngest children, which were run by people like Romana Wysznacka and Estera Markin. Before the war, they had been assistants of Professor Władysław Witwicki, a renowned psychologist at the University of Warsaw. The professor was interested in the fate of his former students and their work as teachers in the ghetto. He helped them by sending toys for the children (dolls he had carved himself) and food.

7

The Great Action

In the winter of 1942, living conditions in the ghetto deteriorated even more. Adults and children were dying of hunger, the cold, and disease. In January, the Social Welfare Department undertook an action to stamp down on children begging in various parts of Warsaw. As described by Jan Dobraczyński after the war, the initiative actually came from the German police. "[The German police] commandant drew attention to the fact that there was an enormous number of child beggars on Warsaw's streets. The action was prepared in the following way. One cold and snowy January day we sent out a few municipal trucks. In each there were two social workers from the department, accompanied by a blue [Polish] police constable. All the urchins encountered on the way were collected and delivered to the Distribution Office in Przebieg Street. There they were to be washed, given new clothes, and fed. They were to spend the next three days there. In that time, physicians, psychologists, and nurses were to examine the whole group. The lorries had barely started returning with the first children when I discovered something quite shocking—almost half of the delivered urchins were Jewish! The whole of Warsaw knew that Jewish children were slipping out of the ghetto to beg, and people willingly helped them. By the end of the action, over 30 Jewish children had been collected. They were fed and spent a few hours in the warmth. I telephoned Janusz Korczak (at the time there was still a telephone connection with the ghetto), and told him about the children. He replied he was ready to take them in. We agreed that the children would return to the ghetto through a hole in the wall very near the Office (the children themselves told me about this hole). When it was quite dark, half an hour before curfew, I went out with the children. The hole was concealed behind a heap of black, iced-over snow. One of ours called out quietly. A voice answered: "We're here from the Doctor." The children, one after another, disappeared into the hole; they approached the pile of snow and suddenly melted away in the darkness. "The last one's coming!" I called. "She's gone through, okay," came the answer from the other side of the wall. And then I also heard the child call, the last one, a pretty, perhaps nine-year-old girl who had been standing beside me all the time and informing me of various matters concerning life in the ghetto: "Goodbye, sir."[1]

I ask Mrs. Sendler if she remembers this action. "I certainly do," she replies. "This was a major controversy between us. It even turned into a very unpleasant argument. I could not understand why all those children had not been sent to one of the children's homes we were cooperating with [on the Aryan side]. Dobraczyński explained that he was following the instructions of his superiors, who had received a very explicit order from the Germans. Dobraczyński had been promised that if the children returned to the ghetto that very same day, no harm would come to them."

Such was the winter. A few months later, the situation for both adults and children in the ghetto took an even more dramatic turn for the worse. "Both my colleagues and I observed their living conditions deteriorate literally from day to day," recalls Irena Sendler. "One day in the summer, I received instructions to serve as guide for a man visiting the ghetto. He was led into the ghetto by a trusted person through a tunnel under Muranowska Street. His objective was to witness, first hand but undercover, the tragic conditions of the Jews' daily lives, and I was one of several people to accompany him inside the ghetto. Each of us had a white handkerchief by which he could recognize us. Thus the man would follow one guide until another guide took over.

The objective was to maintain safety precautions, so that the visitor would never find himself in a situation without any means of escape. This visitor was Jan Karski,[2] the courier of the commander of the Polish Home Army (AK). But I only found out about this after the war.[3]

Various underground organizations on the Aryan side tried to help the powerless Jewish population in the Warsaw ghetto. However, this help was always insufficient. There was also some professional solidarity; for instance, artists saved other artists, lawyers rescued lawyers and doctors rescued doctors.

"On the night of Wednesday, July 22, 1942, the Germans (SS units and a Ukrainian detachment) began the Great Action of transporting Jews to Treblinka, which lasted until September 21, 1942. Every day over 6,000 women, children, and old people were sent out in transports from the ghetto's Umschlagplatz. In that period, over 300,000 Jews were murdered."

After the war, when he was already in exile, Stefan Korboński[4] recalled the mistrust and lack of understanding encountered by all those who not without great difficulty and risking their own lives had tried to inform the world of what was happening in the Warsaw ghetto: "It started when I sent to London a series of dispatches, one after the other, informing them that the liquidation of the ghetto had started on July 22, 1942. In batches of 7,000, people were loaded into freight cars in Stawki Street and transported east to Majdanek, where they were all gassed. I was greatly surprised when, contrary to their regular practice, the BBC made absolutely no use of these dispatches and not a single word was mentioned about this in news broadcasts. I therefore sent a separate message in which I demanded an explanation for their silence. To my even greater astonishment this message also remained unanswered. But I was not going to give up so easily and personally saw to it that each time they contacted London, the telegraphers would request a reply to all the aforementioned despatches. This game continued for a few days and then, presumably on account of the daily alerts from the radio station, the government finally answered. But their message did not explain much. In full it stated the following: 'Not all your dispatches are suitable for publication.'

"I was racking my brains to make any sense of it. Here they are shipping out and murdering 7,000 people a day, and in London they believe that this information is not suitable for broadcasting?! It was only after a month that the BBC aired the news based on our information. It was many months later that a government emissary, who had parachuted into the country, explained: 'No one believed your dispatches. The government didn't believe you and nor did the British. They said you had exaggerated with the anti-German propaganda. It was only when the British received confirmation from their own sources that consternation ensued and the BBC broadcast your news.' "[5]

Many eyewitness accounts from this period have survived in Ringelblum's Archive. They do not require any comments.

Nathan, a worker at Ostdeutsche Bautischlerei-Werkstätte, wrote:

"On the night of September 5th/6th [1942] the tragic news spread. All the 'shops,' i.e., work brigades sent out to work for the Germans on the 'Aryan side' were to be disbanded. By 10:00 in the morning of Sunday September 6th everyone was to leave their home and assemble in a rectangle between Miła, Lubeckiego, and Stawki streets. There a new segregation of workers would be conducted and only those who passed the selection would be allowed to return home. I myself live in Miła Street: on September 6th I stood in the window from the morning onward and observed. No words, no picture can express the horror of that morning.

"Tens of thousands of emaciated, distraught, unwashed faces. Mothers with children in their arms, crying children torn away from their mothers. Masses, masses, and yet more masses of people moving to and fro, helplessness in their eyes. The endless procession just keeps on going. And the continual segregation; some are turned back, but most, tens of thousands, are led to Umschlagplatz."[6]

Notes

1. Jan Dobraczyński, *Tylko w jednym życiu*, Warszawa, 1970, pp. 231–232.

2. Jan Karski (original surname Kozielewski, 1914–2000), during the war, served two times as a courier in occupied Poland. Between August 20 and 25, 1942, Karski twice visited the ghetto. On October 1, he travelled to the West (he reached London in November!) with a mission to tell the world the truth about the tragic fate of the Jews. "He met representatives of the Polish Government [in Exile] as well as English politicians and journalists. His report made an enormous impression, but did not change Allied war policy, even if the Polish Government offered him strategic advice on how to stop the German genocidal madness. From London, Karski travelled to the United States of America, where he was granted a long meeting with President Roosevelt. But even the Jews, including Morgenthau, could not believe what he was saying. In June 1982 a tree bearing Jan Karski's name was planted in the Avenue of the Righteous Among the Nations," thus wrote Nathan Gross in an article entitled "Irena and Jan," which came out in the Polish language weekly *Nowiny – Kurier* in Tel Aviv on August 1, 2003.

After the war he became a distinguished historian and political scientist, a professor at Georgetown University in Washington, D.C., and the author of a number of publications, including *The Secret State*.

3. "Since the end of 1941 the government [in exile in London] started receiving reports on the mass murder of Jews, and in June 1942 it sent a report to the governments of Allied states concerning this matter. . . . In December 1942 Minister [Edward] Raczyński sent Allied governments an extensive report on the mass exterminations of Jews up to that point. Detailed accounts of the situation in the ghettos and the perpetrated murders were reported by Jan Karski, the AK commander's courier, to the Polish government, and next to the governments of Britain and America. Thanks to Karski's many statements and interviews, public opinion in the English speaking world learned of the ongoing extermination of Jews. The Polish government tried to persuade their Western Allies to answer Nazi terror by retaliating against the German civilian population. They

frequently repeated this appeal, but the Allies consistently refused. Yet despite requests from Jewish leaders, the Polish government delayed issuing an appeal for compatriots in occupied Poland to help the Jews. So great was their fear not to deepen the discord within the government, and especially the underground movement, of which a significant part comprised groups that were unsympathetic or even hostile toward the Jews." – Andrzej Friszke, *Polska. Losy państwa i narodu 1939–1989*, Warsaw, 2003.

We know that already in 1940, during his first courier mission to the West, Jan Karski submitted a report to the Polish Government-in-Exile on the "mounting threat to the Jewish people." His first report constituted "a rare and historically valuable documentation of the terror in its early stages." His "account of the Jewish problem in the homeland" was a shocking particularization of the cruelties and humiliations the Jews were being subjected to in occupied Poland. It included descriptions of incidents he had personally witnessed. The report also contains a review of the living conditions of Jews in every part of the occupied country." The emissary stated that: "in the western parts of the country which have been annexed by Germany the situation of the Jews is clear and easy to understand: they are beyond the law. . . . The Jews are practically deprived of any means of survival. In turn in central Poland, i.e., the General Government, the Germans would like to create a type of Jewish reservation." E. Thomas Wood and Stanisław M. Jankowski, *Karski. Opowieść o emisariuszu*, Kraków-Oświęcim, 1996, p. 73.

4. Stefan Korboński (1903–1989), prose writer and journalist. He was one of the organizers of the Polish Underground Movement in Warsaw. From mid-1941 he was the head of the Directorate of Civil Resistance (KWC). From March 1945, he became a deputy prime minister in the underground government and the last Government Delegate at Home to be nominated by the Polish Government-in-Exile.

5. Stefan Korboński, *W imieniu Rzeczypospolitej . . .*, Paris, 1954, pp. 253–255.

6. *Ringelblum Archive*, "Dzień po dniu Zagłady." Selected and submitted to print by Katarzyna Madoń-Mitzner in collaboration with Agnieszka Jarzębowska and Tadeusz Epsztein, *Karta*, nr 39/2003, p. 52.

8

I Saw It

German cruelty knew no bounds. In the tragic days of that sweltering summer of 1942, "to every party that was deported were added children from nurseries and orphanages." [1]

Teresa Prekerowa cites a fragment from a pamphlet published by the Polish Home Army in December 1942 and entitled *Liquidation of the Warsaw Ghetto* (Likwidacja getta warszawskiego), in which under the date August 19, Antoni Szymanowski wrote:

"Yesterday an order was issued for all the Jewish children to assemble tomorrow morning at Umschlagplatz. So too all those who do not have a work card. Their determination to persecute small children is dumbfounding. This evening on the corner of Gęsia and Okopowa Streets I saw a cluster of 150–200 small children huddled tightly together. Opposite them stood a pair of Germans, their guns levelled at this throng of tiny individuals. The children were most visibly crazed with fear, they were crying, cowering, biting their fingers. A short distance away stood a small group of women—probably their mothers. One of them broke away and ran up to the German to explain something, she was gesticulating with her hands, pointing to a child. The German roared at her, the way only they can, and ordered her to return to the other women. He was threatening her with his gun. She turned and started running back—he fired the gun and she fell to the ground, dead."[2]

Irena Sendler described how she remembered Korczak[3] proceed with the children of his orphanage to their death. By then he was very sick, but he nevertheless walked very erect, his face resembling a mask, ostensibly composed:

"He walked at the head of this tragic procession. He held the youngest child in his arm and with his other hand he was leading another infant. That's how various people have recorded it in their memoirs, whereas others record it differently, but this doesn't mean anyone has made a mistake. One has only to remember that the route from the orphanage to the Umschlagplatz was long. It lasted four hours. I saw them when they were turning from Żelazna Street into Leszno Street.

The children were very neatly dressed. They wore blue cotton uniforms. The whole procession marched in fours, quite sprightly, with dignity and in step to Umschlagplatz; to the square of death!

"Who had a right to pass such a sentence, one quite unprecedented in history? That all-powerful master of Germany, Adolf Hitler, had condemned Jewish children, just like the adults, the old and the sick, to the gas chambers.

"And how did the world respond? Those mighty powers? The world was silent! And silence may sometimes be understood as tacit consent to what is actually happening.

"So how did it happen, how could it be that tiny children and a beautiful youth, who are the bright hope of every country's future, here in Poland, in Warsaw on a hot summer's day, on August 5th or 6th are collectively going to die? Because before them other children from other orphanages and dormitories have already gone. They go to a death that was planned for them far away by wonderful scholars of the great German state—the creators of the greatest invention of those days: Zyklon B! The pride of their nation!

"And as the children proceed, they think about Rabindranath Tagore's play *The Post Office*,[4] which they so recently performed in their orphanage. To better understand why the children were told extracts from this story, I will recount the basic plot: A small boy, Amal, is sick. He has to lie in bed. His only recreation is to observe life through the window. Outside his window pass a postman, a girl with flowers, a water carrier, and a dairyman. There, beyond the window, children play. The flowers smell enticingly. Singing can be heard. The small, sick boy absorbs everything and experiences all the events. He yearns for freedom, he wants to escape to the country, enjoy the sun and kiss the flowers. But the stern and thoughtless doctor orders the windows to be closed and lets no sign of autumn or sunlight into the room. For the small boy it seems that the great mountain outside his window has hands, drawn out to the heavens! Amal loves those hands. He strains to break out of the stuffy room and follow the road nobody knows. He is calmed when they assure him the time will come when the doctor will himself lead him out. But instead someone more important, wiser arrives and frees him.

"There are sometimes short breaks in this mournful march. The children need to rest a little bit. And then I imagined the Old Doctor [Korczak] telling them that a letter from the king has just arrived, and in it, as in the story, he invites them to take a long journey on a open road with beautifully blooming flowers and murmuring streams, and with the high mountain raising its hands to the heavens . . .

"After all, the children should not know until the last moment, until the lethal hands of the German criminals close the doors of the evil freight cars bound for Treblinka and death.

The children mustn't know until the very end. In their tiny hands the youngest ones hold the Plasticine dolls that Professor Władysław Witwicki had made and which had been delivered to the orphanage by two of his former assistants, Dr. Romana Wysznacka and Dr. Ester Markinówna.

"Trapped inside the ghetto, these women did not waste time. They ran the so-called play corners for the very youngest infants, thus making sad, tragic childhoods more pleasant. And the infants, clutching their dolls, which were made out of love especially for them by a University of Warsaw professor of psychology, did not yet know that very soon the beastly hands of Hitlerite oppressors would close them inside deadly freight cars, full of carbide and lime, and that they would embark on the last journey of their lives.

"After all, the recently prepared play entitled *The Post Office* was supposed to draw their attention away from what was actually happening outside their windows. And at the time outside their windows the worst possible things were happening!

"The tragic summer of 1942 was a real hell. Frequent roundups of ordinary pedestrians in the street, hunger, and spotted typhus were claiming victims every day. On top of that there were the continual shootings of quite innocent and quite defenseless people.

"The idea of drawing children's attention away from such evident horrors could only have been thought up and realized by someone like Korczak, for no one in the world was more sensitive and loving toward all children. And at the same time, in that ghetto hell his ingenious mind was able to foresee the very worst.

"Indeed, the very worst was now about to happen. It was approaching the ghetto with terrifying speed. And Korczak selected such a play because it ended with a positive accent. 'Because a letter from the king has just arrived,' he told the children, 'who is inviting us to a beautiful, liberated country.'

"I was at the orphanage to see that play. And then, when on August 6, 1942, I saw that tragic parade in the street, those innocent children walking obediently in the procession of death and listening to the doctor's optimistic words, I do not know why for me and for all the other eyewitnesses our hearts did not break.

"But our hearts remained intact, and what also remained were thoughts that to this day cannot be understood by any normal person.

"Of all my wartime experiences, including the tortures in Pawiak Prison and Gestapo headquarters in Szucha Avenue, as well as the dying youths in the hospital where I worked during the Warsaw Uprising, none made as great an impression on me as the sight of Korczak and the children's procession to their appointment with death.

"I cannot understand why that day witnesses of that funeral procession did nothing. People in the street were shocked, but silent. I know onlookers in the street were unable to help.[5] They were unarmed, frightened, terrorized. And tired, having struggled for three years just to survive. An underground movement was already operating inside the ghetto, but it wasn't yet strong enough to challenge German might. They had no weapons.

"One has to state it bluntly and baldly: the ghetto Jews died alone! Not even the Jewish financiers in Great Britain and the United States would believe the words of an eyewitness who saw the crimes committed against Jews every day of the war in Nazi occupied Poland.

I also saw it."

Notes

1. Teresa Prekerowa, *Zarys dziejów Żydów w Polsce w latach 1939–1945*, Warsaw, 1992, p. 103.
2. Teresa Prekerowa, *Konspiracyjna Rada Pomocy Żydom w Warszawie 1942–1945*, Warsaw, 1982, pp. 35–36.
3. Janusz Korczak, real name Henryk Goldszmidt (1978/1979–1942), physician and pedagogue.
4. The play *The Post Office* was performed in the orphanage on Saturday July 18, 1942. It was prepared by one of the teachers, Ester Winogrónówna, who was sent to Treblinka at the end of July.
5. In an interview with Tomasz Szarota, Irena Sendler said: "I usually went to the ghetto in the afternoons, after my normal work. Yet this time I was there before noon. I was going down Leszno Street toward Żelazna Street, heading for the exit between Żelazna Street and Chłodna Street, where the guards were and the gate through which I could leave.... There were few passers-by in the street.

Everyone was heading in their own direction, no one was stopping. People were scared. I was aware that Korczak and the children were going to be killed because before them children from other institutions had been directed to Umschlagplatz."—"'Ostatnia droga Doktora.'" Rozmowa z Ireną Sendlerową – Jolantą, kierowniczką referatu dziecięcego w Żegocie, o ostatnich dniach Janusza Korczaka." *Polityka*, nr 21, May 3–4, 1997.

9

Why Żegota Was Formed

After the Great Action, the only people who remained in the ghetto were the workers employed in plants producing for the Germans and their families, of which there were now very few, as well as a relatively small number of people in hiding—who, of course, were not working. Officially, the ghetto population was reduced to 40,000, but historians estimate that another 30,000 people were there illegally. The action was a massive shock to the terrorized Polish population and underground activists, who felt quite helpless in face of such a major tragedy.

After the Great Action, in October 1942, the Germans increased security measures. The Social Welfare Department was put under stricter supervision. They started checking whether help was actually going to places entered in official records. There was now a great danger of being uncovered, which would mean a tragic end not only for the staff but also for the thousands of Jews who were relying on them for survival. The needs were enormous and yet the already meager resources dwindled.

"One of my colleagues, Stefa Wichlińska,"[1] recalls Mrs. Sendler, "was aware of my difficult situation. She knew I was unofficially helping the Jews. She informed me of a new organization that had been founded on the initiative of, among others, the famous writer Zofia Kossak-Szczucka. The organization was called Żegota.[2] This was already in December 1942. She gave me the address in the Śródmieście district (at 24 Żurawia Street, Flat No. 4 on the third floor) to report to and ask for Trojan. When I went there, the door was opened by a man—Marek Arczyński as I later found out[3]—who led me to a tiny room at the end of the flat (this was a large five-room apartment). There I met Trojan, that is, Julian Grobelny. I told him in detail about the help we were secretly providing to the Jews and about the great problems we had on account of the financial cuts the Germans had imposed on us. Trojan listened to me carefully and then asked a number of questions. Finally, he said: 'We'll work wonderfully together because you have a trusted network of women couriers and we have the money.' Later he appointed me to run the Jewish children's aid section. Thus I became a very active member of the social Konrad Żegota Committee to Aid the Jewish Population."

Zofia Kossak-Szczucka, a famous writer (known for anti-Jewish views before the war!), already in August 1942 wrote: "The world looks on at this crime, which is more terrible than anything history has seen before, and—is silent. The slaughter of millions of defenseless people is conducted amid a worldwide, ominous silence. The perpetrators are silent, they do not boast of what they do. England is silent, so is America, even the international Jewry, previously so sensitive to any harm against its people, is silent."[4]

Those were bitter words uttered too late. So many had already died and could no longer be helped. But awareness of the danger threatening the lives of those who still remained demanded swift and effective action. Effectiveness was limited to what was available, or rather by the desperate scarcity of everything. Many activists now experienced a rude awakening. They realized the need to create a special, secret organization, above political divisions, devoted to helping the Jews. A secret institution was founded that received direct funding from the Polish underground authorities and was answerable to the Government Delegation in Poland for the Polish Government in Exile. It was through these channels that money also came from Jewish organizations in the United States. Zofia Kossak-Szczucka categorically stated: "Those who are silent in the face of murder become the murderer's accomplices. Those who fail to condemn, express consent."

The Provisional Committee to Aid Jews was founded on September 27 and was headed by Zofia Kossak-Szczucka[5] and Wanda Krahelska-Filipowicz.[6] On December 4, 1942, the committee was transformed into the Council to Aid Jews.[7] The council's fictitious patron was Konrad Żegota. The first radioed telegram, which was sent on October 31, 1942 to London to the deputy prime minister of the Polish Government in Exile, Stanisław Mikołajczyk, requested for a 'monthly grant of half a million zlotys'! Such was the scale of needs. Yet by December 4 the Government Delegation in Poland only granted 70,000 zlotys—and that in two installments! The shortage of money lasted until the end of the war, but there was no shortage of excellent organization. The acquisition of extra funds was attempted in many ways. Each Council member had a special function. When Irena Sendler became the head of the Children's Section,[8] its monthly budget amounted to approximately 80,000 zlotys, whereas in the first months of the following year, 1943, it rose to over 100,000. We also know that at the start of the Warsaw Uprising it approached 250,000 zlotys a month.

"I was most amazed to learn of the scrupulous way in which the accounts were kept in those wartime conditions . . .Those responsible for delivering set sums of money (500 zlotys; in exceptional circumstances 1,000 zlotys) were given receipts from the beneficiaries or their guardians, which were next truthfully recorded in special ledgers. These books were run by an associate of Żegota, the prewar defense lawyer Maurycy Herling-Grudziński."[9]

Irena Sendler recalls: "I would collect the money for the children directly from Grobelny and I would bring all the receipts back to him. It was in my interest to collect the receipts as I was answerable to him for the money. Vast sums passed through my hands and it was a great relief to me when I could prove that the money reached the right place.

"Unfortunately, the Children's Section documentation, which was kept in a house in Boerner (today the Warsaw district of Bemowo), disappeared. This was a great pity because it included receipts signed by the older children or guardians, in the case of infants.[10] Today, over 60 years later, it is difficult to establish how many activists there were in the Children's Section."

In her book,[11] Teresa Prekerowa emphasizes that work in Żegota was Irena Sendler's primary concern. Prekerowa attributes the energy and extensive range of activities of the children's section to Irena Sendler's initiative, her self-denial and complete dedication. Of the dozen or so people she worked with only two, perhaps three or four, were oriented in Żegota affairs. The rest, even though they collaborated closely, delivering the money, personally looking after the saved children, knew nothing of Żegota's existence. "Such were the requirements of effective conspiracy," stresses Irena Sendler. "The basic rule was to tell no one about what you were doing. This had certain consequences after the Gestapo arrested me, for it took my close colleagues a very long time to find the only person who could help me in this case. Nevertheless, when I think about it now, many decades later, I believe Żegota's work was of enormous importance to Jews and Poles alike. The founding of this organization provided a vital chance for those who survived the terrible period of the Great Action. And this was not just temporary help. Regular contact with those who delivered the funds gave the survivors a feeling of safety, the comforting thought that someone remembered them and was trying to help in the face of mortal danger. The allowances from Żegota were small, but they came regularly. The sums those under our care received were indeed quite inadequate for their situation, when they continually had to remain in hiding and when prices were constantly rising. I remember a time when pork fat cost as much as 1,400 zlotys a kilo. But in my contacts with those in hiding, I frequently heard that in their tragic situations our help gave them a tiny ray of hope. Some remember the help to this day. They write about it in their memoirs and in the letters they send me.

"But Żegota was also of great significance to Polish society. In the underground press this organization published numerous appeals for the Government Delegation to categorically crack down on blackmailers and szmalcowniks. [Thus] their shameful behavior was made punishable by death.

"Żegota also printed and distributed leaflets calling on the Polish community, though itself frightened and terrorized by the German invader, to help the Jews. With no degree of exaggeration I can responsibly state that saving a single Jew (adult or child) required at least 10 Poles."

If the Elysian Fields
Really exist
I think, o Lord
That in Your goodness
You permitted
Rachela and Yoyne
To sit there peacefully
And wait till their parents
Call them
They might have had a few years
When their wings were attached
And they flew up
To the sun
Driven on by rifle butts
Today no one knows
Where their home was
And on what table the menorah
And if You are angry
At the Son's suffering on earth
Take pity on those
Who from Judah's generation

Grew
The child's face
What could it have done
That the Cross on Golgotha
With God's body was wrapped
Processions of tiny shadows . . .
Abandoned toys . . .
Heaps of tiny garments and shoes . . .
That's all there remains of them
So little
Too little!
To Irena Sendler
With great respect and dedication
Agata Barańska, June 6, 2001

Notes

1. Stefania Wichlińska was courier for Zofia Kossak-Szczucka, but Irena Sendler did not know this at the time.

2. Żegota was an underground social organization founded on the initiative of Zofia Kossak-Szczucka and Wanda Krahelska-Filipowicz. The council included representatives of diverse underground political parties (the Bund, Rebirth of Poland Front, Polish Socialist Party, Polish Democratic Party, and the Union of Polish Syndicalists). Its primary objective was to provide as comprehensive as possible help for the Jews by securing for them places to live beyond the ghetto. Nevertheless, it became apparent that the enormity of the problem was far beyond the founders' financial means. The organization had its regional branches. In Lwów a branch was headed by Władysława Laryssa Chomcowa, whereas in Krakow by Stanisław Wincenty Dobrowolski.

3. Ferdynand Arczyński (1900–1979), an employee of the Krakow Railways Directorate, sports activist, and journalist, from 1939 a member of the Polish Democratic Party. He was in Warsaw from 1942, where he became the treasurer for Żegota. After the war, he continued using his nom de guerre, Marek.

4. It was on the initiative of the Rebirth of Poland Front that Zofia Kossak-Szczucka's Protest was printed and secretly published in leaflet form. Cited from a selection of sources, *Polacy-Żydzi 1939–1945*, ed. Andrzej K. Kunert, with foreword by Władysław Bartoszewski, Warsaw, 2001, p. 213.

5. Zofia Kossak-Szczucka (1890–1968), writer. On account of the fact that she had helped save Jewish children, in June 1945 [the Stalinist minister] Jakub Bergman (the brother of Adolf Bergman!), offered Kossak-Szczucka, who was

wanted by the communist internal security police, a chance to escape from Poland. She left with her daughter first for Sweden, and later moved to Great Britain, from where she returned to Poland on February 21, 1957. Information obtained from: Miroslawa Pałaszewska, *Zofia Kossak*, Warsaw, 1989, p. 187.

6. Wanda Krahelska-Filipowicz (1886–1968), social activist and journalist.

7. Members of the Council to Aid Jews included: Ferdynand Arczyński, Władysław Bartoszewski, Adolf Berman, Witold Bieńkowski, Leon Feiner, Piotr Gajewski, Szymon Gottesman, Julian Grobelny, Emilia Hiżowa, Roman Jabłonowski, Janina Raabe-Wąsowiczowa, Ludwik Rostkowski, Zofia Rudnicka, Tadeusz Sarnecki, and Stefan Sendlak.

8. The first head of the Children's Section was Aleksandra Dargielowa (1890–1959), a teacher and social activist, who had to give up this post because of her work at the Central Welfare Council (RGO). The Section for Child Matters was not officially established until August 16, 1943. But from the very start of its existence, the Żegota organization recognized saving children as one of its most important objectives, and from the very start such help was organized.

9. After the war, Maurycy Herling-Grudziński became a judge in the Supreme Court. Not until 1976 did he reveal his role in Żegota. We know that he helped some 500 Jews. He was the brother of the famous émigré writer Gustaw Herling-Grudziński. [As mentioned by Zdzisław Kudelski, Gustaw Herling-Grudziński's biographer, when commenting on *Studia o Herlingu-Grudzińskim* (Lublin, 1998) in the "Rzecz o Książkach" supplement to *Reczpospolita* nr 155, July 5–6, 2003.] These facts were previously stated by Teresa Prekerowa in a short article entitled "Komórka 'Felicji,'" in *Rocznik Warszawski*, 1979, vol. XV.

10. Teresa Prekerowa citing Helena Grobelna, who told her the Żegota archive was kept at the home of Władysław Lizuraj in Bemowo, writes: "Being situated in peripheral Bemowo, Żegota members considered it to be relatively safe. This was a pity because the lost documents had belonged to the largest and most extensively linked Council cell, that of the PPS-WRN. It was an irreparable loss both for Żegota history as well as for the entire action to save Jews." *Konspiracyjna Rada Pomocy Żydom w Warszawie 1942–1945*, p. 140. In one of her accounts Irena Sendler writes: "For obvious reasons, no applications or other documentation could be produced to obtain material help from the Żegota Council. It was only for the sake of internal discipline as well as a sort of means of monitoring by the Council that the beneficiaries of aid personally wrote receipts using pseudonyms that were known to the couriers." *Biuletyn Żydowskiego Instytutu Historycznego*, 1963, nr 45/46, pp. 234–247.

11. Teresa Prekerowa, *Konspiracyjna Rada Pomocy Żydom w Warszawie, 1942–1945*, Warsaw, 1982, *passim*.

10

How Sister Jolanta Rescued Children from the Warsaw Ghetto

From the very first days of the occupation, Irena Sendler combined two forms of professional work: official work in the City of Warsaw Administration and secret, underground work. Both served the same cause: to save Jews, adults and children, whom the invader had sentenced to total annihilation. The section she was in charge of specialized in helping children of various ages leave the ghetto and live safely on the Aryan side. And it also provided shelter for other children who had managed to escape from the ghetto individually. Depending on their age, sex, and outward appearance, the children were either found Polish families to live with, or were sent to convents, or, alternatively, to secular childcare institutions. The older youths (often not without very considerable problems) joined the partisans. Each case was different. Before a child could be taken out of the ghetto, the family had to be interviewed. Here help was provided by people from the Jewish community or Centos (Ewa Rechtman).

It was important to know whether the child spoke Polish. Each child needed documents, that is, each needed new, fictitious documents regarding his or her birth. Here Catholic parishes helped.

Irena Sendler: "The cruel living conditions in the Jewish district quite literally decimated the inhabitants. There were now many homes where all the adults were dead and only neglected, helpless children remained. One way to help, of course, was to take the children out of the ghetto. But we could not take them all at once. One first needed to organize temporary help, child care, and food. The ghetto streets were full of child beggars. We saw them on entering the ghetto and when, after a couple of hours we returned to leave, lying on the ground there would often already be tiny corpses, covered with newspapers."

"The deaths of adults resulted in a rapid rise of child orphans," wrote Ruta Sakowska,[1] thanks to whom today we know much more about hunger in the Warsaw ghetto. For example, in September 1941, the ghetto inhabitants received ration cards for 2.5 kg of bread a month, whereas in November this was reduced to just 2 kg a month. "The adults shared these paltry rations with their children to the end," stresses Sakowska. In mid-July, just before the Great Action, food prices in the ghetto soared. From 10 zlotys a loaf, bread prices rose steadily to 20, 45, 80, and then 100 zlotys a loaf. Potatoes went from 5 zlotys a kilogram to 300 zlotys. Many distraught Jews actually volunteered for deportation when it was announced that "for the road" every one of them would receive 3 kg of bread and 1 kg of marmalade.[2]

"With my colleagues we also contacted families we knew had children," recalls Mrs. Sendler. "We would tell them we were able to save the children, to get them beyond the wall. Then they would ask the crucial question regarding what guarantees there were of success. We had to honestly answer that we could offer no guarantees. I spoke frankly; I said I couldn't even be certain I would safely leave the ghetto with a child that very day. Scenes from hell ensued. For instance, the father would agree to give us the child, but the mother would refuse. The grandmother, embracing the child most lovingly of all, tears streaming down her face, in between the sobs would declare: 'I'll never give up my granddaughter!' Sometimes I would leave such a family with their child. The next day I would return to see what happened to the family, and frequently it would turn out that the entire family was already in Umschlagplatz."

One of those who refused to hand over her son was Artur Zygielbojm's wife. "Whatever is to be my fate shall also be the fate of my son," she told the courier who wanted to find a safe place for her child. The mother and her son perished in the Warsaw Ghetto Uprising in May 1943.[3]

"Tears welled in the eyes of mothers when they gave us their beloved children," recounts Irena Sendler, "so difficult it was for each mother to let go of the tiny hand of her baby! ... Who could tell whether she would see her child again?"

During one of our many meetings, Katarzyna Meloch, a child of the Holocaust, told me: "Mothers such as those of Grynberg, Głowiński and others, were the real heroes of the war—the ones who gave up their infants to strangers so that their infants could survive."

Irena Sendler: "Some Jewish mothers would spend months preparing their children for the Aryan side. They changed their identities. They would say: 'You're not Icek, but Jacek. You're not Rachela, but Roma. And I'm not your mother, I was just the housemaid. You'll go with this lady and perhaps over there your mummy will be waiting for you.'"

When 40 years later one of those saved children asked Sister Jolanta[4] how his mother could have handed him over to strangers, Irena Sendler replied: "Your mother handed you over out of love."

***

There were several ways to get infants out of the killing zone. In order for such an operation to stand any chance of success, one needed help from the Jewish police.

Irena Sendler: "We needed to know in advance which houses were selected to go first to the Umschlagplatz. We were also helped by the policemen escorting youth brigades sent out to work on the Aryan side. It was difficult to get older children out of the ghetto individually. One needed to find a whole group of young boys and a policeman who, like others, had had enough of the ghetto's cruelties and wanted to leave it permanently. For a few days the boys had to be put up with highly trusted Polish families and then, once the underground resistance authorities had agreed to recruit them, one of us would lead the group out into the forest.

"It was a different matter with small children. We would usually take them out through the court building in Leszno Street. This court had two entrances: one from the ghetto side, and the other from Ogrodowa Street on the Aryan side. Some of the doors were left open and, thanks to the courage of the ushers, through this building one could get out of the ghetto with a child. Children were also driven out in fire engines, ambulances, or by tram, thanks to a befriended tram driver called Leon Szeszko.[5] When he was on duty, before he set off, a child would be taken to his car. Older children left the ghetto in official work brigades."

Stefanek was a few years old when he was saved. Today he is an elderly man who doesn't know exactly how old he is. His birth details had to be recreated. Having survived the war, he now lives near the western border of Poland. He told me how he escaped: under the coat of a fully grown man, his bare feet in the adult's boots. And he clung on to the man's belt. Once they had passed the danger, he was collected by an appointed guardian.

Some children were taken in sacks, boxes, or baskets. Babies were put to sleep and hidden in crates with holes, so that they could breathe. They were driven out in the ambulance that delivered disinfectants to the ghetto (the driver, Antoni Dąbrowski took great risks to help us). That is how three-month-old Elżbieta Ficowska was saved. Now she emotionally recalls that in her life she had three mothers: her Jewish mother, whom she never knew (she doesn't even have her photograph!); her Polish mother, Stanisława Bussoldowa, who raised her; and a third mother, Irena Sendler, who saved her.

Some children were smuggled out though the cellars of houses bordering with other houses on the Aryan side. Sewage canals were also used as an escape route. That is how four-year-old Piotr Zysman (today 70-year-old Piotr Zettinger,[6] an engineer permanently living in Sweden) got out of the ghetto.

In the middle of the night, a courier brought a boy and his sister to Irena Sendler's flat. The children and their clothes needed to be immediately washed. But Irena had run out of soap. Without a moment's hesitation, she went to her neighbor to borrow some. The neighbor duly gave her the soap, but the next day she commented: "You must be crazy. Doing your washing at night?!"

Rescued children and adults all needed documents. The children needed a baptismal certificate, whereas adults needed authentic Kennkarte identification cards, because, among other things, without these you could not get food ration cards. "This was the first condition to fulfill if someone was to be saved. In case of being stopped by the Germans, it was essential to have good ID documents."[7]

Irena Sendler: "We got in touch with the husband of one of the couriers. He worked in the Public Records Office and in a very secret way he was able to issue authentic Kennkartes with the appropriate thumb prints. Next, once again by very secret means, a rescued individual would be registered [as a resident] by Mrs. Stanisława Bussoldowa (a woman who was very dedicated to rescuing both children and adults), the administrator of house No. 5 in Kałuszyńska Street, Praga.

"There were considerable difficulties with hiding adults. Often they failed to appreciate how crucial it was to behave in the least noticeable way in the homes of people who were risking their own lives to hide them. They sometimes did not understand that even leaning out of a window or stepping out onto the balcony was of great danger not only to themselves but also to their hosts.

Those who had so-called good looks, particularly women, were in an easier situation. 'A person with good looks did not arouse suspicions when hiding. It was easier for such people to blend into a crowd, they did not draw attention to themselves and it was easier for them to pretend to be someone they were not.'[8]

"One of the basic principles of successfully hiding Jews was to frequently change locations. This was essential on account of observant neighbors, who would notice when a family suddenly started buying more food, especially bread."

Notes

1. *Archiwum Ringelblum*, vol. 2, p. 302.
2. Aleksander Rowiński, *Zygielbojma śmierć i życie*, Warsaw, 2000, p. 218.
3. Szmul Mordechaj Zygielbojm (1895–1943), Bund Party pseudonym "Artur." From February 1942, he was a member of the National Council of the Polish Government in Exile in London. His wife, the actress Mania Rozen, perished together with their nine-year-old son [in the Warsaw Ghetto Uprising].
4. Most of the saved children knew Irena Sendler only as Sister Jolanta. They discovered her real name only after a few decades had passed!
5. Leon Szeszko was a member of the Polish Home Army (AK) and had good contacts with fellow AK members in the Public Records Office. He was shot dead on November 13, 1943.
6. In an interview given to a Swedish journalist, he said: "'I remember it like a film scene. I see them squeezing me (and my two years younger cousin) into an opening, and there are channels that lead us to the Aryan side. I see the back of the person in front of us with a torch lighting up the way. Then I learned not to think about my old life. I suppressed such thoughts in my mind. I was told to hide, so I hid. As a child I hid in the attic. I knew that no one other than the sisters [nuns] should have contact with me. I understood that they were hiding me, that I was an escapee and not like other children. I accepted this situation, I was able to adapt, such were the conditions of survival." (March 16, 2003).
7. Michał Głowiński, *Czarne sezony*, Kraków, 2002, p. 124.
8. Michał Głowiński, *Czarne sezony*, p. 116.

11

Where the Children Were Taken

The first place of stay was the most important. A young child had to be taught to live in new (and not necessarily immediately safe) circumstances. These were special, private family "emergency care units" managed by very trusted people. Children there were taught Polish, how to pray, sing Polish songs, and recite Polish poems. They were surrounded with the most affectionate care. They were washed, dressed in new clothes, and fed. Considerable trouble was taken to calm them down, to ease the pain of being separated from their loved ones.

There was no fixed time a child had to spend in an "emergency care unit." It all depended on how long it would take for the child to adapt. When they were ready, they were next sent either to the Father Boduen Civic House (orphanage), alternatively to a convent somewhere in occupied Poland,[1] or to live with a trusted family.

The emergency care team included, among others: the teacher Janina Grabowska, who lived at 1 Ludwiki Street in Wola; Jadwiga Piotrowska, her sister, and parents, who cared for children in their home at 9 Lekarska Street; Zofia Wędrychowska (for many years a teacher at Nasz Dom [Our Home]) and Stanisław Papuziński, who risked the lives of his own children to save other people's children; Izabela Kuczkowska and her mother, Kazimiera Trzaskalska, who lived in Gocławek; Wanda Drozdowska-Rogowiczowa from Sadyba; the midwife Stanisława Bussoldowa; Maria Kukulska from 15 Markowska Street in Praga; M. Felińska from 80 Bema Street; A Adamski, who lived near the road to Włochy; the caretakers of houses in 8 Widoki Street and Barkocińska Street in Praga, as well as Janina Waldowa and Róża Zawadzka.

How did the children fare in the care homes? "It varied greatly," recounts Irena Sendler, "depending on whether or not the hosts had an appropriate attitude to the child's tragedy. Older children were more aware of their situation and therefore terrified of being identified. They had witnessed the cruelty of the ghetto and understood that Jews were killed. Therefore, one could not be a Jew! Having to constantly pretend in front of others frequently proved too much for them. Some children adapted with great difficulty and continued to wait for their mother, grandmother, or other close family member.

"A lot depended on the reaction of the guardians and carers, whether or not they would be able to somehow get through to the child, and get a positive response, or whether they became cold and indifferent. Some managed to strike up friendships, which created problems of a different nature. The fastest to adapt to the new situation were the smallest children. They were quick to play and be mischievous, like normal children.

"It was another matter when children were moved from the 'emergency care units' to private families. These were usually very young children. But here too every case was different. Much depended on the atmosphere in the home. The child's adaptation process varied depending on whether or not the foster parents had children of their own. Regardless of whether there were other children or not, the adopted child had frequently to remain hidden from inquisitive surroundings, nosey neighbors, acquaintances, or other family members. Life on the Aryan side was still very much on borrowed time. Occasionally, when there was a danger of the cover being blown, of the German authorities being informed, visits from *szmalcowniks* or even the Gestapo, then a new hideout for the small escapee had to be urgently found. Such a forced change of home meant just another tragedy for the child.

"I was once taking this distressed, sobbing boy to new guardians. In between his tears and sobs, the boy asked me, 'Please, Miss, how many mommies can you have, because I'm going to my third now.'" She also stresses that no child was ever uncovered by the Germans in an orphanage run by nuns. "There is an untrue accusation," states Irena Sendler, "put forward by some Jewish circles that nuns wilfully baptized these children and also made them go to confession and receive communion. But one has to appreciate that there was still a war on and there was a constant threat from various Poles in the vicinity, as well as Germans, who for various reasons often visited the convent. That is why Jewish children could not be in any way different from the Polish children. It was essential for the sake of safety! One has to remember that in the orphanages and care homes run by nuns there were also Polish children, frequently semi-orphans who were visited by their families. People noticed the 'new' kids. There were cases when the families of Polish children argued with the management, fearing that on account of the presence of Jewish children the whole orphanage would 'go up in smoke.' All sorts of threats were made. In such cases the Jewish children had to be moved to yet another home. For this reason, there were cases of Jewish children who had undergone the harrowing experience of escaping from the ghetto, still being in great danger and having to change the place where they lived several times, all of which made their tragedy even worse. The most difficult task was to transport children that had distinctly Semitic physiognomies. Bandages would be put on to cover part of their face. Sometimes, for the sake of safety, it was essential to hide children in wardrobes, coal skips, storage spaces, specially constructed hiding holes in larders or under the floor, and only after it became dark, would the child be transported to another place. A serious problem concerned children who had become accustomed to living in darkness and therefore reacted badly to strong sunlight. They often suffered from various eye inflammations, which required treatment from eye doctors. Not infrequently such children ended up in hospital."

Journalist Katarzyna Meloch, who was rescued from the ghetto at the age of 10 and was later cared for by nuns in the Turkowice orphanage, recalls: "I once made a big mistake that could have had very serious consequences. I had a genuine birth certificate, after a Polish girl of my age who had died. I knew all the most important prayers. And yet I almost gave myself away when I asked if we were going to evening mass. In those days masses were only celebrated in the morning!"

"We had two flats in Otwock," recounts Mrs. Sendler, "and one in Śródborów. There we would house adult Jews whose Warsaw homes were no longer safe. School was organized for boys up to the age of 14—the older ones went to join the partisans! One of my colleagues, a member of the prewar PPS, went through the teaching program with them. I had an agreement with Leon Scheiblet, the headmaster of the Władysław Reymont School in Otwock, by which the Jewish boys would be entered into his school register. What I wanted to do was to make sure that if the children survived the war, they would not have too much education to catch up on. I also arranged for Michał Głowiński's mother to be put up in the house of one of the schoolteachers. Michał Głowiński was at the time in an orphanage run by Felician Sisters. The schoolteacher was very active socially and frequently invited children from the Felician Sisters' orphanage to her garden, and later for refreshments in her house. One day she invited a group of children that included Michał—though he at the time did not know his mother was there. The refreshments were brought to the children by the 'housemaid.' Mother and son were in the same house for one and a half hours, but the mother could not even wink to her son because she could not let anyone know that there was any relationship between them." The ploy worked and nobody suspected how important this moment for these two people was.[2]

***

Even more dramatic adventures were experienced by people transporting Jewish children to safe places. "Jaga Piotrowska was once taking an infant by tram," recounts Mrs. Sendler. "The child, which had been separated from its mother, was crying and calling out in the Jewish language. My courier froze; the interest of the other passengers was immediately aroused. Worse still, there were Germans nearby. On hearing the child's crying, the tram driver realized how dangerous the situation had suddenly become. He stopped the tram and declared that it had broken down; it was returning to the tram depot. Once all the passengers had disembarked, he approached Jaga and asked: 'Where do you want me to drive to?' Jaga also had another adventure. She was travelling by train, taking a rescued girl to the sisters in Chotomów. She got engaged in a conversation with fellow passengers. In the meantime, the train had passed her station and was now bound for the Reich . . . She had to quickly catch a train bound for Warsaw. The one that eventually arrived was terribly overcrowded. The cars for Poles were bursting at the seams and there was no chance of getting in. Then a German who had noticed Jaga's difficulty, came forward and invited her to travel in his compartment."

Notes

1. Irena Sendler believed the key role played by very many church institutions deserves particular emphasis. Teresa Prekerowa published Irena Sendler's recollection in which she stated: "Convents such as that of the Sisters of the Family of Mary in Chotomów near Warsaw and its mother superior, Sister Matylda Getter (1870–1968), or the Little Servant Sisters of the Immaculate Conception, who ran an orphanage in Turkowice, beyond Lublin, deserve to be mentioned in the most positive way. In the latter order, there was Sister Witolda, who on receiving a coded telegram from us (a message ostensibly referring to a clothes parcel), would travel to Warsaw and collect children we could no longer keep in the capital as the house

where they had been staying was 'burnt,' i.e., there had been arrests in the house or informers were blackmailing the residents and there was no more money to give. These children were most usually boys who had very Semitic features, which distinguished them from other boys and thus exposed them to greater danger. It was such boys that Sister Witolda took to Turkowice, having to take the long, dangerous, wartime route through Lublin and Chelm all the way up to the border. These children were subjected to yet more terrible experiences when the front moved through the area in the years 1944–1945." [*Konspiracyjna Rada Pomoczy Żydom w Warszawie 1942–1945*, Warsaw, 1982, p. 209.] "Thirty-six Jewish children were kept in Turkowice alone! No priest or nun ever refused to help me save Jewish children! Quite the opposite, they helped to the very end of the war, putting their own lives and the lives of those around them on the line. Nor did any convent ever refuse to take in any child I sent them," stresses Irena Sendler.

2. Michał Głowiński described this incident as follows: "[Mother] knew that I was also in Otwock, but she could not contact me. (I was not aware of the fact that she was so close.) I was accepted as an orphan and my mother had false documents stating that she was a spinster . . . She understood that she could not reveal her real identity also on account of the fact that she would immediately lose her job . . . That day was exceptionally difficult for her because she naturally wanted to approach me but, of course, she had to steer clear of me. At the same time she had to make sure her behavior did not seem strange or inexplicable in anyway to anyone around her. On this ordinary January day I was quite unaware of all these complications . . . The basic principle of hiding was not to do anything [peculiar], to blend in with the crowd, become someone with no characteristic features, the greyest of the grey." *Czarne sezony*, pp. 105–114.

12

The Ghetto Uprising

Apart from various dramatic surprises that were part and parcel of life in the occupied capital, up to January 1943 the operation of rescuing the now far less numerous ghetto inhabitants had its regular rhythm. Escapes from the "work brigades" occurred on a virtually daily basis. However, from January 18–22, 1943, "while attempting to conduct a successive deportation as part of the January Action,[1] the Jews resisted with firearms for the very first time. Then on April 19, 1943, during yet another attempt to conduct the final liquidation of the ghetto, Jewish soldiers and groups of Jewish civilians put up the organized and sometimes chaotic resistance that after the war became known as the Warsaw Ghetto Uprising," wrote Anka Grupińska.[2]

"At dawn, around 6 A.M., German troops—almost two thousand strong—entered the ghetto through the gate in Nalewki Street. [Already] on April 6 the Polish underground had received information about an imminent German action to raze the ghetto to the ground. This time there was no surprise."[3]

The chronicles record that the spring was very warm. That year Easter came a couple of days after the Jewish Passover.[4] Hiding at the time with his younger brother, Jerzy, in the Warsaw district of Nowe Miasto, Natan Gross recalls those events as follows:

"On Easter Saturday we went to church to have our Easter eggs blessed. It seemed to me that the whole house was looking at us. I sent Jerzy out as a scout, so that he would see and learn how to do it, while I stood in the queue with the basket in my hand and a pain in my heart . . . I stood in that queue, deep in unhappy thoughts, catching snatches of conversation, not always pleasant for my soul, and then Jerzy finally returned from his investigation and declared that there was nothing to it. And indeed there wasn't. The priest just sprinkled some water on the eggs and we went home.

"By then everyone was saying that something was happening in the ghetto. But nobody knew exactly what. You could hear gunshots, sometimes more powerful explosions. Presumably, an action, resettlement. What the word 'action' meant we knew very well.

"The following day there was finally some concrete news from beyond the wall: the Jews were fighting! The Jews were defending themselves! It became the big story of the day, the chief topic of conversation. Rumours followed one after the other, and were immediately confirmed. In Krasińskich Square, close to our small street, the Germans set up a small artillery piece which every couple of minutes fired a shell over the other side of the wall. The ghetto started to burn . . .

The days that followed were ever more difficult to bear. Our neighbors, good people, quite explicitly made it clear that it was time for us to pack our things and move on to another place, while there was still time . . . At every step our ears were assaulted as if with poisoned arrows: 'It is good that Hitler is doing our work for us.' But there were also words of caution: 'Today they, tomorrow we!'

"Some regretted the burning down of property, after all, this was Warsaw burning! Others still could not hide their admiration for the ghetto fighters: 'Look at those Jews, who'd have thought that they could fight with weapons in their hands.' News of the ghetto uprising reverberated in the Polish underground press. Everyone knew about it and everyone was talking about it. For Jews living in Warsaw on Aryan documents, these were days of bloodshed and glory, days of fear and despair."[5]

How did the famous actor from Teatr Polski, Marian Wyrzykowski remember it? During the occupation he worked as a waiter in the U Aktorki café. In his wartime diary[6] he wrote:

April 20, 1943
Business is rather quiet in the café. In the city there is great unease. For two days now a real battle is being fought in the ghetto. There must be a massive number of victims. Horror overcomes you when you consider what times we are living in. No more than a few tram stops away people are being murdered, and here guests are drinking, eating, there's music, a gentleman is singing . . . I went out into the garden for a moment and the terror struck me. The non-stop booming of

artillery and the rattle of machinegun fire. . . . Some apocalyptic demon is running wild in the world.

April 21, 1943
The café is constantly busy. Today I occasionally serve out in the garden because the weather's nice. The cannonade in the ghetto can still be heard. Apparently they're fighting a regular battle. Over the ghetto there's a huge pall of smoke. A massive blaze. I'm terribly depressed.

April 28, 1943
The ghetto's still burning. The wind blows eastwards, so the whole of Warsaw is choking in the smoke, appropriately reminding the inhabitants of the human tragedy. I cannot come to terms with the thought. Those gunshots, that smoke, the news from that terrible place all together create such a ghastly, apocalyptic situation, quite unimaginable.

April 30
The ghetto smoke hangs over me. I just cannot think of anything. I feel so depressed, so dejected, as never before. And the shame of humans being treated so terribly! I went out of the café into the garden for a while. Billowing red clouds of smoke envelope the sky, above them circles a plane, and it drops bombs. Every so often a loud thud, the ground shakes. Over there people are dying. I feel I can hear the cries of those being murdered . . . No, I can't [bear it].

***

After a week, on April 26, when the pall from the constant blaze reminded the inhabitants of other Warsaw neighborhoods of the thousands in the ghetto who were fighting and dying, "a new announcement from the Warsaw district chief of police was plastered on the advertising columns. It threatened not only the death penalty for providing any type of help to Jews outside the ghetto, but also penal camp sentences to those who knew of a Jew outside the ghetto and failed to report this fact to the police," wrote Ludwik Landau, adding that "probably of greater practical consequence was the announcement annulling all passes into the former Jewish district and a warning that anyone found there would be shot on the spot."[7]

***

On May 4, 1943, those (very few) who had concealed radio receivers in their homes, something strictly forbidden by the Germans, were able to hear a speech by General Władysław Sikorski, broadcast by the BBC to the inhabitants of occupied Poland. Even now, after over 60 years, this speech is dramatic. All the more so when we consider that two months later Sikorski was himself dead, killed in a plane crash in Gibraltar on July 4. But earlier, in May, he spoke as follows:

"The Germans are casting children into the fire, they are murdering women. All this has created an impassable rift between Poland and Germany. The Germans are burning corpses en masse to erase evidence of their appalling crimes. In mid-April, at 4 in the morning, the Germans commenced to liquidate the Warsaw ghetto. They enclosed the remainder of the Jews within a police cordon, moved into the centre with their tanks and armoured vehicles and proceeded to carry out their work of destruction. The struggle has continued since then. Bomb explosions, gunfire, blazes persist day and night. The greatest crime in human history is being perpetrated. We know you are helping the Jews insofar as you are able to. Please undertake all efforts to help them and at the same time condemn this terrible cruelty."[8]

Teresa Prekerowa, the author of a book on the work of Żegota, cites a fragment of a declaration by the Republic of Poland Government Homeland Plenipotentiary, which was published in the underground newspaper *Rzeczpospolita Polska* on May 6, 1943. Its part concerning events in the Warsaw ghetto cannot be ignored:

"Over a year has now passed since, after several years of brutal persecution, the Germans started the mass murder of all the Jews in Poland, and are continuing the murder to this day. In recent weeks the capital of Poland has witnessed the bloody liquidation of the remainder of the Warsaw ghetto by the German police and Latvian mercenaries. Currently there is a cruel chase, the hunting down and murdering of Jews hiding in the ghetto ruins or beyond its walls. The Polish nation, steeped in Christian values, refusing to recognize double standards in morality, observes German anti-Jewish barbarities with utter revulsion. And when on April 19 the unequal struggle in the Warsaw ghetto began, they regarded the valiantly defending Jews with sympathy and respect, and the German murderers with contempt. The country's political leadership has already expressed its total denunciation of German anti-Jewish barbarity and today it reiterates these words of condemnation with full force.

"The Polish community is right to feel sorry for the persecuted Jews and to provide them with help. This help should be continued. . . . We call on all Poles to follow the instructions contained in these words. Not for a moment should we forget that in committing their crime the Germans are simultaneously striving to show the world that Poles are participating in the murder and the robbing of Jews. In these circumstances any direct or indirect help provided to the Germans in their heinous actions is the most serious offence against Poland. Any Pole who collaborates in such homicidal actions, blackmails or denounces Jews, exploits their appalling predicament or participates in the robbing of Jews is thus committing a serious crime against the Republic of Poland and shall be immediately punished. And if at present such a person manages to escape punishment or gains the protection of the criminal powers occupying our country, let him be sure that the time is near when he will answer before a court of Reborn Poland."[9]

On May 13, 1943, English society and the Polish émigré community were shocked by news of the suicide of Szmul Zygielbojm, the Bund delegate at the National Council in London, which was appointed by the Polish Government in Exile as an advisory body replacing the Sejm [Polish parliament]. Symbolically and in reality this was a tragic protest of someone who represented a forlorn nation, lonely in their mass extermination, the Jews. The listlessness of the free world, the lack of response to desperate cries for help, the indifferent attitude in face of evidence of Nazi crimes, provided with such difficulty by couriers, all contributed to this tragic decision.

In his testament he wrote: "I cannot remain silent and live when the remnants of Jewry are being murdered."

Three days later, on May 16, General Jürgen Stroop reported to his superiors that the "former Jewish quarter" had ceased to exist.[10] This was actually not true. Difficult as it is to believe, amid the smouldering ruins and rubble, without the basic means of survival (water, food, medicines), people somehow managed to exist. After the war they were called the "ghetto Robinsons." The bravest survived there until liberation.

***

And what was Sister Jolanta doing during that tragic period?

"Not for a moment did we interrupt our vigil outside the ghetto walls," answered Mrs. Sendler when I asked her this question. "On Julian Grobelny's instructions, we immediately went into action. We waited at various manhole covers. I organized several more child care points. I widened the exit routes, which were usually through the basements of adjoining houses. My team had their work cut out. And whatever proved unachievable for the rest, in this difficult and dangerous work, was entrusted to Irena Schultz,[11] who was exceptionally successful in rescuing children from the burning ghetto. When it was no longer possible to help those inside the ghetto who had stayed to fight, we concentrated on helping those who had managed to escape that hell. Unfortunately, our aid could only be limited and quite inadequate. The pulling out of children and adults, especially the sick and old, was only possible for a few days. Later, even with passes, we could not enter the ghetto. And when the ghetto fell, the searching for Jews on the Aryan side nevertheless continued. In fact it actually increased. And it should be remembered that 'our help was not limited to saving children.'" Thus wrote Irena Sendler in *Biuletyn Żydowskiego Instytutu Historycznego* in 1963.

"A separate group of people needing our help were youths. They too had to be put up in private homes or sent to the forest to join the partisans. How did we deal with this problem? Like in the case of the children, through Trojan we let the units fighting inside the ghetto know the addresses of points/homes where those who decided to leave could report. For the 'arranging' of this—as it used to be termed—we recruited several new people from various backgrounds. We were helped by, among others, Joanna Waldowa, a social worker whose tiny, poky flat in the Grochów neighborhood was open to us day and night. Moreover, we rented two flats, one in Świder and the other in Otwock. Superficially, the latter was supposed to be for people with lung ailments, but in fact it served mainly as a stopover point for those intending to join the partisans in the forest. We arranged for elderly, and ostensibly sick, ladies to live in these flats as permanent residents, and under this cover we could use the flats for their real purpose. For those who remained in Warsaw, formal matters were settled the same way as in the case of the children. A given young man or women would spend a few days in an Emergency Allocation Family Unit, and in that time our couriers (in each of the 10 social welfare centers there would be such a trusted person) would arrange appropriate clothes, a welfare allowance and money from Żegota (every zloty counted), as well as necessary contacts with family, friends, acquaintances or a political organization concerning the fugitive's future plans. Moreover, it was a matter of urgency to produce appropriate Aryan identity documents, including work permits, without which it was impossible to move around Warsaw. There were not infrequent cases where we arranged for hospitals to produce certificates stating that an escapee had been a patient or had had an operation in order to provide an alibi against possible blackmailers. However, the most important thing was to find a place where that person could live. Without any exaggeration one can say that every saved individual has a history that could be the subject of a thick book.

Once they had all the necessary documents—in accordance with the strictest German regulations—and a place where they could live, the person under our charge was properly 'arranged.' Every single one of them had a file bearing their pseudonym. These had to be kept for very practical reasons, because Żegota paid out money once a month and the couriers needed to know to whom and where to deliver it. Every escapee under our charge also had a courier-cum-guardian who was responsible for maintaining contact with the escapee and settling their diverse matters."

For example, Maria Krasnodębska was the courier-cum-guardian for the famous pianist Władysław Szpilman, who had been hiding on the Aryan side since the winter of 1943. A colleague of Irena Sendler's from the Social Welfare Department, for many months Maria Krasnodębska provided Szpilman with food and money, which she took directly to the flat where he was hiding.[12]

"Those who went to join the partisans were granted a larger lump sum of money, clothes, various medicines, as well as appropriate documents before they were taken to the forest. There they would be collected by Trojan's specially appointed couriers."[13]

For Irena Sendler the greatest concern was the fate of the children, whose safety in hiding she and her colleagues continually monitored. "I visited them regularly," she recounted over 60 years later, "and in the case of any danger I had to swiftly find them a new home."

***

Even during the war consideration was given as to what would happen after it ended. It was understood that the situation of the rescued children would also change. A lot depended on whether any of their relatives survived. For the rescuers it was important that these children should not be lost to the Jewish community. For the sake of families eventually finding their children, it was deemed necessary for every child to have a file and for their location to be traced not only in Warsaw but also in the whole of Poland.

Irena Sendler was the person who ran the personal files system for several years. This was a very difficult task as any list with names, surnames, and addresses could get into the wrong hands. But, nevertheless, lists of one sort or another had to be made. In brackets, next to the name "Marysia Kowalska" would be the name "Regina Lubliner," and the coded address to where the child had been sent. The elevated name of "file" referred to a roll of narrow strips of very thin paper.¹⁴

"For safety's sake, I was the only person who kept and managed the files," states Irena Sendler. "But where was I to keep them? This was the fourth year of the war and by then the Germans were aware of the most likely places; wardrobes, storage compartments, ovens, and spaces under floorboards—all were now routinely searched. So I thought of something different. My idea of hiding the files was as follows: In the middle of a room that partly overlooked the courtyard and a small garden was a table. I therefore decided that each time before I went to bed, I would place the tiny, tightly rolled up scroll in the center of that table. If I heard knocking on my front door, I planned to throw the scroll of top secret information through the window into the bushes in the small garden. I practiced many times to do it swiftly in the eventuality of unwelcome visitors."

And then that day came.

Notes

1. On January 31, 1943, Żegota issued a letter to the Polish Government Plenipotentiary requesting a special grant in the face of new dangers threatening the ghetto inhabitants in which we read among other things: "The action was undoubtedly a signal that the Germans are preparing for the final liquidation of the Warsaw ghetto, to murder the already greatly depleted remainder of the Jewish population in Warsaw. Within just a few days they shipped 5–6,000 people to the Treblinka death camp. Among those taken were most of the community's surviving staff, 400 persons from the supplies unit, some 300 doctors and health department workers as well as a number of distinguished social activists and intellectuals. For the time being, probably on account of the armed resistance put up by the ghetto's inhabitants, the eviction action has been halted. Nevertheless, the fate of remaining ghetto residents is already sealed. Imminently, one can expect a continued and complete liquidation of the Warsaw ghetto. Making use of this temporary lull, mass escapes from the ghetto have begun, the number of people for whom getting out of the ghetto is the only hope of survival is rising day by day. Taking care of such people is becoming an urgent problem today. Providing them with places to stay, documents, financial means and food are things that have to be organized immediately and on a massive scale. Many valuable individuals from the world of social affairs, culture, science and art are still in the ghetto and they should be rescued at once! There are still a few thousand children, survivors of the previous massacre, which was especially ruthless and cruel toward children; this small remainder of children who are still alive need to be pulled out of the ghetto and saved." From Teresa Prekerowa, *Konspiracyjna Rada Pomocy Żydom w Warszawie 1942–1945*, Warsaw, 1982, p. 369.

2. *Getto warszawskie*, Warsaw, 2002, pp. 9-10.

3. Marian Apfelbaum, *Dwa sztandary. Rzecz opowstaniu w getcie warszawskim*, Krakow, 2003, pp. 184–185.

4. "The Passover began on the evening of Monday 19th April. At 1 A.M. in the night from Sunday to Monday the ghetto was surrounded by a cordon of German gendarmes and Polish blue police. After half an hour of fighting, the Germans withdrew. In the afternoon they entered the ghetto a second time."–B. Engelking and J. Leociak, *Getto warszawskie. Przewodnik po nieistniejącym mieście*, Warsaw, 2001, p. 733.

5. Natan Gross, *Kim pan jest, panie Grymek?* Krakow, 1991, pp. 276–277.

6. Marian Wyrzykowski, *Dziennik 1938–1969*, Warsaw, 1995, pp. 79–80.

7. Ludwik Landau, *Kronika lat wojny i okupacji*, vol. 2 (December 1942–June 1943), Warsaw, 1962, p. 369.

8. Cited from Teresa Prekerowa's invaluable book, *Konspiracyjna Rada Pomocy Żydom w Warszawie 1942–1945*, Warsaw, 1982, pp. 374–375.

9. Original leaflet in Władysław Bartoszewski's collection. First edition in: *Ten jest z ojczyzny mojej*, 1st edition, 1966. Reprint from T. Prekerowa, pp. 375–376.

10. Barbara Engelking and Jacek Leociak, *Getto warszawskie. Przewodnik po nieistniejącym mieście*, Warsaw, 2001, p. 744; "Raport Stroopa o likwidacji getta warszawskiego w 1943 roku," edited by J.Gumkowski and K. Leszczyński, in *Biuletyn Głównej Komisji Badania Zbrodni Hitlerowskich*, vol. XI, Warsaw, 1960.

11. Irena Schultz (1902–1983), journalist. "It deserves to be remembered that in October 1942 Irena Schulz travelled to Lwów, where she received from Father Pokiziak a large number of blank birth certificates. These certificates were used in Warsaw to acquire Kennkartes [IDs]." M. Grynberg, *Księga Sprawiedliwych*, Warsaw, 1993, pp. 477–478.

12. Unfortunately, the famous composer and outstanding pianist Władysław Szpilman (1911–2000) never wrote anything in his memoir about the person who had done so much to save him—neither in his 1946 *Śmierć miasta*, nor in the re-edited version published 50 years later. His book has been published in many languages and is now even more famous thanks to Roman Polanski's film *The Pianist*. I write this because Mrs. Sendler was upset that people who risked their own lives to save others should be forgotten. Maria Krasnodębska certainly deserves to be remembered, because it was on her initiative that the outstanding artist Władysław Szpilman was put on the list of people protected by Żegota, from where he received 500 zlotys a month up to the Warsaw Uprising. These are facts Szpilman never mentioned.

13. Irena Sendler, "Ci, którzy pomagali Żydom," *Biuletyn Żydowskiego Instytutu Historycznego*, 1963, nr 45/46, pp. 234–347.

14. Despite the considerable risks involved, the importance of preserving such records was borne out after the war. The need to know one's true identity

is universal, as is testified by a remarkable letter Irena Sendler received in 2008:

Sonja Sun Johnsen
Diskusvagen 9
SE-19248 Sollentuna   2008-02-13
Sweden

Dear Ms. Irena Sendler

Through this humble letter I would like to personally thank you for your efforts during World War II. My apologies for not being able to write to you in Polish, but I hope someone can translate my heartfelt gratitude. My name is Sonja and I am 32 years old. I do not have any personal connection to the Holocaust or to war, since I was born some 20 years after the end of the Korean War and 30 years after the end of World War 2. Still, Ms. Sendler, I feel the need to thank you for what you did.

Last month I had the opportunity of attending a public lecture in Stockholm. Ms. Anna Mieszkowska presented the biography she wrote about you and your efforts during the war. The presentation touched me tremendously, and during some very emotional parts of the story I felt shivers going down my spine. When Ms. Mieszkowska told the audience about how you went out of your way to keep track of the rescued Jewish children's real identities, about the carefully folded notes with real and "new" names you and your colleagues hid in the jar in your home, protecting them with your own life, I felt tears coming to my eyes. After the lecture I had the opportunity to talk to Ms. Mieszkowsk (through a translator) and tell her how much your story had affected me and why. She kindly provided me with your address so that I could convey my feelings to you directly.

I was adopted from Korea to Norway when I was 1 ½ years old. I currently reside in a suburb of Stockholm, Sweden. I grew up with an empty space inside, not knowing anything about my background or true identity, and feeling like a vital part of me was missing. In 1999, as an adult I went to Korea, and without knowing my real name or even an accurate birth date (since I was too young at the age of adoption to have any memories from my life in Korea), I thought that I had no chance of ever finding out who I really was. Thanks to a big portion of luck and the aid of Korean media, I was, however, able to track down my biological family in 2000. It turns out that I have an older brother who was adopted to a family in the USA, and a younger sister who remained with our biological parents in Korea. While the tragedy which led to our separation was in itself traumatic, and despite the fact that my adoptive parents in Norway provided me with both their love and made sure all my physical needs were met, I have all my life felt the emptiness and pain stemming from not knowing who I really was, where I came from and who my biological relatives were.

I guess that is the reason why I was so touched by the fact that you and your colleagues in Zegota went to such effort to keep records of the true identities of the many thousand children you rescued. You realized that a child and human being need more than merely food and shelter in order to live, you understood the importance of being able to reunite families after the war, or at least give the survivors knowledge of their background. The fact that you did prioritize all of this in the middle of the war, in a time where physical survival was everyone's prime focus, tells me that you are an extraordinary person. And for that, Ms. Sendler, I want to thank you. Dziękuje!

With gratitude and love,

Sonja Sun Johnsen (born as Young-Joo Park in Korea 1975).

13

The Arrest

Irena Sendler: "October 20, 1943, was my name day. During the war, name days weren't really celebrated. People had other things on their mind. Despite this, that day an elderly aunt of mine and Janina Grabowska—one of my best couriers—did visit flat 82 at No. 6 Ludwiki Street in Wola, where Mother and I lived. We talked till three in the morning. My aunt and my courier stayed for the night, because curfew had started at 8 in the evening. The frightful bang and pounding on the door first woke my mother. When I finally was also fully awake and about to throw the small scroll out of the window, it turned out that the house was totally surrounded by the Gestapo. I tossed the small scroll, that is, the entire filing system, to my courier, and went to open the door. They burst in, eleven of them. The search lasted three hours, with the lifting of floorboards and pillows being ripped open. Throughout that time I did not once look at my friend, or at my mother, for fear of any of us giving anything away. We knew that the rolled-up lists were the most important thing. Janina had managed to hide them in her undergarments, under her armpit to be precise. She was wearing my large dressing gown, whose long sleeves covered everything—good, dependable Janka Grabowska.

"When the Gestapo officers ordered me to get dressed, incredible as it might seem, I felt happy because I knew the list of children was not in their hands. I was in such a hurry for those murderers to get out of my flat that I left the house in my morning slippers. Janka ran after me with my shoes. The Germans let me put them on.

"I walked down the long courtyard thinking only about how I had to stay composed, so that my face would not reveal to them any traces of fear, even though fear was clutching my throat. Yet in that time three miracles occurred. The first was that the Gestapo did not find the lists—the children were safe! The second miracle . . . That day I had a large sum of money at home, the allowances for the escapees, and their addresses. There were also Kennkartes and birth certificates, both real and false ones. All this was under my bed, which collapsed during the search. The Germans were so preoccupied with ripping up pillows and casting clothes out of the wardrobe that they, fortunately, took no notice of the broken bed. Thus in such a difficult situation I was able to maintain an internal calm. After all, this was just the first night . . . The third miracle was my successful destruction of an important list of children for whom I was due to deliver money the next day. This I managed to do on the way to Szucha. It was in my jacket pocket, the one I was wearing. There was no doubt that I would be striped naked and searched again. So I quietly tore the incriminating card into tiny pieces and furtively disposed of them through a slight opening in the car window. It was six in the morning, it was dark, and the Germans were so tired they were virtually snoozing. No one's suspicion was aroused. I no longer had to fear for those children. What I did not yet know was my own fate."

14

Jesus, I Trust in You. A Hundred Days in Pawiak Prison

At the Gestapo headquarters in Szucha Avenue, Irena Sendler was put in the so-called "tram". There—terrified and dismayed—she saw she was not alone. That night some of her colleagues from social welfare centers had also been arrested.

"During the investigation I realized," she later wrote in her memoir, "that one of our 'post boxes,'[1] as we called our contact points, was uncovered. The 'post box' was in a laundry in Bracka Street (between Aleje Jerozolimskie and Three Crosses Square). The owner had been arrested for some unrelated matter, broke down during torture, and gave my name away. During interrogations I was asked to name the organization I worked for and its leader. The Germans knew there was a secret organization helping Jews. But they did not know the details: its name, its headquarters, and members. They promised me that if I told them everything, I would be immediately released."

In Pawiak Prison[2] they interrogated and tortured Irena Sendler for many days and nights, but she gave no one away. "I was silent," she would say years later, "because I preferred to die rather than reveal our activity. What did my life mean compared with so many other people's lives, lives that I could have endangered?"

The Gestapo interrogator (a handsome and elegant man who spoke perfect Polish) considered her to be a mere pawn. He wanted addresses and the names of her superiors. The Germans did not realize they had arrested such an important member of the underground movement. They showed her a file with informants' reports. "I was shocked," she told the journalist interviewing her.³ "They showed me a whole file with information about the times and places. They also showed me the files of people who had informed on me. After three months, I received a sentence: I was to be shot. I received secret letters from Żegota, telling me to stay calm because they were doing everything to save me. This was comforting; it allowed me to believe in humanity. But I also knew that other condemned inmates were also encouraged to feel that there was still a chance.

Awareness that I was not alone, not abandoned by friends from the organization, helped me survive the most difficult moments . . . It reinforced the will to fight, it gave hope for the near future."

Irena Sendler: "I am in a Pawiak cell. A medical team enters, including prisoners. Among them is someone I know, Jadwiga Jędrzejewska.⁴ She noticed me. She came in again and threw me an apple. The medical team also included inmate doctors. 'Sendler, to the dentist,' I heard. She said it twice. 'But I don't have a toothache,' I replied. When she repeated it a third time, I realized this was conspiratorial. The German female warder escorted me to the 'surgery.' The dentist was prisoner Hania Sipowicz.⁵ The 'dental surgery' was a narrow room at the end of which sat a Gestapo man. There was also a dentist's chair. 'I'm going to drill a hole and insert a large filling.' (I understood this to mean a secret message!) She quietly warned me that in each cell there was an informant. During my stay I was in three cells. In one there were six of us, in another four (the other three were prostitutes!), and then I was in a cell for 12. The last one was the worst. Toilets? Four holes (craters) in the concrete floor, and seated opposite a Gestapo man. For four days I just couldn't do it.

"The most amusing incident? In the cell with the four prostitutes. Jadwiga once gave me a packet of cigarettes. I gave them to my cellmates, and they smoked them even though it was strictly prohibited. The cell was thick with smoke. A Gestapo man burst into the cell and started shouting, but my cellmates did not reveal that they had received the cigarettes from me. I am grateful to them for that. And what were they in for? Can't prostitutes be patriots, too?"⁶

***

Irena Sendler was not forgotten. They thought about how to get her out of prison because she was the only person who knew where the rescued children were. They were thinking about the children as well. Inside Pawiak Prison she witnessed some cruel scenes. She worked in the laundry, which had windows overlooking the courtyard. Seated in the middle of this courtyard there would be one, sometimes two Gestapo men. "One day I saw a three- or four-year-old boy playing in the courtyard. This was a Jewish boy. Sometimes, when arresting a mother, the Gestapo would also take her children. There were occasions when the 'good' female warder would let the children play out in the courtyard. I remember such an incident. The Gestapo man beckons for the boy to come to him. The small boy is scared, he doesn't want to approach, but is eventually enticed by a sweet. He is given a sweet into his small hand, and then another sweet into the other hand. Visibly happy, the boy returns. But once he has turned around, the Gestapo man shoots the infant in the back." Irena Sendler wrote down this shocking scene decades later.

Another scene from the laundry: "In the prison there were two laundries: the black one where the inmates' clothes were washed, and the white one, where the Gestapo's undergarments were washed. I had suffered from allergies since childhood and had nosebleeds whenever I washed clothes. One of my colleagues offered to do the washing for me. In all there were 20 of us women prisoners working in the laundry. The worst thing to wash was the terribly soiled underwear. The ingrained and dried feces just wouldn't come off. (We were actually happy that the Germans were soiling themselves out of fright . . .) The 'old' prisoners, washerwomen, advised us to use tough scrubbing brushes, the ones for cleaning floors. After some time, this abrasive action wore holes through the underpants. The Germans were furious, and it ended tragically. One day four of those brigands came to the laundry and ordered everyone out. We were made to stand in a row and then every second one of us was ordered to step forward. Before our eyes, every second woman was shot dead. We couldn't take it, we were crying. And then came Dr. Hanna Czuperska,[7] the head of the medical team, and seeing the state we were in, said: 'Girls, what's this? Do I hear someone's had a nervous breakdown? Dears, this is an ordinary Pawiak day!'

"Starvation was avoided in prison thanks to the presence of small children, the ones who were arrested together with their mothers. The 'good' female warders sometimes let the children go down to the cellars for some potatoes and carrots. We made an agreement with the boys, who would bring some potatoes to our laundry. When we boiled the undergarments, we would also boil the potatoes. Once a Gestapo man suddenly appeared. I quickly ran with the pot of potatoes to the toilet and sat on it, pretending to be answering the call of nature."

In the Pawiak Prison there were two types of execution by shooting. "The first type was on orders from Gestapo headquarters in Szucha Avenue. In such cases, prisoners were led out of their cells and shot, nearly always on the site of the former ghetto. The other procedure involved two Gestapo men entering the cell at five in the morning with an Alsatian dog. We would have to stand in a row and they would say who was to step forward. One of the cellmates was Barbara Dietrich, the manager of a children's playground and by profession a nursery school teacher. She sang beautifully. On days when a large number of death sentences were passed, she would sing patriotic songs with us. But one evening Barbara did not want to sing. We asked her to sing, but she refused because the next day she was to be shot. Indeed, this happened. In the morning the Gestapo men came. One of them said: 'Barbara Dietrich, sentenced to death, step forward . . .' She was shot together with another woman prisoner in Nowy Świat Street (today their memorial plaque is in nearby Foksal Street). After the war it turned out that both of them had been Soviet agents. When we were together in that 12-inmate cell, we would say to one another: 'In case I live to be free, in case that miracle happens . . . give me your address, I'll take care of your children, your family . . .' After the war, I did look after Barbara's children and mother."

***

A period of mass executions began at Pawiak Prison. Every morning the cell doors opened, and those called out never returned. "I once found a small, damaged picture with the words 'Jesus, I trust in You!' I hid it, and had it with me all the time."[8]

On January 20, 1944, among those called out, Irena Sendler also heard her own name. "What did you do then? You quickly handed out to remaining cellmates all you had received in parcels from the family or the Polish Red Cross. What did you feel? This no one is able to describe in writing; all the descriptions I have ever read failed to reflect how it really felt. There were a lot of us, 30, perhaps 40 people. We were being taken to their headquarters in Szucha Avenue," she recalls. "I realized this was my final journey. And then something quite unbelievable happened. They read out the names, and every person called out was told to go to a room on the left. Everyone except me; I was told to go to a room on the right. Quite unexpectedly a Gestapo man appeared, apparently to take me for further interrogation. He escorted me out of the Gestapo headquarters toward the Polish Sejm (parliament) building in Wiejska Street. On the corner of today's Wyzwolenia Avenue, Aleje Ujazdowskie, and Na Rozdrożu Square (where there is now a fountain, and not far from where until recently I used to live) he told me in Polish: 'You're free! Get out of here at once !' I was bewildered, but out of some naivety or stupidity, I asked for my Kennkarte—the most essential document to have in those days. In response he just repeated: 'Go away!' But I was persistent in demanding the return of my identity document. So he hit me in the face, knocking me to the ground, and left. I was bleeding profusely. With difficulty I reached a nearby chemist's or pharmacy. Fortunately, when I entered, there were no customers. Seeing the state I was in and how I was dressed (prison uniform), the owner took me to the back of the shop. Asking no questions, she gave me a glass of water and some droplets to calm me down. She also offered to help. I asked for a coat (this was winter) and money for the tram. She gave me these things. So I got on the tram with the intention to get home. But when it reached Młynarska Street, a newspaper boy (those wonderful, unmatched boys) jumped on and yelled: 'Get off, Gestapo round-up round the corner!' I disembarked with everyone else and with considerable effort and pain finally reached home.

"The happiness and joy at my return and my reunion with Mother cannot be described. An hour later one of my couriers arrived and said, 'Sleep here tonight, but tomorrow you must go into hiding.' A few days later, Żegota gave me new documents for a new name: Klara Dąbrowska."

***

The action of rescuing Sister Jolanta was organized by Julian Grobelny and Maria Palester.[9] Grobelny's initial efforts to free Irena Sendler proved unsuccessful. Maria, however, had a friend from Poznań, Władysław Pozowski, who spoke excellent German and was able bribe a Gestapo officer. Everything was carefully planned. A mother, Małgorzata Palester, left a rucksack stuffed with wads of dollars hidden beneath packets of macaroni and kasha (Maria was in charge of feeding infants in the Social Welfare Department) at the agreed spot. The money was picked up and the deal made. The bribed Gestapo man entered Irena Sendler as "executed" in all the relevant documents. He paid dearly for this, for when the ruse was uncovered, he and his colleagues who were also implicated, were sent to the Eastern Front as a punishment for betraying the Third Reich.

For Irena Sendler this was a return to a quite different world. She could no longer contact anyone in the Warsaw Civic Administration, where she had worked. But she could resume her underground activities as before, though now she was in hiding, just like the people she was trying to help. News of her execution was officially released. She even read about her own death on advertising columns in the street. In addition, the street megaphones announced it. It was not until a few weeks later that the truth came out.[10] The underground authorities themselves forbade her to sleep in her flat. The Gestapo did not make daytime arrests, so in that time Irena could be with her mother, but she had to stay at her neighbor's flat during the nighttime curfew. Eventually her mother's condition became so acute that in great secrecy Irena had to take her out of their flat. But then the Gestapo came and started asking after, Irena Sendler's mother. That was when Irena Sendler turned to the invaluable Dr. Majkowski, who as the chief of a medical office was able to send an ambulance to take her mother away. "They drove her to the hospital in Płocka Street. She was carried in on stretchers, only, after a while, to be carried out again. They took her to another hospital, The Child Jesus, but there the same thing happened. So from there we drove to the tram depot in Kawęczyńska Street, where our friends the Wichliński family worked. Stefania Wichlińska, my dear colleague from work, had been very active in underground work, for which she was arrested by the Gestapo in a confectioner's shop in Trębacka Street. They tortured her for many weeks. Then, in a very critical state, they carried her out on a stretcher to an area next to the ghetto, and shot her dead. Her husband, Stefan, who was an engineer, worked in the tram depot. They had two children, a daughter and a son. He agreed to hide my mother and me in his home at No. 2 Kawęczyńska Street," recalled Irena Sendler in her memoir.

On March 30, 1944, Irena Sendler's mother felt much worse. She asked for their friend Dr. Ropek. Her daughter had failed to tell her that Dr. Mieczysław Ropek had been arrested for his involvement in the issuing of phoney death certificates. "There was no telephone in Wichliński's home, so I went downstairs to the shop," recounts Mrs. Sendler over 60 years after the event, but with such precision as if it happened only very recently, "To my total amazement, the telephone was answered by Dr. Ropek! I was quite taken aback. I informed him of my mother's condition and he promised to come at once. When he came, Mother smiled. The doctor knew she was dying. I held Mother in my arms, and she just managed to say: 'Promise me you won't attend my funeral, the Gestapo will be looking for you . . .' Those were her last words."

Irena Sendler kept her promise and did not attend the funeral. The Gestapo asked questions about her at the church and then at Powązki Cemetery. They were told that the daughter of the deceased was in Pawiak Prison. "She was, and has now disappeared!" growled one of the furious German officers.

***

The ruins of Pawiak Prison in 1945. (From the collection of Anna Mieszkowska)

Irena Sendler: "After what I experienced in Pawiak Prison, I know we cannot condemn those who broke down under torture and betrayed others. In the Pawiak museum there is an exhibit with the instruments of torture. One should also be very careful not to be too hasty in accusing people of collaboration. Some time before my arrest I had been warned about a certain woman medical practitioner suspected of collaborating with the Germans. Inside Pawiak Prison I was quite surprised to meet that very person. We slept in the same bunk; we worked in the same laundry. But I was very careful. There was no doubt in my mind that she was an informant. A couple of years after the liberation, I discovered that before the war she had studied medicine in Vienna. Her husband had been a [Polish] officer who died in the defense of Warsaw. She lived in Śródmieście district, in Żurawia Street. Some time after the Germans had entered the city, she met two German officers near her home who greeted her very affectionately. These were her old colleagues from student days. Terrified (because nosey neighbors immediately drew their own conclusions), and not knowing what else to do in this extraordinary situation, she invited them into her home. She didn't want to arouse suspicions and provoke comments. In fact, she was helping Jews and came to the conclusion that her acquaintance with these Germans could come in useful. Indeed, it did. There were occasions when she was hiding a Jewish family in one room and entertaining her former colleagues in another. And from these colleagues she was able to extract all sorts of information that was useful in working out German plans with regard to Jews and Poles.

"I learned the truth about her wartime activities many years later when she turned to me for help in applying for a job. Before helping her, I told her about what she had been suspected of during the war. It was only then that she told me her full story. From Pawiak Prison she had been sent to Ravensbrück concentration camp. And there she was held until the end of the war, helping Jewish fellow inmates, who later submitted very positive opinions about her."

Notes

1. The so-called "post boxes" played an invaluable role in Żegota activity, recalls Irena Sendler.
These were the premises of very trusted people where Żegota activists could meet. They were places where important and urgent instructions or money for those who needed it could be left. "Żegota had the following premises where I could meet members of the presidium and receive instructions: 24 Żurawia, Marszałkowska, Radna, Bracka (I do not remember the house numbers), and Lekarska (the house of Prof. Mieczysław Michałowicz), at the place of the Ursuline Sisters in Powiśle near Gęsta Street, and in Praga at 15 Markowska St., in teacher Maria Kukulska's home, where apart from a 'post box' there was also an emergency care unit for children and adults who had been brought directly from the ghetto."

2. Pawiak was a prison built in the nineteenth century in Warsaw between Dzielna and Pawia streets. (The name is derived from the latter street.) During the Nazi occupation, it was one of the chief investigative jails for the German security forces in the so-called General Government. It was destroyed on August 21, 1944, by a Sonderkommando. In her book *Pawiak–kaźń i heroism*, Regina Domańska wrote: "'From 16th October 1943 to 15th February 1944 the terror increased sharply both in Warsaw and in Pawiak Prison. There were massive round-ups throughout the city. Those captured were taken to Pawiak Prison. They started executing Pawiak inmates in the streets of Warsaw. At the same time there were also secret executions carried out amid the ruins of the ghetto. The names of those executed were announced through megaphones in the street and on posters." (Warsaw, 1988, p. 37) In another of her books, the author wrote: "And although transports were constantly leaving Pawiak, bound for concentration camps and other prisons, or taking prisoners to do forced labor in the Reich, and despite all

the shootings, the prison remained overcrowded because the arrests never stopped," *Pawiak był etapem. Wspomnienia z lat 1939–1944*, Warsaw, 1987, p. 20.

3. Thomas Rose, "Sendlers Liste," *Frankfurter Rundschau*, April 19, 2003.

4. Jadwiga Jędrzejowska had been arrested on November 13, 1942. In April 1943, she worked in the medical team and was thus able to secretly help fellow inmates as well as pass on secret letters and reports. On July 30, 1944, the Germans transferred her to Ravensbrück concentration camp. She died in 1978.

5. Anna Sipowicz-Gościcka, dentist. Arrested together with her husband on May 17, 1941. She worked as a doctor in the "Serbia" ward of the women's prison section as well as the male hospital. She was an important messenger for the underground movement. A very courageous woman, who was committed to helping prisoners. Released from Pawiak Prison on July 31, 1944, she next participated in the Warsaw Uprising.

6. Irena Sendler said that the clients of these prostitutes were communists of underground resistance who happened to be out of the house when the arrests happened.

7. After the war, Anna Czuperska-Śliwicka published a book about Pawiak Prison entitled *Cztery lata ostrego dyżuru* (published twice).

8. This picture, which she described as the most valuable object in her life, Irena Sendler posted in a letter (describing its history but not leaving a return address) to Pope John Paul II during his first visit to Poland.

9. Maria Szulisławska-Palester (1897–1991), a Romanist. Her husband, Henryk (who died in a tragic accident at the age of 75 on November 19, 1944) was a doctor. They lived in flat 8 at 53 Łowicka Street. They had two children: the elder, a son, Krzysztof, died in the Warsaw Uprising, and a daughter, Małgorzata, is now a doctor and lives in Warsaw. At various times during the war they hid a total of 12 Jews in their flat. It was Maria who managed to contact the Żegota presidium directly (which was far from easy in the difficult conditions of wartime conspiracy). This she did thanks to the help of the prewar Democratic Party activist Andrzej Klimowicz, who contacted his party colleague Emilia Hiżowa (1895–1970), the head of the housing section and later medical section in Żegota.

10. On February 1, 1944, Polish Home Army soldiers of the Pegaz detachment (previously called Agat and afterward Parasol) carried out the death sentence on the SS and Police General for the Warsaw District, Franz Kutschera. The decision to execute Kutschera (who had done a lot to increase actions of terror in Warsaw, including public executions in the streets) was made by the Directorate of Civil Resistance of the Polish Secret State. A few days after this famous operation, the Gestapo came to Irena Sendler's Wola District home.

15

April–August 1944

Irena Sendler: "My husband was in a camp. After the death of my mother, I was alone and devoted all my energies to work for the Council to Aid Jews (Żegota). I also continued to work for a secret PPS cell. My tasks included delivering money to the families of activists who had been arrested. I also transported medicines to those hiding in the forests. Despite my changed name, I had no fixed abode. For my own safety and theirs, I never stayed at a friend's home for more than a few days at a time. I had just a bag with toiletries and a change of underwear."

Once she was returning from a mission and the train, she was on stopped for a while at Skierniewice. The Germans were conducting a thorough search of all the passengers; they were checking documents and looking though the baggage. They were looking for someone. The gendarme had a list of wanted people. "I was calm, because I had good documents for my new name," Irena Sendler recalls. "Feeling confident, I looked over the gendarme's shoulder, and froze. On the wanted list I saw my name: Irena Sendler.

"In July, the atmosphere in the city was becoming increasingly tense. One could feel a general expectation that something extraordinary was about to happen. I personally did not believe in an uprising. I did not think there was any chance of victory through armed struggle. Although the streets of Warsaw now saw German soldiers retreating from the Eastern Front, one still felt the might of the German Reich and its army.

"After my escape from prison, I put the lists with children's names into a jar, which I then buried. During the uprising, I transferred the lists to a bottle and buried it almost in exactly the same place—in the garden of

9 Lekarska Street, where my courier and friend lived, so that she would be able to give it to the right people if I died."

The old apple tree beneath which Irena Sendler and Jadwiga Piotrowska buried the bottle grows to this day.

***

When the uprising started, Irena Sendler (like many Varsovians) was out in the street, in the district of Mokotów. She eventually reached the home of her friends Maria and Henryk Palester at 51/53 Łowicka Street. Staying there was also Stefan Zgrzembski, a lawyer and prewar PPS activist who had previously been in Otwock and Praga. Irena had known him since before the war, and for a few years, they had worked together in the underground movement. They married two years after the war.

16

What Sister Jolanta Did during the 63 Days of the Warsaw Uprising

Having completed a six-month Polish Red Cross course in nursing, Irena Sendler reported to the nearest dressing station, which was in the courtyard of the house where the Palester family lived. Soon after the uprising had begun, the dressing station was full of wounded people. "With our own eyes we saw all the inhabitants being thrown out of the surrounding houses, and the courtyard of 51/53 Łowiecka Street suddenly teeming with people," recalled Irena Sendler in 2003, 59 years after the event. "After a few days, the dressing station had turned into a large hospital with dozens of wounded patients. Among them we hid five adult Jews (three men and two women, with all of whom to this day I remain in touch!).[1] Ostensibly wounded, they had bandaged faces. Toward the end of September 1944, when all the inhabitants of Warsaw were expelled from their homes and all the first aid points were closed, our outpost found itself in great danger. Our evacuation was impossible because for the dozens of wounded people we only had one stretcher.

"Quite unexpectedly, one of the Germans approached the chief doctor of our improvised hospital, Maria Skokowska-Rudolf, and said in Polish: 'Follow me.' Those who were in a slightly better state proceeded on foot, whereas the badly wounded ones were carried on whatever was available— doors taken out of their hinges or large municipal dustpans. We were joined by a group of able-bodied residents from the house, and we all followed the

German. On the same street opposite our home there was another house, still under construction; it had no windows and no roof!

"This was where the German took us and said: 'My father is German, but my mother is Polish. When the war began and I was called up, I had to promise my mother that I would never kill a Pole, and that whenever I could I would help Poles. That is why I have taken you here. All the inhabitants of Warsaw are being sent to a camp in Pruszków, where terrible things are happening. I want you to be spared such suffering and that's why I'm leaving you here. If the Germans find you, say that you are here on the instructions of Major Patz.'

"We moved into the empty house where there was nothing. We slept on planks and ate what the healthy residents who had joined our group had brought with them for the road. This food quickly ran out and for a few days all we had to eat were the tomatoes growing in surrounding gardens. Among our patients there was a housemaid from a nearby residence. The residence was bombed out, but the cellar remained intact. And in that cellar there were huge supplies of food: sacks of rice, flour, sugar, as well as smoked meats and pickled meats in jars. We went there together. As we were packing everything, a German entered the cellar. He was as frightened of us as we were of him. In a blind rage he attacked me with his bayonet, deeply wounding my leg. It turned out that this was a deserter looking for civilian clothes. He told us he had had enough of war. For five years he had been killing and he did not want to kill anymore. He said he had a large family and had to live for their sake. He wanted to run away from this hell. He was actually asking us for help!

"Marysia Dziedzic, the woman who was with me, gave him a complete set of the owner's clothes, which she had found hidden in the cellar. After getting the clothes, he left us alone. When we returned with bags full of precious food, Dr. Skokowska greeted us with an exclamation of delight, but then her expression changed to one of concern when she noticed my leg. The wound became infected. For a couple of days I had a very high fever and was struggling with death. We had no antiseptics. It was with considerable difficulty, thanks to the enormous efforts of Dr. Skokowska, that I pulled through.

"Warsaw was still being bombed. A bomb fragment struck a woman, tearing off her right arm. It was a matter of life and death—she had to be operated on at once. Dr. Skokowska-Rudolf specialized in child tuberculosis, whereas Dr. Henryk Palester was an epidemiologist; neither of them were surgeons, and neither had ever carried out an operation. It was decided that Maria Skokowska-Rudolf would do it, as she was 30 years younger.

Dr. Maria Skokowska-Rudolf after the war. (Courtesy of the Janina Zgrzembska family archives)

My task was to return to the now burnt-out house where we had previously stayed and boil some ordinary kitchen knives for the operation.

"As I was crossing the garden, a bullet grazed my head, cutting through my hair on the left side.

We laid the woman on a improvised operating table, made of planks, and Dr. Skokowska started making the first incision (without anaesthetic!). My job was to hand her the improvised surgical instruments, that is, the kitchen knives. Two other 'nurses' were entrusted with keeping the flies away. While this operation was being carried out, there were over 60 people in the room. Suddenly we heard Germans shouting and scuffling with the other doctor, Henryk Palester, who, carrying a Red Cross flag, had gone out to speak to them. The German yelled: 'Who are you? How did you get here?' Dr. Palester calmly explained that we were there on the instructions of Major Patz. This astonished the German, and then made him even more enraged. He demanded to know on what authority the

Polish doctor was using his name?! He struck the doctor and broke his flag staff, then with submachine gun ready to fire, burst into the room. Dr. Skokowska, who was still operating, calmly told the major: 'Allow me, sir, to finish this operation, and then I'll explain everything.' The German lowered his gun and waited. Once the operation was completed, he ordered Dr. Skokowska to follow him. Accompanying them were four other German soldiers. Our team, including Skokowska's husband, who was a professor at the Warsaw University of Technology, and their 15-year-old son, huddled together and waited on tenterhooks to hear the shots. For two hours there was total silence. Then through the glassless windows we saw the four soldiers carrying two large laundry baskets. One was full of bread, and the other full of medical dressings. Walking alongside them, very much alive, was Dr. Skokowska. She told us that Major Patz had taken her to his quarters, where she explained to him how we had ended up in the deserted house. She did not mention the German who had led us this place, but said that it was the state of the patients and the lack of stretchers that prevented us from leaving Warsaw.

"Major Patz admitted that he had been ready to have us all killed, but the sight of that operation being carried out in such incredible circumstances, as well as Dr. Skokowska's determination and heroism made him change his mind.

"I also remember another dramatic incident. One day a distraught woman came to us begging for help. By some miracle she had pulled out of a pile of corpses her still-living son as well as her husband, and she brought them to us. It turned out that at the start of the uprising a large number of people had been out on their allotments in Mokotów Field and found shelter in a Jesuit monastery in Rakowiecka Street, not far from where we were. They remained there because they could not return to their homes. One day the Germans set fire to the building. Almost everyone was killed. This woman, perhaps with some supernatural intuition, heard the groans of those still alive, and among them she found her loved ones. In desperation she was now trying to find help for them in our improvised, insurgent hospital.

"In mid-September the remainder of Warsaw's inhabitants, including ourselves, were herded out of the city. We had to go across Mokotów Field. There we were joined by the inhabitants of surrounding streets who had had nothing to do with our 'hospital.' Suddenly we heard a woman crying out loud; she was in labor. Also crying beside her was a small child and its elder brother.[2] Several people stopped. I searched in the crowd for Dr. Skokowska. Two men carried the pregnant woman in their arms. It was with difficulty that we reached the fork junction where one road was for Krakow and the other for Pruszków. The Germans escorting us were already on the Pruszków road. One of our patients approached them. They talked for a long time. He offered them a large sum of money so that we could take the road leading to Okęcie. They agreed. We reached the site of a marmalade factory. Seeing the crowd of sick people, cripples, and crying infants, the factory's German director told his workers to bring out for the children containers of marmalade, bread, and milk. He also provided transport, so that our escorts could take us to where they wanted. The local authorities put us in some barracks. We set about accommodating the sick. The barracks were filthy, infested with lice and other pests. Previously they had held Soviet prisoners of war. The pregnant woman was sent to a nearby hospital. The next day the local authorities moved us to a housing cooperative building that had been deserted by residents fearing the fighting in nearby Warsaw. It was then that a priest from a local parish took very good care of us. He provided us with meals of soup and bread.[3]

"I remember our last wartime Christmas Eve. Sitting around a modest supper in a festive mood, we were suddenly startled by furious pounding on the door. It was a German, wounded and quite drunk. Without asking questions, Dr. Skokowska and I took care of him. Once his wounds were treated, Stefan Zgrzembski took him as far from the house as possible. In the meantime the rest of us set about scrubbing his blood off the floor; we had to remove all traces of his presence."

Notes

1. One of the women, Jaga Rosenholc, now lives in Canada. Mrs. Sendler says she was the bravest of the group. Under German fire, she would get across three barricades to bring a bucket of water.

2. Mrs. Moszyńska [(the woman in labor)] found Irena Sendler decades later thanks to an article in *Gazeta Wyborcza*. She reminded Mrs. Sendler of the dramatic way they had met that day and described the later fortunes of her two children.

3. Irena Sendler: "On September 14, 1944, some 150 people, including those who were sick or wounded, were thrown out of Insurgent First Aid and Rescue Point No. 2 at 4 Fałata Street and taken on a penal march west. Thanks to a coincidental stroke of fortune, the doctors of the point were able to take their patients not to Dworzec Zachodni, but to Okęcie. Barracks that had previously held maltreated Jews and next Soviet POWs became the first base for Red Cross Hospital No. 2 (the later Dom Dziecka [Children's Home–orphanage] in Warsaw), whose objective was to rescue as many people as possible from the columns

being marched to Pruszków. In order to accommodate an ever-increasing number of patients as well as protect the building from the Germans, at the end of September 1944, the Okęcie local authorities gave the Warsaw evictees a new base at No. 21 Bandurskiego Street. In November, child victims of the fighting in the capital started arriving at the orphanage. Moreover, Polish Social Welfare Authorities began gradually withdrawing children from the countryside as conditions there deteriorated. In January and February 1945, the youngest children started arriving, ones who, separated from their parents during the uprising, had been taken in by strangers and were now being sent on to orphanages. Finally, the most tragic group of children arrived, those from the German camps, who had witnessed rapes, mass murders, and mass executions—children who were constantly talking about crematoriums. In August 1945, there were still 120 children aged 3–18 in the Dom Dziecka orphanage."

17

Warsaw Free!

Irena Sendler: "After the liberation of Warsaw, on January 17, 1945 (I remember that the first troops entered Okęcie at 15:00 hrs, the Soviet Army and our Army!), the hospital was converted into an orphanage—Dom Dziecka. One day they delivered some children from Auschwitz. These were very small children, perhaps three or four years old. They had been in the camp with their mothers, but just before the Red Army liberated it, their mothers were . . . burned. The children knew this, and the only reason they weren't also burned was the lack of time. They were saved by the arrival of the Soviet Army.

"All the orphanage staff surrounded these unfortunate beings with their most tender and loving care. And this concerned not only health and general hygiene (they were all infested with lice!) or a proper diet (they were very weak from hunger and living conditions in the camp), but above all moral and emotional support. They suffered from a serious post-camp neurosis that wouldn't let them sleep at nights. They'd wake up crying. Each child had to be hugged and gently rocked back to sleep. One little girl once asked me, 'Did it hurt mummy very much when she was being burned?' I was shocked, but I couldn't let the girl see that. 'No, it didn't hurt because an angel took her straight to heaven,' I replied. A few days later the same girl asked me to draw her an angel. This I did, but it was one of my most difficult experiences from that period.

"The shortage of food posed a great problem for the hospital. It was a stroke of luck that helped us to survive this difficult time. I was on a commuter train that ran between Milanówek and Opacza (a tiny hamlet a few kilometers from Okęcie) when I met Dziatka (Władysława)

Dr. Maria Skokowska-Rudolf Irena Sendler, and Irena Wojdowska, 1945. (Courtesy of the Janina Zgrzembska family archives)

Michałowiczowa. She was involved in Żegota thanks to her father-in-law, Professor Mieczysław Michałowicz, whose home was always open to Jews seeking help. On that train Dziatka immediately informed me that the Social Welfare Department, the Central Welfare Council, and part of the Żegota presidium were now all based in Milanówek. So I went there and almost at once received from Adolf Berman and Marek Arczyński financial aid for our children. Today I do not remember the exact sum, but I know that back then it was considered substantial and it certainly helped us survive that most difficult winter. The last time I had contact with the illegal Żegota organization was on the morning of January 17, 1945. When the Soviet army took over, there was an immediate change of currency and the entire hospital, including some 300 patients as well as a large number of medical, nursing, and ancillary staff, was again without food. Toward the end of January, I was delegated to Lublin, to the new government. There I obtained help from the new Health Ministry. They gave us 100,000 zlotys (in the new currency) as well as a whole lorry full of food and medicines. During my stay of several days I learned that the vice-chairman of Żegota, Leon Feiner,[1] was lying seriously ill in a Lublin hospital. He thought he was suffering from pneumonia, but the doctors didn't tell him that they had actually diagnosed lung cancer. I visited him. It was then that he said to me: 'Jolanta, the war is almost over, we shall keep our word, you shall have your monument in Israel.'"

***

Soon afterward, the newly founded City of Warsaw National Council summoned Irena Sendler to work for the Health and Welfare Department. "For the first few weeks I refused to go to Warsaw," recounts Mrs. Sendler. "I shared with my close companions experiences from the uprising. I could not imagine leaving either my colleagues or the children, for whom I was a nurse, guardian, and teacher. I finally relented when the first [postwar] mayor of Warsaw, Marian Spychalski,[2] promised to quickly build a new orphanage—for indeed the former residents of the house where the Okęcie orphanage was located had started returning home.

My unhappiness at having to part company with the children was mitigated by the fact that I was leaving them under the good care of Maria Palester. At a general staff meeting, we decided that she should become the director of the orphanage. After the tragic death of her husband (Henryk Palester, a distinguished member of the Polish Home Army) and of her son, who was killed in action during the uprising, she was deeply heartbroken. Knowing her, I realized that the terrible pain after such a loss could only be eased through work for the benefit of children.

"I arrived in Warsaw on March 15. There I was made deputy head of the Health and Welfare Department at 10 Bagatela Street. A month later, I became the head of this department. The work was interesting, but extremely hard. Thousands of expelled inhabitants were returning to their hometown, or rather what was left of it. The whole of Warsaw was in ruins. The houses were burned-out, there was no electricity, effective sewage and drainage system, or running water. Those coming back, often on foot, had no means of subsistence. It was the Health and Welfare Department that had to supply them with at least the minimum to survive. This task seemed impossible, but the enthusiasm of the staff, not only the young but also the old and experienced, helped to overcome many difficulties. We worked day and night, hungry and cold, living, like others returning to Warsaw, in basements, frequently with rats for company. My first monthly salary was a loaf of bread. Help was provided by peasants, who delivered food from the surrounding countryside. Within a short space of time, 10 welfare centers were set up.[3] Moreover, we created emergency care units for street urchins, most of whom had lost their parents in the war. These needed some upbringing, as well as being dressed and given three meals a day. Similar treatment was provided to adults who applied for help. Many were in a very bad state of health, as well as having had terrible wartime experiences. For many we needed to find a place to live and work. Another problem was with old people, frequently infirm and lonely after they had lost their families in the war. Apart from physical sickness, war trauma led to total nervous breakdowns. Such people required quite different living conditions. They were usually accommodated in the prewar old people's home in Góra Kalwaria or in a new home that we set up in Lesznowola.

"A great tragedy of that period were young girls returning from various concentration camps or forced labor camps in Germany who had no family in Warsaw. They lived in the rubble, so they were called the "rubble girls" [in Polish *gruzinki*, which is derived from the word for rubble, *gruzy*, but can also mean Georgian females]. They earned what money they could out of prostitution. Finding a way to tackle this shameful problem became a priority for our social welfare staff.

"In Henryków, near Warsaw, there was a special home for girls with such problems that had already existed before the war and was run by nuns. The director was Sister Benigna,[4] who had herself had an extraordinarily tragic past. Our Warsaw Health and Welfare Department took over this home and created a new institution for the 'rubble girls' [or 'Georgian girls']. It was decided that the home would be open but organized in such a way that the girls would not want to escape. Our task was to give them back a relatively normal youth, to love them and surround them with great affection. There was a school there where they could complete the elementary education they had been deprived of. The war had robbed them of their formative years; it had orphaned them and led them to depravity. Our home was an enormous chance for them to return to normality through study and work. Apart from school lessons and work in the garden, they were encouraged to learn new skills. Thus they could attend workshops in horticulture (flowers, fruits, and vegetables); toy making; sewing underwear; and tailoring. A rota was also established for work in the kitchen, but the rule was that all of them had to be engaged in other types of work as well. We also cared for their state of health. The staff were a wonderful team; they were dedicated and there was a good, loving atmosphere.

The girls did not run away. They understood what we were doing for them and they were grateful. In five years, up until I stopping being the director on March 15, 1950, only one girl ever left the home. I remember how when my daughter was born (in 1947), three girls brought me a basket of tomatoes from their garden and a pot with a fern they had grown themselves. The fern grew and grew to become very big. It lived 40 years, until 1987, which according to gardeners was exceptionally long. After I had gone, my successors destroyed what we had created in Henryków. It eventually became a home for the aged."

Notes

1. Leon Feiner (1888–1945), lawyer, Krakow solicitor, member of the Bund and its representative in the Polish underground resistance. From January 1943 to July 1944, he was the vice chairman of Żegota and from November or December 1944 its last chairman.

2. Marian Spychalski (1906–1980), workers' movement activist, Marshal of Poland, architect, and in 1945 mayor of Warsaw.

3. There were 10 welfare centers before the war, 12 during the war and 10 social cooperative centers after the war. The author of the new name was Wanda Weltstaub-Wawrzyńska, a cooperative studies graduate of the Free Polish University Pedagogy Faculty.

4. Sister Benigna, formerly Stanisława Umińska (1901–1977), actress. In 1924 in a hospital in Paris, she shot dead her fiancé (Jan Żyznowski, painter, novelist, and art critic), who was dying of cancer. In 1925, a French court acquitted her. After her return to Poland, she gave up her career in the theatre and instead worked in hospitals. She joined the Benedictine Sisters' Order of the Good Samaritan, and became Sister Benigna. She took her solemn vows in 1936. In the years 1939–1945, she was the mother superior of the home for problem girls and fallen women in Henryków. [Information from: *Słownik biograficzny teatru polskiego*, Warsaw, 1994.]

18

Fulfilled Vocation. The Postwar Fates of Rescued Jewish Children

In her already frequently cited book on the Council to Aid Jews (Żegota), Teresa Prekerowa published a statement on efforts to help Jewish children in the years 1939–1945. It was written in March 1979 by four of the most active carers of Jewish children: Irena Sendler, Jadwiga Piotrowska, Izabela Kuczowska, and Wanda Drozdowska-Rogowiczowa. This invaluable historic document is cited below in full:

"We the undersigned state that during the 1939–1945 war as workers of the Social Welfare Department and its agencies, the Health and Welfare Centers, we were simultaneously members of the Żegota Council to Aid Jews, though at the time we did not know the organization's full name or who the other members were. It was through our membership that we participated in the saving of Jewish children from mass murder and as members we were in close contact with Irena Sendler, who was then the head of the children's section in Żegota. We fully confirm her report on the number of children saved. Today, almost 40 years later, it is difficult to provide an exact figure, but we estimate the total number of children helped one way or another by Żegota to have been around 2,500. Thus:

1. Approximately 500 children were accommodated, via the Social Welfare Department, in monastic institutions (Jan Dobraczyński, Jadwiga Piotrowska).
2. Some 200 children were accommodated in the Emergency Civic Care Unit of Father Boduen's Orphanage (Maria Krasnodębska and Stanisława Zybertówna).

3. Some 500 children were accommodated in institutions run by the RGO [Central Welfare Council] (Aleksandra Dargielowa).
4. Approximately 100 youths aged 15–16 were sent to the forests to join the partisans (Andrzej Klimowicz, Jadwiga Koszustka, Jadwiga Bilwin, and the Żegota chairman, Grobelny).
5. Some 1,300 were helped and cared for by so-called foster families. Here the most active were: Helena Grobelna (wife of the Żegota chairman), Maria Palester and her daughter Małgorzata Palester, Stanisław Papuziński, Zofia Wędrychowska, Izabela Kuczkowska and her mother Kazimiera Trzaskalska, Maria Kukulska, Wanda Drozdowska-Rogowiczowa, Wincenty Ferster, Janina Grabowska, Joanna Waldowa, Jadwiga Bilwin, Jadwiga Kosztulska, Irena Schultz, Lucyna Franciszkiewicz, and Helena Małuszyńska.

Among these children were:

1. Those for whom Żegota found a family (guardians) and provided them with a regular money allowance, documents, clothes, food parcels, and so forth.
2. A group of children who needed only limited help in the form of a registration document, birth certificate or, for example, medical help; alternatively, if threatened by szmalcowniks, an immediate change of address or money to pay off the blackmailer.
3. Children taken in by families who did not ask for money, in which case our organization's help was usually limited to providing a birth certificate.
4. Families that had used their own contacts to take children out of the ghetto or off the streets (this concerned children who begged around private houses). These families out of their own initiative undertook full responsibility for Jewish children. Such children only sometimes required medical treatment, medicines or, in some cases, a bed in hospital. Here we were greatly helped by Dr. Juliusz Majkowski, Dr. Mieczysław Ropek, Dr. Zofia Franio, Prof. Andrzej Trojanowski, Dr. Hanna Kołodziejska, and Nurse Helena Szeszko.

Moreover, we believe that many more children than the number stated here were actually rescued from the Warsaw ghetto because they certainly were also rescued in other, sometimes very surprising ways, which did not involve Żegota."

***

In the period from August to December 1944, only 25 percent of the Jewish children's list secured by Irena Sendler was destroyed; and these losses were soon restored by Irena Sendler's couriers. After liberation, the list was deciphered and, once complete, submitted to Adolf Berman,[1] who in the years 1947–1949 was chairman of the Central Committee of Polish Jewry. Why? Because activists from this committee were taking Jewish children away from their foster parents. In some cases their original families were reclaiming them. However, children with no surviving relatives were also taken away and temporarily put into Jewish orphanages,[2] after which a large number of them were sent to the Palestine, later Israel. Irena Sendler believes that the vast majority of the 2,000 children featured on the Warsaw list were found after the war.

***

Unfortunately, all this did not happen without problems of a psychological nature. Contrary to Mrs. Sendler's wishes and instructions, the children were frequently snatched from the foster parents without due consideration in preparing both children and guardians for such an abrupt change. "It was a harrowing experience for the small heroes!" recalls Irena Sendler, deeply agitated even today, after so many years. "Mothers and relatives started reclaiming their children. Some of the reunions were beautiful and happy events. But others were very difficult, indeed. For both sides, because some of the younger children did not remember their wartime past, and the foster parents also suffered because it was difficult for them to part with children they had had, in some cases, for a few years! Knowing the fate of so many Jews, some foster parents had assumed that the adopted child's entire family was dead. For the children's own good they did not tell them where they had really come from. And then, all of a sudden, there was this surprise. Everything now had to be explained. And to tell a child the truth can be extremely difficult. Sometimes these complex problems resulted in legal proceedings."[3]

***

There were cases where representatives of the Central Committee of Polish Jewry could not trace saved Jewish children in Poland. Raised in Polish families, some children discovered their true history at a very late stage (if ever!). All Jewish children who lived through the hell on both sides of the ghetto wall continue to be its victims, no matter how many years have passed since then. The cruel experiences have affected their psyches permanently, for the rest of their lives. The youngest of the saved children are now aged over 60, whereas the oldest is 83. All, regardless of sex, age, or place of residence, share one thing in common: trauma. Many of them united at the start of the 1990s, when they founded the Association of "Children of the Holocaust" in Poland. There they learn to cope with the burden of their memories. They support each other. Relationships among them have become close and they need each other. Those who have had similar experiences but have not yet united with the others suffer more.

The Association of "Children of the Holocaust" has published in Warsaw three volumes of narratives and recollections under the collective title *Dzieci Holocaustu mówią* (Children of the Holocaust Speak). This is the cruellest collection of memoirs and yet it is deeply moving to read. It is all the more disturbing because these narratives, although written after many years of relatively "normal" life, have lost none of the horror of those events. It appears that there is no escaping from one's memories. The pain can only be alleviated by sharing your experiences with others. It is for this purpose that therapeutic workshops have been formed, where those saved as children from the Holocaust meet in their own circle. Do they realize what a miracle it was that they survived? They probably do. But not all of them have been able to accept the miracle of survival, to come to terms with it. Some are unable to cope with their nightmarish memories and resent the fact that they are still alive. They resent the fact that only they survived, abandoned, given away by their family. It is with such problems, kept suppressed for years, that they turn to Irena Sendler. And Irena Sendler always tells them that it was not she who saved them but the determination and courage of their mothers and fathers, grandmothers and grandfathers who were able to part with them. They were able to overcome the love of keeping with the love of giving. Today, after over 60 years, they know more about themselves. But they do not always wish others, particularly their children and grandchildren, to know all of the terrible truth. Thus for so many years survivors have been running away from their memories. And yet it sometimes happens that the past catches up with them in the most unusual of places. It turns out that after decades, somewhere in Israel, Australia, Canada, the United States, or alternatively somewhere much closer in Europe, someone is looking for them—a cousin or some other distant relative. There are sometimes wonderful reunions of cousins. Sometimes they do not wish to talk about it. "Why?" some ask. Every story is different.

In 1945, "they emerged out of nowhere, large or small, but each similar to the rest: emaciated, tattered clothes, frequently shoeless, matted hair, aged children with grey skin and a dull gaze," writes Maria Thau (Weczer) in her moving book *Powroty* (Returns). "Such were the ones who emerged from the ground, from the sewers or other hiding places, from holes without daylight or from ruins such as those in the Warsaw ghetto. There were also others who looked healthy, those from the countryside or the partisans. But all of them without exception had something in common in the way they looked and behaved: avoiding eye contact, the expression on their faces and their posture, as if they were about to escape, a latent fear, readiness at any moment to retreat back into their holes, to the ruins, the basements; that was still their place, they belonged there, not among the upright people and the noisy, confident children. They actually avoided other children: they feared their otherness, their normality. People said of them: 'They have come out into the light.' Others much less kindly said, 'They have come out of their holes, like rats.'"

"The life of a single Jewish child had to be looked after by many people, sometimes representing more than one organization or institution," wrote Teresa Prekerowa. One should add that in peacetime these were organizations and institutions had never collaborated with each other. What united them was the Holocaust. The cause of rescuing those in the gravest danger: the Jews.

***

For Irena Sendler the action of helping Jews, something she participated in with such great devotion, has never ended. It persists thanks to continued contact with the rescued children, their children, and grandchildren. They write to her from all parts of the world. They remember. She is the last person that knows who they were before they left the Warsaw ghetto. Sometimes she knew their parents or grandparents, sometimes their siblings. She is the only person whom these now quite elderly people can ask certain questions, such as: "What did my mother look like?" "What did my father do?" "Did I have a brother, a sister?"

You cannot escape from yourself. That is why they return from distant parts of the world to places they will always remember. They fear these returns, but they desire them. After several decades, they finally decide to try and confront their past—a past they had previously tried to erase from their memories. It can happen that they return to a place they barely remember and search for people who might be able to help establish the details, find the traces of their house or just their street. Sometimes, thanks to the Association of "Children of the Holocaust," they immediately contact

Irena Sendler. Such was the case, for example, with the daughter of Achilles Rosenkranc. After over 60 years, she decided to find her father's grave at the Jewish Cemetery in Warsaw. Achilles Rosenkranc, an outstanding expert on treasury law, had died of typhus in the Warsaw ghetto in 1942. No one from his family was present at his funeral. Among the few who were, was Irena Sendler, who had smuggled in under her coat a branch of white lilacs and placed it on his tomb. And it was only she who could know where he was buried. It was only thanks to Irena Sendler that after so many years the daughter could ease the painful memories and salve her conscience.[4]

Irena Sendler's invaluable list let many orphaned children find distant relatives. Adolf Berman took the list with him to Israel. To this day copies of it are circulated among many private homes.

Irena Sendler: "I know that the lives of those saved children are very complicated. Every one of them has had to live through their individual drama of being saved. They were brought up by strangers, with other families or in orphanages. They were given a roof over their heads, they were fed, cared for, and given an education. That is a lot. But never again were they in their real home with their real parents, with their real family. Frequently an agonizing notion persisted in their minds that if they had stayed together in the ghetto, a miracle would have occurred and they would have somehow survived together with their parents, and their brothers and sisters. Throughout all those postwar years they nurtured in their hearts a tiny glimmer of hope that never died. Despite numerous searches all over the world, many to this day do not know their roots. They know nothing about their families: grandparents, relatives, even parents and siblings. But they have painful memories of separation. The tragedy of those times concerns them all. It concerns the children just as it concerned their mothers who handed them over to strangers. It also concerns their adopted mothers, who took them in and assumed the burden of raising them.

"It often happened that the latter were not treated well by their adopted children, despite themselves treating the saved child as best as they possibly could, sometimes even better than their own children!

"Not infrequently, despite the greatest care being taken to surround them with affection and using all possible means to provide them with what they would have had at home, despite all this love and warmth, the adopted children felt pain and regret that, instead of their real mother, they had to have an adopted one. It sometimes happened that this pain and regret turned into resentment and rebellion. 'Why are you alive when my mother had to die?' When such a question was posed, it was very difficult to give a good, tactful answer; one that would placate the anger and resolve the dilemma.

"I witnessed such behavior more than once. I experienced it myself with my adopted child, whom I treated not only as well as my own daughter but quite consciously tried to show her even more feeling, and yet in response I was confronted not only with reluctance but even with outright hostility. Despite my completed studies in pedagogy and many years' experience of working with children and youths, I was unable to understand such behavior. I was quite at a loss as to what to do. Quite simply, contemporary pedagogy and psychology had not yet considered such problems, the problems of children who had survived the Holocaust."

***

So many years after the war. The streets and houses rebuilt. Life returned to the ruined cities. Yet in the hearts of the saved children there is still despair, sorrow, and longing. They were educated, many moved to other countries, many had outstanding professional careers, and many set up their own families. Today they are grandparents. And yet as long as they live they will still be "children'" searching for their past. They search for it, but they also run away from it—from the memories, which with age become even more vivid. Memories that are like a disease, a memory disease for which no cure has yet been found. Does anyone understand them? Perhaps only they, themselves, because no one else has had such experiences. These experiences never go away—they are a part of them.

Elżbieta Ficowska recounts: "In our Association there are almost 800 people with very similar life histories. The main differences may depend on how old the child was when it was rescued by one of Mrs. Sendler's agents or by Irena Sendler herself. There is a group, a relatively small group of people my age, who were born during the war and who do not remember anything that happened then. They have a 'black hole' in their memories. They know nothing about themselves. For instance, a child found somewhere under a fence, with no information about who it is. These people usually find out from their adopted parents that they are actually not their biological parents. And such people, now usually well into their sixties, are quite alone in the world. There is no one they can ask: 'Who am I?' 'How did it happen that I survived?' I am fortunate to have avoided this. I have no memory of those days, those years. I have no conscious experience of it, and, I think perhaps it is good that I have no lasting impression of all those terrible things that were going on then. For me it is like a film, like a read book; it doesn't hurt me to talk about it. Nevertheless I know, I know everything . . . In 1942, I was transported out on a brick laden cart that was being taken from the ghetto to the Aryan side. In between the bricks they hid a wooden box with holes in it. I was placed inside this box, at the time probably a six-month-old baby, and put to sleep with luminal. They also put in a silver spoon for luck. Engraved on this spoon was my name and date of birth. Earlier, also thanks to Irena Sendler's contacts, my several-year-old cousin was also taken out of the ghetto. I ended up at the emergency care unit of Stanisława Bussoldowa, Irena Sendler's friend and a midwife who would go to the ghetto to help deliver births. I was supposed to stay there for a few weeks, but I stayed there for good. She decided to keep me as no one in my family had survived and she did not want to give me away anywhere else. I know from her that my real mother had left the ghetto a few times to see me. She would telephone to hear my voice. She 'looked good,' so she could have been saved, but she did not want to leave her parents and my grandparents. I don't even have their photographs. I've been looking for them throughout my adult life, in Poland and in Israel. For me this will always be an unrequited longing—something unfulfilled, although I have personally experienced family happiness."

***

Elżbieta Ficowska's spoon. (Courtesy of the Janina Zgrzembska family archives)

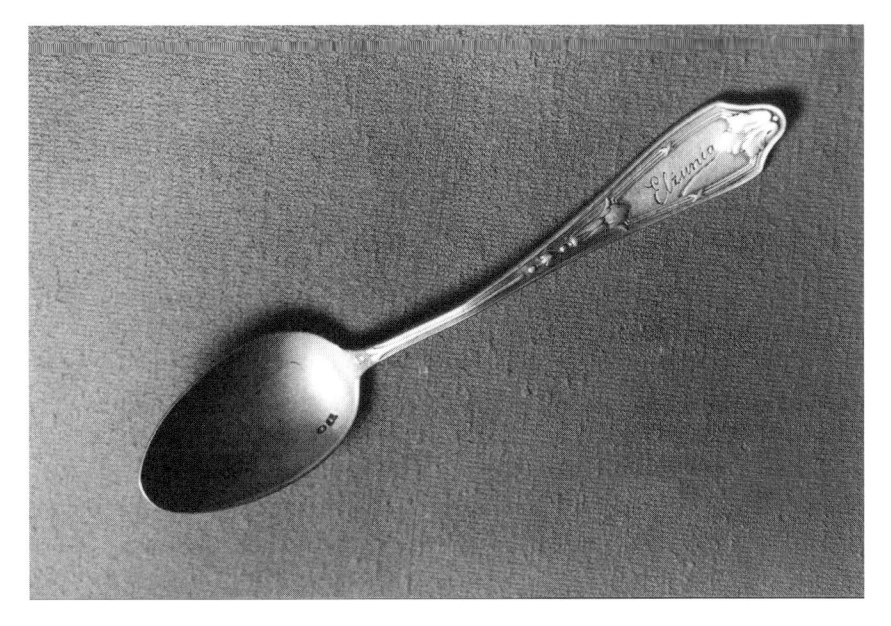

FULFILLED VOCATION

Elżbieta Ficowska's spoon. (Courtesy of the Janina Zgrzembska family archives)

Some of the rescued children have agreed to speak with me, but they wish to remain anonymous.

Helena K., journalist: "I left Warsaw at the last moment, in December 1939. Via Berlin, I arrived in Bucharest. I 'looked good' and my documents were good. I survived. My father and my younger brother died in the Warsaw ghetto. For years I could not think about them. I ran away from the memories of my youth spent in Warsaw. After the war, I settled in London. I did not have the courage to return until 1993. I attended the 50th anniversary commemoration of the Warsaw Ghetto Uprising. I stood in the crowd and cried for many hours. This was my return to the past, a return to the history I had been trying to escape from. I then went to the Jewish Cemetery to search for the grave of my mother, who had died before the war. Accompanying me was a friend, a child of the Holocaust, who told me with envy: 'How happy you must be, you have your mother's grave. I have nothing.'"

***

Jerzy K., lawyer: "I do not know exactly how old I am. When the war broke out, I may have been four, perhaps five. I only remember that we lived in Lwów. My father died of heart failure when the Russians entered the city in 1939. Together with my mother and her younger brother we travelled first to Krakow and then to Warsaw, where another brother of my mother's lived. But we missed each other, because meanwhile he, not knowing of our arrival, had set out for Lwów. We wandered from place to place for a while. Then mother and I settled in the ghetto. The uncle who had travelled with us all the way from Lwów got involved in some underground organization. He went into hiding somewhere around Warsaw. For a time my mother kept in touch with him. The summer of 1942 was exceedingly hot. For entire days I had to sit in an attic, hidden among eiderdowns and pillows. I had to be quiet. Mother worked in a canteen, from where she would every day bring me a small pot of soup. One day she told me that someone would come for me. And so it happened. He was calling out my name. I left the ghetto when it was dark. Never again did I see my mother. A Polish family took me in, but I could no longer stand this life of constant hiding. I ran away. Not knowing Warsaw, I had nowhere to go. I stood beneath a street lamp and cried. Someone stopped, and took me to their home. Later I was sent to an orphanage run by nuns. Before the [Warsaw] uprising they moved us to Otwock. After the war, I was recognized as a war orphan. They moved me from one home to another, all over Poland. For many years I did not know who I was. On my rewritten birth certificate I had a different name. No one was looking for me. And I was looking for no one. In 1958, after completing my studies in Poznań, I travelled to Warsaw. And there I met someone who recognized me. He knew my real name and he had known my parents. Gradually I learned of my past. I started discovering facts about my early life. But this gave me no peace. For over 50 years now I have been searching within myself. And when after some time I find a trace, a faint, distant recollection, it doesn't bring any sense of relief. On the contrary, I find it increasingly more difficult to live with these remnants. All I have are gradually picked up snippets of information that only very incompletely reveal the unattainable truth. I sometimes regret ever having picked up the trail and started the search. Perhaps it would have been better for me if I had continued to know nothing about myself? When I told one of my sons about my past, he replied: 'Dad, I don't want to know any of this.' His words caused me pain. I read an article about Irena Sendler. Since then I can't stop thinking about her. Was it she who organized my escape from the ghetto? Did she know my mother? I know how old she is and where she lives, but I lack the courage to go to her and ask her these questions. Perhaps it's better not to know?"

***

Jolanta G., librarian, lives near Warsaw. Born in 1947. "My parents were hiding in the Warsaw region during the war. That is how they met. Father died in 1953. Mother was much younger than he; she died 10 years ago. For many years I thought I had no other, more distant relatives. My grandparents perished in the war. But in the 1960s, a cousin turned up. Twelve years older than me, he [Jerzy] was the son of my father's sister. Mother took him in but was mistrustful. He tried very hard to befriend us. He told us about an uncle who after the war had settled in London. For many years this uncle failed to get in touch with us, 'for our own safety' as my mother would frequently explain. Probably on account of my mother's cold reception, Jerzy left as suddenly as when he had appeared, and we had no contact for many years. He turned up again after my mother's death. He wishes to stay in touch, stressing that we are very close family. His mother and her brother, that is, my father, loved each other very much. Together they escaped from Lwów, leaving behind their mother, our grandmother. But in every other respect we are different. Quite different life experiences have shaped us. He is so nervous . . . Despite undertaken efforts, we seem unable to find a common language. During our infrequent meetings he always repeats how lucky I was to have such a happy childhood: a normal home, both parents. Yes, I reply, but I knew nothing about my parents. For all those years mother never told me anything about her past. After my father's death, she lived in constant fear of being observed, she felt threatened. Any letter that arrived from abroad she would receive with a sense of foreboding. I learned the truth about my father's family and about what happened to them during the war many years later. There are some letters, documents, which I had never looked into. Although I am of a postwar generation, I feel I have inherited the tragedy of the wartime experiences of both my parents."

***

"After the war, it wasn't easy to put your life in order," says Basia, a teacher. "I was five when it broke out. We lived in a small town and our parents decided to divide my brother and myself between them. I went to the [Warsaw] ghetto with mother, while father with his brother and my older brother travelled to more distant relatives in the country—and next, once it became even more unsafe, to the forest. No one other than I survived the war. When I understood this, for a long time I could not be happy. I was still waiting for them. In fact, I'm waiting all the time. The worst time is around Christmas, the exchanging of wishes and gifts, the get-togethers.

I have had two failed marriages—problems with my own children, who I did not understand. Perhaps I shouldn't have got married and started a family. Today I am alone. But I have two friends with similar histories. It's in their company that I feel the best. They, too, have been unhappy in their adult, mature lives. We understand each other without words. Although we never talk about it, we are united by this secret wartime experience that is never discussed with anyone. I read in some scientific journal that Holocaust survivors suffer from a post-traumatic stress disorder. This is true. I think that every one of us Holocaust children bears the stigma of wartime experiences. I suffer from a severe neurosis that just gets worse with old age. The recurring nightmares are now troubling me more frequently than before. I do not read any war literature, memoirs or narratives. I don't watch war films, whereas war comedies I find unethical, and just in bad taste."

***

I met Stanisław a few years ago in London. I knew his story and when I started working on this book, he immediately sprang to mind. I telephoned him so that he would once again repeat what he had previously told me:

"I escaped from Poland in 1956," he began, "as soon as it became possible to partake in a holiday cruise on the M/S Batory to Denmark. We all had a collective passport and the ship did not enter the port but lay at anchor in the roadstead. We were able to get to shore in motorboats. Of the holiday group we had joined perhaps half of them returned. It was easier for me because I had an uncle in London. I informed him where I was, and, after a few weeks, he came to collect me. It was another few months before I could officially enter England."

"Why did you risk an escape?" I asked. "You see, madam," he replied, "a person cannot be alone in the world. And after the war, I was quite alone. My grandparents, my parents, both my sisters were all dead. It was only I, hiding in the countryside, who survived. I worked for a miller. Among my siblings I had the slimmest chances of escaping death. My sisters were pretty blondes, whereas I had dark hair. Unfortunately, I was similar to my father, who had very Semitic features. That is why I was sent to the countryside. Everyone else went to the ghetto and only I was taken away by persons my parents knew. But in 1942, when people had already heard of Treblinka, they themselves began to feel frightened. They passed me on to others. Next, after a few months, these other people now suggested that the best place for me would be with the miller. And that was where I stayed until the liberation. The war was over, and I was a healthy, well-fed, fit (I did a lot of cycling), 17-year-old boy. I knew about the uprising in Warsaw. From the winter of 1943, I no longer had any news from my family. For a long time I could not believe that only I had survived. I wrote letters to the Polish Red Cross. I deluded myself with the hope that perhaps some family member had ended up in a camp, to do forced labor. In 1954, I received news that my father's brother, who was in Lwów when the war started, had left Russia thanks to General Anders army and was now living in London. Although before the war he had obtained a university degree in law, in London he worked in a restaurant, and later in the London Underground. He married an English woman and they had children. When he discovered that I was alive, he helped me get away. He was the one who planned everything. When I read an article in the London *Tydzień Polski* about Irena Sendler, I thought to myself: why didn't the Good Lord direct her to my parents' home? Perhaps one of my sisters could have been saved? Throughout all these years I still ask myself the question, why am I the only one to survive?"

***

"The Time of Annihilation was ended, but it still persisted in the hearts of every single one of those who survived. It existed all the more so because only after it was over could the losses be counted, that is the silent roll call of those murdered," wrote Michał Głowiński in his *Czarne sezony*. Elsewhere he added: "Time takes away hope, but it does not heal wounds."[5]

Notes

1. Adolf Berman (1906–1978), doctor of psychology. An activist of the Poale Zion Left. In the ghetto he was the director of Centos. In 1942, the party instructed him to cross over to the Aryan side. He cooperated with Żegota and became its secretary. After the war, he became chairman of the Central Committee of Polish Jewry. From 1950 onward, he lived in Israel. He was the author of collections of documents and witness accounts.

2. "In 1945 Jewish orphanages (Żydowskie Domy Dziecka) were springing up throughout liberated Poland. According to the Jewish Historical Institute (ŻIH), up to December 1945, Jewish orphanages were founded in Krakow, Częstochowa, Lublin, Zatrzebie, Otwock, Przyborów, Helenówek near Łódź, Przemyśl, Warsaw, Chorzów, Toruń, Ostrowiec, Staszów, Radomsk, Garwolin, Krzeszów, Pietrolesie. Katowice and Kielce. The vast majority of children were

aged between 4 and 16, with a few exceptions who were slightly younger or slightly older. Frequently in very poor health and malnourished, they suffered from sick lungs (tuberculosis), all sorts of skin diseases, lice, their limbs often covered with festering wounds, they had eye and ear infections as well as 4 to 6 years missed out on education—these were 10-year-old illiterates, But above all they were frightened, mistrustful, ready to escape," writes Maria Thau (Weczer) in her excellent book *Powroty*, Krakow, 2002. According to Mrs. Sendler, the Jewish children did not arrive at the orphanages in such a state from Polish homes but because they had been hiding elsewhere.

3. From a letter written to Kaya Ploss (director of the American Center of Polish Culture in Washington, D.C., on August 30, 2003): "Chairman Berman and I agreed that the taking of children from orphanages run by nuns or private homes had to be conducted in a calm and tactful manner. And the children had be duly prepared because for them this would be the third traumatic experience in their short lives. The first was being torn from their family and relatives and having their identities changed. The second was their being taken from the care point. And the third was when soon after the war they were taken from a children's home or family home to which they had become attached. At the time I was the head of the Social Welfare Department in Warsaw, and therefore, I was able to appoint my very best inspector, while also asking Berman to select a member of his staff who loved children, so that the two of them together would take the children from their temporary guardians and pass them on to Jewish orphanages. This subsequent change in the lives of children who had been saved from death was always very hard and sometimes even tragic. Children who had gotten used to their new families, guardians, or nuns in orphanages found having to be separated yet again very distressing, especially if it turned out that none of their original family had survived. These changes were also a terrible experience for the foster families that had looked after children for the last few years and frequently regarded them as their own. . . .

The list that we here submit includes the names of children saved from the Warsaw ghetto, with most of whom we stay in touch to this day. They are the children from two orphanages run by nuns as well as the children of friends or fellow workers from before the war.

Turkowice–an orphanage run by the Little Sister Servants of the Blessed Virgin Mary:

1. Stach Janowski, living in the United States of America, doctor, prewar name Hadasa Anichimowicz
2. Joanna S., lives in Poland, married to a Pole, has children, entirely different circle of friends, Roman Catholic
3. Stefa Rybczyńska, emigrated
4. Katarzyna Meloch, during the occupation called Irena Dąbrowska, lives in Warsaw, writer
5. Joanna Mieczyk, lives in Israel, now called Ilana Nachsoni
6. Fredzia Rotbard, wartime surname Kowalska, lives in Israel

7. Feliksa B., deceased, lived in Poland
8. Ludwik, Zdzisław B., lives in Poland
9. "Zetem," lives in Poland, does not reveal his Jewish origins
10. Chaim Sternbach, wartime name Stefan Borzęcki (or Borzeński), lives in Israel
11. Andrzej Nowicki (Wengbauer), lives in USA

Chotomów–Sisters of the Family of the Virgin Mary (head office in Hoża Street, Warsaw):
1. Joanna Majerczyk, lives in London
2. The girl "X," does not wish to reveal name, has changed circle of friends.
3. Ida G., changed name, lives in Israel
4. Anna Paprocka, the protagonist in Jan Dobraczyński's book, Ewa
5. Halina W.
6. Jadwiga Cz.
7. Irena and Anna Monatówna, wartime surname Michalska
8. Janina L.
9. Danuta R.

Some of the saved children have requested not to have their real names or full names revealed. After tragic wartime experiences, these people decided to start new lives and change their circle of acquaintances. Many converted to Catholicism and set up families, whose members sometimes do not know of their Jewish origins and tragic past.

List of saved children who are currently Irena Sendler's friends and acquaintances:
1. Michał Głowiński (b. 1934), wartime surname Piotrowski, lives in Warsaw, writer, essayist, outstanding critic and historian of literature, professor at the Polish Academy of Sciences Institute of Literary Research
2. Piotr Zettinger (Michal Głowiński's cousin), prewar surname Zysman, the son of a famous lawyer, himself an engineer, lives in Sweden
3. Irenka Wojdowska, used to live in Szczecin, now lives in Warsaw
4. Bogdan Wojdowski, brother of Irenka, writer, deceased (d. 1994)
5. Elżbieta Ficowska, pedagogue, author of children's books, for two terms chairperson of the Association of "Children of the Holocaust" in Poland, lives in Warsaw
6. Ala Grynberg, lives in the United States
7. Margarita Turkow, daughter of social activist in the [Warsaw] ghetto, lives in Israel
8. Teresa Korner, dentist, lives in Israel
9. Regina Epsztein, daughter of [Warsaw] ghetto journalist, doctor, lives in the United States

4. Aniela Uziembło published an article about Achilles Rosenkranc in *Gazeta Wyborcza* on February 16, 2004.

5. Michał Głowiński, *Czarne sezony*, pp. 174 and 181.

19

The Director—Postwar Professional and Social Work

Irena Sendler: "In prewar Poland the Warsaw city authorities set up two complexes of shelters for destitute people who had been evicted from their homes for not paying rent. One comprised barracks in Annopol, while the other was located in Praga, in a former shoe factory called Polus. These were large factory halls housing scores of people who had to share a kitchen and toilets. Constant arguments and fights made life miserable. Therefore we decided to close this site of the shame of a bygone epoch and instead set up a few welfare institutions. This task I entrusted to two of my subordinates, very brave and devoted social workers. I instructed them to arrange, in cooperation with the voivodeship (provincial) authorities, the relocation of the inhabitants of Polus to what was now western Poland. There they would have better housing conditions, in residential blocks abandoned by the Germans, and work. Meanwhile, Polus was renovated, and there we founded: a nursery, flats for the aged, a school for social workers with a beautiful library, and also several flats for some of our staff. There we also set up a central UNRRA[1] clothes depot.

"The work of the Social Welfare Department in that period was inordinately difficult. All those who returned to the ruined capital needed our help. Realization of our tasks went in two directions. On the one hand, it concerned providing the inhabitants of Warsaw, downtrodden and maltreated by war, with temporary help in the form of meals or food parcels as well as a means of finding work and shelter. On the other hand, we faced the much more challenging task of formulating a new concept of social welfare activity in a fundamentally changed political system. I travelled to Łódź, to Professor Helena Radlińska, for advice and help in fulfilling this daunting task as I felt I was inadequately prepared for it.

"While at first, right after the war, the Communist Party authorities did not interfere in welfare issues (at the time being more engaged in politicizing Polish society), five years later they also became interested in our work. Thus I was instructed to close all 10 of our Social Cooperative Centers (the name was thought up by Wanda Wawrzyńska) and henceforth the aid they provided was to be put under the supervision of the local administrator (*starosta*). Next, social welfare was divided into three categories. Matters concerning children aged from zero to three were the concern of the Ministry of Health, children aged three to eighteen were the responsibility of the Ministry of Education, whereas the Social Welfare Ministry was only to look after the aged and the disabled.

"On the basis of many years of experience, I believed that social welfare aid should encompass entire families, naturally insofar as a particular ailment, accident, or other pathology permitted. This was because most aspects of a given individual's daily life usually also concerned the rest of that person's family. In my opinion, the new policy was wrong. I therefore struggled to convince the authorities that the above changes would worsen rather than improve the situation of those who needed help. They would simply make it impossible for us social workers to provide effective aid. I lost this battle and thus, after five years' service, on March 15, 1950, I left the Social Welfare Department. I thought I would find a better understanding in other social aid organizations. Thus I started working in the Welfare Department of the Union of War Invalids. There, however, aid was basically restricted to those who were suffering as a direct result of the war, and so I was unable to help the much broader group of people in genuine need.

I left this job under the illusion that I might be able to persuade the Women's League to organize a welfare section and that there I would be able to realize what was really most important at the time. Unfortunately, here politics also proved to be more important than society's most pressing needs.

"Consequently, in 1952, I started working for the Ministry of Education, where I became the head of pedagogical supervision. This proved to be very interesting work, but required a lot of travelling around the country, which greatly complicated my family life. At the time I had two small children, both very sickly.

"In 1954, I became a deputy head teacher at the High School for Hospital Attendants, which was an evening school. This was a decision made for the sake of convenience, it was dictated by conditions at home. I was now able to spend more time with my family during the day. Over the subsequent few years, I worked in various medical schools for nurses (especially pediatric nurses), for midwives, and for medical laboratory workers. These were vocational schools where the teaching program was strictly focused on a given medical profession, but it virtually ignored teaching methods that specifically applied to adolescents. I reached an agreement with the Ministry of Health Medical Education Department and, thanks to their very positive attitude, I was able to place greater emphasis on teaching methods concerning youths. This was important because the teachers were doctors and nurses who were good in their professions but had almost no idea of how to teach. The trick was to prepare them for their jobs as teachers.

"On October 1, 1958, Dr. Aleksander Pacho, the then Vice Minister for Health, appointed me to the post of director of the Department of Medical Secondary Schools at the Ministry of Health. I held this post until 1962. That year I became the deputy head of education at the Teaching College for Dentistry and Pharmaceutical Technicians.

"In 1967, I was forced into early retirement. At the time I was only 57! The cause was the fact that Israel had won a war against the Arabs and I was accused of loudly celebrating this victory in the teachers' room. This was a time of increased intolerance toward the Jews in Poland. Not wishing to lose touch with youths, work with whom had given me so much joy, contentment, and satisfaction over the years, I took up a job in the school library, where I worked until 1984. From 1932 to 1984, I had worked in total for 52 years!

"Apart from my professional work, throughout my life I was also always engaged in social work. In secondary school, I was an active member of the girl guides; I went to the girl guide camps and acquired various merit badges. Scouting had a very positive effect on my approach to life and character. There we were taught to distinguish good from bad, as well as how to look after the sick and old. These skills and experiences paid off in later life.

"During my university studies, I joined the Union of Democratic Youth. In this organization we fought against unfair decisions made by the university authorities, including the so-called ghetto bench system and registration restrictions for students with peasant backgrounds. When I worked in the Civic Welfare Committee and later the Social Welfare Department, I also belonged to the Polish Socialist Party (PPS). In that time, I was engaged in distributing to various factories our party newspapers, leaflets, appeals, and other propaganda materials.

"I also belonged to the PPS[2] during the war. In that time, I was responsible for providing material help to the families of those imprisoned by the Germans as well as people hiding in the forests.

"After the war, in 1948, the leadership of the then Polish Workers' Party (PPR) decided to also incorporate the PPS and create the Polish United Workers' Party (PZPR). Thus I involuntarily became a member of this new [communist] party. But I soon realized that it had nothing to do with the prewar PPS, which had on its standards the slogans 'Independence' and 'Justice.' Before the war the word *socialism* did not mean so much a specific doctrine or political program as a sort of social compassion and opposition to the money culture. This is what appealed to me in the movement. When after 1948 it all changed, I handed in my party booklet, and as a result experienced a lot of unpleasantness. This 'unpleasantness' followed me for many, many postwar years! When I was still working in the Civic Administration Welfare Department, people were informing against me, claiming that among my staff I was hiding Polish Home Army (AK) activists. I was many times summoned to the State Security Office. I was constantly receiving threats. At the time I was in my seventh month of pregnancy. The birth was very premature and the child was very weak; my baby son lived for just over a dozen days. With the medical knowledge of those days they were unable to save him. This was a terrible tragedy for me.

"It was a miracle that in those terrible Stalinist times I was not arrested and thus spared the most serious consequences. I owed this to one of the many people I had saved, a Jewess called Irena M. P., who after the war married Colonel P., the chief of the State Security Office in Warsaw. I did not know anything about her marriage at the time because we had lost contact with one another after the Warsaw Uprising. It was many years later, after her husband had died, that she found me and said, 'During the occupation you saved my life, and after the war I saved yours . . . You were to be arrested, which in that time was synonymous with a death sentence. One day my husband was off sick. His subordinates came to our home to discuss with him some urgent matters. I was entering the room with coffee when I heard my husband conclude: 'on the basis of this evidence Irena Sendler will have to be arrested.' After the men had gone, I told my husband about how I had been hiding during the occupation and your role in saving my life. With tears in my eyes I persuaded him to reverse his decision regarding the arrest. My husband loved me, we had two small children. When he learned the truth, he realized it could not be done.'"

***

THE DIRECTOR

Irena Sendler with her family: (from the left) Janina Zgrzembska (daughter), Iwona Zgrzembska (daughter-in-law), Agnieszka Zgrzembska (granddaughter) and Adam Zgrzembski (son). During the ceremony of being awarded the Order of Polonia Restituta Commander's Cross in 1997. (Courtesy of the Janina Zgrzembska family archives)

Irena Sendler: "As the head of the Social Welfare Department I organized the publication of a monthly magazine entitled *Opiekun Społeczny* (Social Guardian), which came out for five years.

For many years, I was a member of the review committee for the Polish Red Cross (PCK) Board. I was also one of the founders of the League for the Struggle Against Racism, which included many former Żegota activists. But this organization did not last long as the Communist Party soon had it disbanded.

"For a short time, I was also a member of the Warsaw board of the Society of Children's Friends (TPD). Moreover, I belonged to the Secular School Society as well as the Polish Teachers' Union. For two terms I was a counselor in the Capital's National Council and the head of its Health Commission.

"When *Solidarność* (Solidarity) emerged in 1980, I was so delighted with its ideals that I left the Polish Teachers' Union and became a member of the Solidarity Trade Union, with other staff members of the school where I worked following my example. I remained a member of Solidarity until my retirement.

"From the start, I have been a member of the 'Open Republic' Association Against Anti-Semitism and Xenophobia. For many years now I have also been a member of the Association of War Invalids and the War Veterans' Union.

"For my many years of social work, I have received many awards,[3] the most precious of which for me is the Righteous Among the Nations medal, which was granted to me by the Yad Vashem Institute in Jerusalem on December 15, 1965."

***

Irena Sendler's tree was not planted in the Avenue of the Righteous Among the Nations until 1983, as for many years until that time, despite invitations from the Israeli government, the communist authorities had refused to issue her a passport. In Israel in 1983, she was met by the children she had saved, who were by then mothers and grandmothers. Virtually all of them had important jobs, such as professors, doctors, lawyers, and artists. They all greeted her with great warmth and affection, as did Israeli teenagers at numerous public meetings.

Notes

1. UNRRA (United Nations Relief and Rehabilitation Administration) was created in Atlantic City in 1943 on the initiative of the USA, Great Britain, the USSR and China. Its aim was to provide aid, after the fighting was over, to those Allied countries most affected by the war, including Poland.

2. During the war, Irena Sendler belonged to PPS-WRN (Polish Socialist Party—Freedom, Equality, Independence), but thanks to her prewar contacts, in the rescuing of Jews she cooperated with many members of the [pro-communist] RPPS (Workers' Polish Socialist Party). These acquaintances and wartime cooperation were to later have tragic consequences for her and to this day are a cause of many misunderstandings, even slander.

3. In September 1997, Irena Sendler was awarded the Order of Polonia Restituta Commander's Cross, whereas on November 11, 2001, "in recognition of having provided help to those in need," the Order of Polonia Restituta Commander's Cross with Star. On June 16, 2002, Janina Zgrzembska received on her mother's, Irena Sendler's, behalf the ECCE HOMO Order (awarded to those who through their altruistic deeds have confirmed that one can be *Proud To Be Human*).

20

Grateful Memories

Irena Sendler is deeply hurt by the fact that the people who were the most engaged in the rescuing of Jews during the occupation are today forgotten. Among such people she includes Julian Grobelny and his wife Helena. Her beautiful recollection of them was published in *Gazeta Wyborcza* on April 18, 2003.

It reads as follows:

"In association with last year's celebration of the 60th anniversary of the founding of the Council to Aid Jews and this year's 60th anniversary of the Warsaw Ghetto Uprising, I wish to recount my recollections of a chief figure in the Council, Chairman Julian Grobelny, whose pseudonym was Trojan, and his wife, Helena, pseudonym Halina. For many years they were leading PPS activists in the Łódź region. Julian worked in social welfare. Soon after the outbreak of war, when the Germans entered Łódź, they both found themselves on the list of enemies of the Third Reich. Thus they had to immediately leave their hometown and settle in a small house they had in Cegłów near Mińsk Mazowiecki. From there they continued their Polish leftwing political activity in the underground PPS. When Julian Grobelny became the chairman of Żegota, he and his wife moved to Warsaw, where they stayed in the homes of various people they knew. For their own and their hosts' safety they never spent more than a night or two at a time in a particular flat.

The tortuous course of underground life led me one December afternoon in 1942 to the third floor of No. 24 Żurawia Street. On giving the agreed password, the door opened and I stood before Trojan. The reason for the meeting was to see if we could work together. I was already engaged in rescuing Jews, working in a secret cell of five and later ten people at the Welfare and Health Department of the City Administration. But we found it increasingly more difficult to provide those persecuted people with material support. Already in mid-October 1939 the Germans ordered the sacking of all workers of Jewish origin and the withdrawal of welfare aid for the Jewish poor, to which, on the basis of a 1923 Act, they had been entitled to no less an extent than the Poles.

"We went to the ghetto and tried to smuggle out as many children as possible, because the situation there was getting worse day by day. Working with me in the department was, among others, Stefania Wichlińska, who was also a courier for Zofia Kossak-Szczucka, and this was how I found out that a new organization called Żegota was receiving money from the Government Delegation for Poland. On learning of our already three-year experience in rescuing Jews, Julian Grobelny, who always had a sense of humor, said: 'Well then, Jolanta (that was my wartime pseudonym in the PPS cell), let's do business together: you have a team of trusted people, and we shall have the necessary funds to help the ever greater number of persecuted people.' Thus began a new chapter in my underground work. After a month, I became head of the Children's Section. My predecessor, Aleksandra Dargielowa, had to resign because her post in the Central Welfare Council (RGO) did not allow her to also engage in the extremely absorbing work with Żegota.

"I remember Julian Grobelny as a great individual and a patriot. He had fought in the three Silesian uprisings. He respected and always helped national minorities, he argued for their rights, and for these rights to be respected. He worked tirelessly, demanding always much more from himself than from his subordinates.

"He was a very upright person and someone who possessed a rare quality among people in high positions—modesty. While being engaged in very complex and important matters, he always took every individual into consideration. He was always interested to help if anyone turned to him in need. There were times when he would make urgent telephone calls for me to report to him at once. I would hurry on the presumption that I was to be entrusted with a very important mission because this actually happened in some cases. However, when I arrived, I could be told that I had to urgently and with exceptional affection take care of a Jewish child that had witnessed the murder of its parents. Another time he instructed me to travel immediately with a trusted physician and medicines to a forest between Otwock and Celestynów, where in a hole, amid rubbish, a mother and her baby were hiding. The baby was very ill and therefore needed medical attention.

"The way in which Trojan put so much heart into his work as chairman of Żegota not only endeared him to others but also earned him great respect. He worked tirelessly for days on end, frequently burning the candle at both ends. He was very cheerful by nature and even seemed to also have some supernatural powers. Despite the obvious dangers and the menacing atmosphere that prevailed all around us, everyone somehow felt safe in his company.

"Trojan was the initiator of some powerful appeals in the underground press. Among other things, on many occasions he called on the Government Delegation for Poland to systematically combat blackmailers. He appealed for warnings to be issued, threatening blackmailers with the death penalty. He demanded that Żegota should be able to pass cases of blackmail on to a special court. For this purpose also, Żegota issued leaflets calling on the Polish community to help Jews. He passionately fought against the szmalcowniks. Despite being responsible for the Żegota organization in its entirety, both he and his wife, Helena, also provided shelter to over a dozen Jews, colleagues from the PPS.

"He cared for everyone in our team, the best evidence of which was his involvement in my release from prison. When I was in Pawiak Prison, on several occasions he sent me secret letters to raise my morale and assure me that Żegota would do everything to get me out of that hell. When the opportunity arose to bribe one of the Gestapo men and buy me out prison (despite the already issued death sentence), Julian Grobelny and the entire Żegota council did not hesitate to provide the necessary sum of money.

"When in April 1943 the ghetto's inhabitants rose up to fight, it is to Trojan's credit that he did everything he possibly could to provide the insurgents with firearms.

"His natural tact and ability to be with people always produced results. It made it possible for the Council to Aid Jews to function harmoniously, despite the fact that it comprised representatives of all political parties—with the exception of the National Party and the Polish Workers' Party.

Throughout the occupation, Julian and Helena lived in poverty. There were even times when they suffered from hunger. As active members of the PPS, like the rest of us, they received only very small allowances. They also had a small income from the garden of their house in Cegłów. But all this was not sufficient to feed themselves properly as prices were constantly rising. Having no home of their own in Warsaw and frequently moving locations, they had to eat out in the town, for which they did not always have enough money. As a result, Julian's health, and he was suffering from tuberculosis, steadily deteriorated.

"When in the spring of 1944 they arrested him in Mińsk Mazowiecki, he was to an extent fortunate in his misfortune. The Gestapo had not arrested him for being the chairman of Żegota but because they believed him to be a dangerous Polish leftist activist. This was of colossal significance because the Germans issued the severest punishments, including that of death, for any form of help provided to Jews. For example, there was a lesser punishment for hiding a firearm in your home than for hiding a Jew.

"Our entire circle knew that with the advanced state of his illness and general wartime exhaustion, Trojan would hardly be able to withstand torture or the daily grind of prison life. Therefore, everything was done to provide him with medicines and nutritious food. Help came from, among others, doctors who were deeply involved in underground resistance, such as Dr. Zofia Franio, the head of a tuberculosis treatment clinic; Dr. Mieczysław Ropek of the Hospital for the Treatment of Pulmonary Diseases at 15 Spokojna Street in Warsaw; and Dr. Jan Rutkiewicz, a member of the PPS. Thanks to these efforts, Trojan survived the war to be liberated from prison.

"He became the first [postwar] *starosta* administrator of Mińsk Mazowiecki. However, his illness, made worse by the systematic wasting of his constitution during the over five years of occupation, meant that after only half a year of admirable work in this new office, in 1946, he died. This great activist was buried with full honors in a funeral attended by many friends from the PPS and Żegota. School students and Citizen Pawlak, a local activist, to this day look after his grave in the Mińsk Mazowiecki cemetery.

"For a long time, his wife, Helena, could not come to terms with the loss of her husband. She sold their house in Cegłów and for some of the money bought a one-room apartment in Łódź. She started having serious health problems. Like all those recognized as Righteous Among the Nations, she received a nominal sum of money from the New York foundation and some medicines from the Anne Frank Foundation in Basel.

"I travelled to Łódź many times to visit her. Exhausted by her wartime experiences of living in constant fear for her husband, Helena died in 1993. Her funeral was attended by mgr Halina Grubowska, representing the Jewish Historical Institute, as well as a numerous friends and colleagues from the PPS. For us Helena will always be remembered as her husband's faithful companion in all his social activities and achievements.

"We should never forget that throughout his life, Julian Grobelny, alias Trojan, fought for social welfare and justice for all the inhabitants of Poland, regardless of nationality or religion."

***

In Irena Sendler's archive, there is a copy of an invaluable document. Helena Grobelny's statement made on April 20, 1963, reads as follows:

"I hereby testify that from my husband Julian Grobelny, alias Trojan, chairman of the Council to Aid Jews during occupation, the following facts are known to me:

1. Citizen Irena Sendler, alias Jolanta, was his close colleague in the Council to Aid Jews presidium.
2. On account of the above activity, the Gestapo arrested her in the autumn of 1943; she was held in Pawiak Prison and sentenced to death.
3. The Council to Aid Jews undertook persistent efforts to rescue Sendler because in her flat she had part of the Council's archive. Moreover, she had been extensively engaged in the rescuing of children and was the only person to have memorized their hiding places. The efforts of my husband and other presidium members led to the Sendler's release from Pawiak Prison the very day she was to be executed. That day the enemy invader read out through megaphones the names of those who had been shot dead, including the name of Irena Sendler.
4. From that time on, Sendler had to use false documents, move out of her flat, and go into hiding.

Despite this, she continued to carry out extensive activities for the Council to Aid School right up to the end of the war.

21

Do We Remember? We Will Remember!

Michał Dudziewicz made a documentary film entitled *Lista Sendlerowej* (Sendler's List),[1] which won prizes at two festivals, in Stockholm and Niepokalanów.

"In Poland it has always been easier to talk about martyrs than about heroes. It is easier to talk about Janusz Korczak than about Irena Sendler because she makes us realize what we have not done but could have done," says Leszek Kantor, a political scientist at Stockholm University and organizer of the International Festival of Documentary Films.[2]

Professor Tomasz Szarota: "In the summer [of 2002] I entertained in my house a group of American girls from Uniontown in Kansas who had written a play about Irena Sendler. In our conversation I could not tell them much about how a woman who helped save several hundred Jews in Poland is respected by her own compatriots."[3]

***

In an interview with a female journalist from the weekly *Wprost*, the Israeli ambassador in Poland, Professor Shewah Weiss, said: "People are not born to be heroes. Mothers give birth to children and raise them simply so that they may live. That is why there are no greater heroes, no more courageous people in the world than the Righteous Among the Nations. This is an examination in humanity which we Jews have not yet passed."[4]

In his conversation with Joanna Szwedowska, Ambassador Weiss also confessed: "Being in Poland I have become aware that in these two countries, here and in Israel, the Holocaust still exists. In people's minds, in their memories, in the memories of children. In moral problems which somehow have to be solved. There is hope in future generations. . . . I have met many people who tell me of how during the war they had rescued Jews. And yet for many years in Poland this was not discussed. It was as if the hiding of Jews was a shameful subject."[5]

After the showing of Michał Dudziewicz's film, which also featured the visit of the four American students to Poland, Irena Sendler spoke: "As long as I live, as long as I have the strength, I shall always say that the most important thing in the world and in life is Goodness."

Before returning to the United States, when they were saying goodbye to the hero of their play, the American girls told her: "We will remember!"[6]

Notes

1. Broadcast on TVP2 in April 2003.
2. Aleksandra Zawłocka, "Dzieci Sendlerowej," *Wprost*, nr 7, February 16, 2003.
3. Tomasz Szarota: "Cisi bohaterowie," *Tygodnik Powszechny*, nr 51–52, December 22–29, 2002.
4. Aleksandra Zawłocka, "Dzieci Sendlerowej," op.cit.
5. Cited from an extensive interview conducted by Joanna Szwedowska with Shewah Weiss, published in book form and entitled *Ziemia i chmury*, Sejny, 2002, pp. 107 and 120.
6. When preparing this book, all the people I spoke to consistently stressed the fact that global interest (not only international, but also in Poland!) in Irena Sendler was actually aroused by this group of American students. And only later was it popularized by the American media with the bestowing of the Jan Karski Award. Elżbieta Ficowska, Elżbieta Zielińska-Mundlak (from Caracas), and Renata Skotnicka-Zajdman (from Montreal) all also spoke publicly about it at the conference of the Polish-Jewish Heritage Foundation in Montreal on October 24, 2002. In the proceedings we read: "The purpose of this meeting was to honor Irena Sendler. She is the living symbol of all those for whom the entire evening has been dedicated: the members of Żegota, the secret Council to Aid Jews in Poland in the years 1942–1945, as well as all the people of good will who, risking their own lives and the lives of their families, rescued their Jewish neighbors from extermination. The examples of these people's lives allow us all to be proud of being part of the human race."

22

Why Memories Were Revived So Late

"I constantly think that I have encountered a real miracle: I was bestowed the gift of life," says Michał Głowiński, a professor of literature and the author of a memoir he has called "ordering experiences and liberation."[1]
"This was a social phenomenon in Poland, Israel, and almost everywhere. The subject of the Holocaust was avoided, it was not discussed. Interest began some twenty years ago. Yet today there are fewer and fewer of its survivors.

"It is only now that people realize what happened and want to speak and write about it. A similar process was observed in Poland as well as in Israel and also in America. . . . At home a muffle was put on it, one was obliged to be taciturn. Besides, I said very little to my colleagues and other acquaintances. I was still fearful inside. I only liberated myself from this fear after 1989. . . . The ghetto area is a mystery to me, I simply cannot get my head around it, even though I have looked at the maps. . . . It seems to me everything that happened there cannot be religiously justified. And that is regardless of what religion. Theodicy, that is, the justification of God's behavior, is hardly possible in the enormity of evil in the world."[2]

"I put a seal of silence on everything that was important to me," he wrote in one of the tales in his autobiographical book *Historia jednej topoli* (The history of one poplar tree).[3] Elsewhere in the same book he recounts terrible experiences: "I distinctly remember the sealed trains setting off, bound for death. I was then aware that I was not on one of those trains only thanks to an extraordinary set of coincidences, which years later I can define without a degree of exaggeration as a miracle." It was also a miracle that almost all of Professor Głowiński's family survived. His parents and grandparents survived the war, separately, each hiding in a different place. After liberation, they reunited and lived together in one house. Those family members, friends, and acquaintances who had perished "were rarely and almost unwillingly mentioned. Every reminiscence was associated with pain. It reopened wounds, revived those terrible experiences, renewed the sense of loss, one which none of us could ever come to terms with. It demonstrated that you could not escape the burden of what had happened, and that this was a crushing weight, no less painful than that of a millstone. There was no way of casting it off. Everyone who had the experience carried it with them, and if they are still alive, they are still carrying it today. The experiences sink in and grow inside you, they become part of you and no treatment, not even the most complex surgery, will remove this growth."

In another autobiographical book, *Czarne sezony* (Black Seasons), Michał Głowiński shares some very personal reflections: "I think I'm still hiding in the cellar to this day." "I cannot chronologically order my vicissitudes on the Aryan side, I cannot accurately sequence the events . . . ," ". . . I had a very efficient early warning system which immediately switched on whenever a situation arose in which I might say something that could, even very indirectly, betray my origins. The rules of hiding became deeply ingrained in me. They were always in my mind and I was very careful never to break them." The author of these words was only five when the war broke out. He experienced being moved from the Pruszków ghetto to the Jewish district in Warsaw. He was an eyewitness of the terror in Umschlagplatz, the family's living conditions after the Great Action, and the escape with his parents on a cold winter morning, the day after New Year's Day in 1943.

The terror of Głowiński's experiences is best testified by his words: "For years I had hoped to find an appropriate description of fear in great literature, but not finding it anywhere, I now believe it simply might not exist." It was also Michał Głowiński who wrote: "In the season of great dying Irena Sendler dedicated her entire life to saving Jews."[4]

Jadwiga Kotowska, an author and the protagonist in a description of a child's terrible experiences, writes: "There are wounds that stopped bleeding, and then, when the events are recounted, they start bleeding again. When that happens, it is so difficult. It all appears before your eyes. You see everything and experience it anew."[5]

***

WHY MEMORIES WERE REVIVED SO LATE   153

For several years, I explored Polish émigré theatre. My research took me to London, New York, Los Angeles, Chicago, and Washington, D.C. In all these places, I met people who throughout their postwar lives had been running away from their wartime experiences, quite literally to the other side of the world! They were not only running away from terrible memories, they were also running away from themselves. In California, someone told me: "You know, as a child I was for four years kept in hiding. I was saved, but I don't know what for. Because for over 50 years now I am still hiding. In order to live, I had to forget everything. What was most difficult for me was trying to forget about my mother. I never wanted to know how she died. I blocked it all out of my mind and out of my heart. No one in my present family knows my wartime history—neither my wife, nor my son, nor his family. I thought that if I had not left Poland, it might have been easier. So I travelled to Poland. I entered the house where I was born and lived until September 1939. It was a strange feeling. Though badly damaged, the house had survived the uprising. Today it is quite dilapidated, but people still live there: the old and the poor. Before the war the building had had some very wealthy owners. It gleamed with cleanliness and it smelt fresh. I remember that smell! And I also remember another smell, that of fresh, home-cooked chicken broth! All this was gone . . . But I nevertheless returned from that journey changed, in a lighter frame of mind. I had come to terms with my past and with my own memories. I even wanted to tell my wife and son everything. But then I decided against it. This was my world, one which no longer exists, and those who did not experience it will never be able to understand."

I understood the speaker (who wishes to remain anonymous), for I had read the words of Shewah Weiss, who is himself also a child of the Holocaust: "When in Israel I missed Poland and wanted to return to the places of my childhood; my thoughts and recollections were sad. But sadness is attractive to humans. . . . Inside a person, inside his soul there are many hues, and these hues reflect feelings. . . . Remaining silent about the Holocaust is humanity's greatest sin. For many years the subject was not talked about in Israel. The same was true in Poland. But in both our countries it is now being discussed more and more. This is a third generation phenomenon. The first generation comprised people who were in the very center of events, who survived the war and whose life experiences were tragic and traumatic. Their lives were turned upside-down by the Holocaust, war and emigration. The second generation, their children, is so close that they do not always have the courage to learn about the past, to ask questions. Probably symbolic here is the common expression: 'we didn't talk about it at home.' The second generation, like the first, the one of survivors, has tried to build normal, everyday lives: home, work, studies, normality. Normality is what the first generation remembers from before the tragedy. The third generation, the grandchildren, is living normal, calm, everyday human lives. It is only then that you can ask questions and search for answers. And now they are starting to study the subject, to describe the history of the first generation."[6]

This reminded me of what Irena Sendler's teenage granddaughter, Agnieszka, said when surprised by the presence of a foreign TV crew, she asked: "Grandmother, what is it you did that now you are going to be famous?" And to this question Irena Sendler has a very simple and short answer: "I did as my conscience dictated. I could not have survived the war otherwise." That is the answer I heard in one of my many interviews, during which with my numerous questions I opened up in her memory unhealed wounds. But there was no way I could avoid asking her another very simple question, one Irena Sendler did not like at all: "Were you scared?" "Yes," she answered, "I was scared, but my hatred and anger were stronger than my fear." Yet another time I asked her that question, she replied: "It was as if I was deprived of all feelings. Something drove me to do this work, to make the effort. It was stronger than fear. I knew this was what I had to do, this was it, there was no other way I could live. I had moments of weakness, of apprehension and fear, like everyone else, but did I have any other option?"

Once in my presence she turned down yet another request for an interview. The person requesting used the argument that she was one of the last living witnesses of those events and her testimony was necessary for the sake of history, for the world. "For the world?" asks Irena Sendler incredulously. "And where was the world when I rescued children?" she continues bitterly, "When I walked in the streets and cried because of my helplessness?"

"I feared not for myself, but for the rescued child. I often wondered about their future. I persistently asked myself whether I had done everything to ensure their safety. I knew that the horror of wartime experiences was bound to affect them in their future lives. Everyone who has lived through that war suffers from a certain type of neurosis."

***

In his book *Życie surowo wzbromnione* (Life severely prohibited) Antoni Marianowicz revealed: "A [certain] type of fear is with me to this day. For example, I cannot sit in a café with my back to the door. These are irrational fears, most probably born in those times [when] every saved Jew's life was virtually a miracle. And the trauma resulted in many complexes. . . . Those who never experienced it themselves are not in a position to judge others in such matters."

Irena Sendler's friend Magdalena Grodzka-Gużkowska wrote in her book *Szczęściara* (The lucky one): "Bookshops today are inundated with Holocaust memoirs. Why after so many years? A question for psychologists and sociologists." At the age of 78, this author had the courage to "loudly state reminiscences that had never left her." During the war she was a teenager. In May 1942, she secretly passed her *matura* end of school exam. She dreamed of studying medicine. She was active in the underground resistance. The Gestapo were looking for her. Jaga Piotrowska (Irena Sendler's best courier) entrusted her with a "small but very special task." She was "one of those who took ashen Jewish children, who had spent months hidden in dark nooks and crannies, out into the sunlight. If they went out into the street looking so pallid, everyone would know. I transported them from A to B. I brought them food. And I taught them how not to reveal to the Germans and szmalcowniks that they were Jews."[7]

Magdalena Grodzka-Gużkowska would take the pale and anaemic children out to the banks of the Vistula, out into the sunlight, and tell them to play and swim in the water. After several such trips, the children regained their normal healthy look. This was important for survival, so that they could have a relatively safe life. In order to live, they could not appear to be different from Polish children their age. Someone had to think of all this, to think it through and actually organize it. Who? Of course it was Irena Sendler.

***

In an article entitled "Irena and Jan," which appeared in the Tel Aviv weekly *Nowiny-Kurier*, Natan Gross wrote:

"Irena Sendler is a wonderful woman who has been described as the brightest star in the dark sky of occupied Poland. The Jan Karski Award which she received may be called a prize of conscience. In my opinion, Irena Sendler and Jan Karski are two great names deserving the Jewish nation's eternal remembrance."

In one of our last conversations before the original Polish edition manuscript was submitted to the publishers, Irena Sendler told me: "When analyzing contacts with the rescued children, one can baldly say that their lives are lived in a permanent state of disassociation. The disasters experienced so early in life, the loss of those closest to them, parents, grandparents, and siblings, despite the extensive efforts of nuns, orphanages, or private families where the children stayed, despite the great personal risks undertaken to ease their interrupted childhoods, those tragic moments leave a permanent mark. The sorrow of their distressing childhood and the inability to accept the loss of their dearest ones persist, as does the constant sense of disassociation of identity. Despite many years of trying, many of the children fail to find their roots. Throughout their adult lives they search for the slightest traces of their families and their origins, frequently to no avail. Their anonymity is tiring and unremittingly poisons their otherwise frequently settled lives. This state can be observed in all those who survived the hell of Nazi crimes, and even if frequently they have had in other respects very successful lives (the hoped for education, stable family life, and good jobs), generally speaking, they give the impression of being people for whom the tragedy of the war continues to this day."

Notes

1. Professor Michal Głowiński is also the author of: *Czarne sezony*, *Magdalenka z razowego chleba*, and *Historia jednej topoli*.

2. Dorota Szuszkiewicz's interview with Prof. M. Głowiński, entitled "Kolor czerpienia" in *Stolica* (magazine supplement to *Życie Warszawy*), nr 16, April 19, 2003.

3. Michal Głowiński, *Hitoria jednej topolo*, Krakow, 2003, pp. 69 and 212.

4. Michał Głowiński, *Czarne sezony*, Krakow, 2002, pp. 19, 102, 116, 122, and 144.

5. Jadwiga Kotowska, "Mała szmuglerka," in *Dzieci Holocaustu mówią*, vol. 2, p. 95.

6. *Ziemia i chmury*, Joanna Szwedowska's interview with Shewah Weiss, Sejny, 2002, p. 123.

7. Magdalena Grodzka-Gużkowska, *Szczęściara*, Krakow, 2003, pp. 130–131.

23

Postwar Family Life

Irena Sendler: "My grandparents from my father's side died before World War I. I didn't know them. My grandmother from my mother's side died a few months after my birth, so I didn't know her, either. However, Grandfather Ksawery Grzybowski died in 1923, when I was 13. His passing away deeply affected me because after my father's death in 1917, and ever since his return from Russia, he had stood in for my father."

Janina Zgrzembska: "My parents had known each other since before the war. Father finished law at the University of Warsaw, and after the war, he also completed studies in history at the Jagiellonian University. He was a PPS activist and it was probably in this organization that my parents met. During the war, he lived in Praga and Otwock. His wartime pseudonym was "Adam." Mother helped him in some way. Shortly they got married, as soon as it was possible. We lived in Belwederska Street. I remember that father typed and read a lot. He taught history at school and loved Warsaw. To this day, I remember how when I was merely three or four he would take me on long walks in the town, telling me about the houses, streets, and squares. At the time, I found it tiring and boring. My parents' marriage proved to be failure. There were probably various reasons for this. Most probably both sides were to blame, which is normally the case, as in life. They separated when I was 14 and my brother 10. Soon afterward, father died of a stroke; he was 49.

"Home was always open to those in need; it was full of strangers. Some were young, others somewhat older—though for me at the time they seemed very old. All my questions about who these people were, mother cut short: 'my courier' or 'my friend from the war.' Later, I stopped asking.

The house was well cared for; there was a housemaid who saw to the daily matters. But my brother and I were constantly yearning after mother. And she always only had time for others—work, and after work, meetings, conferences, as well as visits to various social welfare institutions. When I was three, I asked her to take me to the orphanage she was always visiting. Surprised, she asked why? 'Because then I'll see more of you,' I replied. I used to leave notes on the table, informing mother that in my school there was also a parents' evening. I dreamed that mother (not the housemaid!) would take me for the start of the school year on September 1. She practised 'telephone pedagogy': she'd phone from work and ask if everything was okay, then she'd give instructions on what we were to eat and what we were to do.

"In 1965, mother was awarded the Yad Vashem medal. I was 18 by then and so I knew why she had been awarded this distinction. In March 1968, mother was very unwell; she was suffering from heart disease. But she got up, saying: 'They are beating Jews again, we have to set up another Żegota!' She gave my brother and me 100 zlotys each. 'That's for the prison warder if they stop you, so that someone will inform me.' I was at university and my brother was still at school. Life became really hard.

"But there were also pleasant surprises. One year we received a parcel from America, full of delicatessen products. The sender was someone we didn't know, Frank Morgens,[1] who had been rescued from the Holocaust. He had been rescued by someone else (a woman called Wala Żak, who I met in Israel in 1988), but he had heard about my mother and wanted to express his gratitude in this way. On the other side of his enclosed photograph he wrote:

'. . . so that it might make it easier, knowing you have a friend in me.'

"My mother has had many friends, and still has! In Poland, Israel, Sweden, Denmark, Canada, Venezuela, and everywhere else where there are Jews who survived the Holocaust. They write letters, send books, and visit her. When I travelled to Israel for the first time in 1988, mother's tree was already five years old; today it is 20 years old! Everywhere people greeted me, invited me to their homes, I was regaled. It was only then that I really realized what she had done. In Israel I have friends who introduced me to their families because I am Irena Sendler's daughter. I was happy and proud. Mother told me how during her four-week stay in Israel she experienced an extraordinary incident. One Saturday she was being driven around Jerusalem. The driver got engaged in a conversation with her and thus inadvertently they entered a predominantly Jewish Orthodox district. Suddenly stones started being thrown at the car. Her friend sped off and

From a family album: Irena Sendler, Stefan Zgrzembski, little Janina, and Adam. (Courtesy of the Janina Zgrzembska family archives)

said, laughing: 'During the war you were the one saving Jews, and now they are stoning you.'"

Irena Sendler: "I sometimes think I was a bad daughter, a bad mother, and not a good wife. I had two failed marriages. I was frequently absent from home. My deep involvement in professional and social work had a decidedly negative effect on my family life.

"During the war, I realized that what I was doing to save the Jews also exposed to danger my ailing mother, who was suffering from heart disease. If anything went wrong (and it eventually did), she was in grave danger of dying from the lack of care. But my mother never told me: 'Don't do it! Don't take risks, look after yourself.' She knew I was serving a just cause and tacitly approved of what I was doing. I had her assent and her moral support. After my arrest, my colleagues from the organization looked after her. I knew I could rely on them, and this gave me strength. I didn't break. Later, her death and the fact that I could not attend her funeral affected me deeply. For a long time after the war, I would visit her grave every day.

"Today I know that if you are a mother, trying to combine professional and social work with family life is wrong. The children will always suffer as a result. I know that my children were always waiting for me; they told me after many years.

"After the war, despite numerous professional and social responsibilities, I decided to give birth to three children. It was only after I had turned thirty, that I felt ready to make this decision. My daughter, called Janina after my mother, was born on March 31, 1947. My first son, Andrzej, was born on November 9, 1949. Unfortunately, due to stressful experiences (relentless interrogations at the State Security Office), it was a premature birth. He lived for only 11 days. My second son, Adam, was born on March 25, 1951.

"I am aware that my wartime activities had an effect on my children's professional careers. When, despite passing the entrance exam and qualifying for the first year of Polish literature studies, after a few days my daughter, Janina, was mysteriously struck off the students register, she asked me: 'Mother, what was it in your life that you did wrong?' Subsequently, she took up part-time studies. A few years later, the same thing happened to my son. To this day I remember his eyes, full of despair, helplessness, and the feeling of being wronged. And that question: 'Mother, why?' He also ended up doing part-time studies—librarianship in Wrocław.

I remember when he told me that in childhood he almost smashed a window pane because he had been waiting for me for hours, gazing through the window to see me come. When he was four or five, a friend observed him enthusiastically talking about something, and she asked him: 'Why don't you tell mummy about it?' 'Because I can only talk to mummy's soles,' was his reply. 'When I talk, mummy leaves.' Adam left suddenly, in the night, on September 23, 1999. I cannot come to terms with it. I keep thinking about him."

***

"Apart from my own children, I had two older foster children. That is a separate story. Back then, during the war, at the time of the mass extermination of Jews and my efforts to save them, there once occurred the necessity to take particularly affectionate care of two girls who had had exceptionally painful experiences of the German occupation. One of them, Teresa, was 12 at the time, and she lived with her parents and younger sister in Cegłów (Mińsk Mazowiecki *powiat* [administration area]). To her utter horror she saw with her own eyes the murder of her father and younger sister. With Julian Grobelny's help, Teresa and her mother moved to Warsaw. Her mother was put up with a family in Praga, whereas little Teresa was put under the care of a fellow PPS activist. She didn't stay there long, however, because the activist, Szymon Zaremba, was wanted by the Gestapo and had to flee from Poland. Before leaving, he contacted Grobelny and asked him to find a new guardian for the girl. For a couple of days, this terrified child, was in my home. I couldn't keep her any longer on account of my work, which meant the constant danger of the Gestapo coming to the flat. Two days later, I took her to an the emergency care point with a family at 3 Mątwicka Street in the Ochota district. The couple, Zofia Wędrychowska and Stanisław Papuziński,[2] already had four children of their own, but always accepted the Jewish children I sent them with great love and affection.

"Two months later, tragedy struck the family. On February 21, 1944, a Gestapo officer entered their house when Papuziński's sons were conducting a scout group gun training meeting. On seeing this, the Gestapo man fired a few shots and ran to get backup. He very seriously wounded a friend of one of the sons. Zofia Wędrychowska instructed Teresa, as the oldest, to run away with the other children to people they knew in Krucza Street, while she took care of the wounded boy. Soon over a dozen Gestapo men arrived. They took the wounded boy and Zofia to their van. 'Fortunately,' the boy died on the way, whereas Zofia was taken first to Gestapo Headquarters in Szucha Avenue, and next to Pawiak Prison. A few days later, on April 26, 1944, she was shot. In the days that followed, I took the family's own four children and another four Jewish children they had been taking care of to a summer colony near Garwolin. The manager of this colony was Ola Majewska, later a professor at the University of Łódź.

"The children stayed there until the end of the war. I collected the four Papuziński children together with the four Jewish children, including Teresa, and accommodated them in a house in Okęcie, which we had converted into an insurgents' hospital. When on March 15, 1945, I returned to Warsaw, Teresa came with me. She went to school, passed her school final *matura* exam, and went on to study dentistry. She married and in 1956 moved to Israel. There she gave birth to two children. We keep in touch, write letters. When she was in Poland with her sons, she visited me, and when I visited Israel in 1983, I stayed in their house.

"The other girl I treated as my own daughter was Irenka [diminutive of Irena]. Before the war her parents had been wealthy merchants and they were doing business with a Pole when they were forced to move to the ghetto. For a large sum of money, this Pole had promised to look after their children on the Aryan side. In a very roundabout way, one of my couriers learned of these two children. She took care of the boy, and the girl ended up with me. Sadly, their parents died in the ghetto.

"When I worked in the insurgents' hospital, I presented her as my own daughter. I looked after Irenka and she lived with us until the mid 1950s, when her aunt, her mother's sister, returned from the Soviet Union. She went to school. On completing technical college, she went to a summer camp, where she met a boy. Soon they married and later moved to Szczecin, where she completed part-time studies at the College of Agriculture. Her daughter is a doctor, an oncologist, and lives in Warsaw.

"Years later, one of my foster children, Teresa, wrote to me: 'Do you know why I was bad to you, so peevish and disobedient? Because your goodness was breaking my heart. I would then think to myself, what right do you have to replace my mother?'"

Notes

1. Frank Morgens (Mieczysław Morgenstern), b. 1911 in Łódź, lived in New York from 1948 until his death in August 2004. In 1994, in Warsaw, he read out his war memoir *Lata na skraju przepaści* (Years on the verge). In it he wrote among other things: "I am not sure whether people who have not experienced [the Holocaust] are able to imagine what it means to find yourself on the verge of existence and see the face of death day and night, year after year. For years on end, the merciless hunger of body and soul, when the rare good moments providing the strength and will to live, remain abstract. . . . It is my firm belief that we who have survived the Holocaust have an eternal debt of gratitude to those who had the courage to help even when it meant risking their own lives. We have an obligation to assure them that, despite the 50 years that have passed, their heroism will not be forgotten." (pp. 206, 208)

2. Irena Sendler wrote an extensive account of Zofia Wędrychowska (1901–1944) and Stanisław Papuziński (1903–1982), which was published on November 26, 1999, in *Gazeta Wyborcza* (*Gazeta Stołeczna* obituaries and recollections supplement).

24

As Remembered by a Witness

Jerzy Korczak, a historian, was 16 when he first met Jolanta in a flat at 15 Markowska Street, Praga, in mid-1943. He recalls that 'hiding in that ugly tenement house was Stefan Zgrzembski, her future husband and close collaborator. . . . He could hardly contain himself, he was straining at the leash, so eager was he to act. It cost Mrs. Sendler a lot of effort and nerves to find appropriate tasks for him, ones in which he could be useful without leaving the flat. Therefore, he helped in dividing up the allowances, sorting out documents, and figuring out where to accommodate the ever larger number of children under Jolanta's care. . . . The people from Mrs. Sendler's circle, under whose wardship I was placed, simply ordered me to learn. For my education, I went to secret gymnasium (middle school) classes in Otwock. There I was provided with lodgings, food, and washing facilities."

Mrs. Sendler he remembers as "slender, not very tall, with short, smoothly brushed hair and always modestly dressed, all of which made her blend perfectly into the street landscape of wartime Warsaw. Only those who came into closer contact with her could notice some characteristic features. Certainly the eyes—large, bright, always attentively directed at the speaker. It was basically on her decisions that everything else depended: the hiding of hunted individuals, an appropriate selection of documents, or an intelligently invented life story. She saved more than only children smuggled out of the ghetto. Saving children was the basic task the underground movement had commissioned her to do. But time and again she also saved adults, people in grave danger because of their origins. Whatever the difficulties, she never refused. She was more than professional, she was a natural-born social worker. As a worker of the Warsaw City Administration Social Welfare Department, she had to deal with hundreds of people's intensely complex problems and life tragedies."[1]

Notes

1. Jerzy Korczak, 'Oswajanie strachu' [Taming fear], *Tygodnik Powszechny*, nr 33, August 17, 2003.

25

Voices of the Saved Children

This chapter has been included at the request of Irena Sendler. From the very large number of "children" she had saved, Irena Sendler asked a few of those who were particularly close to write about her, themselves, and about those times. They were asked to write about their experiences, what they felt then, and how the past has affected their later lives. The way they wrote it and how many words they used was left for them to decide. It turned out that writing such personal accounts about themselves and Irena Sendler was far from an easy task. It opened up old wounds. But without their personal reflections, the tender memories, the testimonies of their gratitude and attachment to Irena Sendler, this book would be incomplete.

***

Teresa Körner (Israel)

"I was born on February 14, 1929, in Cegłów and given the name Chaja Estera Sztajn. The name on the birth certificate prepared for me by Irena Sendler during the German occupation was Teresa Tucholska. I was saved by Irena Sendler and Julian Grobelny, who was a friend of my father's. They left me under the care of their friends Zofia and Stanisław Papuziński, with whom I shared occupation vicissitudes. After the war, Irena found me and in the years that followed I lived in her home, until I finished secondary school. With Irena and her family I shared the cramped conditions of the flat, the lack of bread, and of fuel during the winter. Irena's over-protectiveness irritated me, as I felt she wanted to replace my

Teresa Körner with her son. (Courtesy of the Janina Zgrzembska family archives)

mother. After finishing school, I wanted to be among my peers. When I started studying dentistry, I moved to a students' hostel. For many years now I have lived in Israel, but I continue to stay in touch with Irena. She was my guest in Newe Monosson in 1983, when she came to plant her tree at Yad Vashem. Irena's daughter was also a guest in our home. When I travel to Poland, alone or with my sons, I always visit Irena. I remember her birthdays and her name days."

***

Irena Wojdowska (Szczecin)
"I first met Irena Sendler in the summer of 1943, in Praga. I was there thanks to her mediation. My stay, I presume, was financed by the Żegota fund. This was a place where people persecuted by the [German] invader found shelter. Previously, I had been in hiding together with my brother, Bogdan, at the home of Jadwiga Bilwin and Jadwiga Koszutska in the Kolo housing estate near Obozowa Street in the Wola district of Warsaw. Through that tiny, one room flat passed a whole host of Jews, leftwing activists, and persons waiting to establish contact with the partisans. This safe haven got 'burnt' when it was uncovered by some [Polish] 'blue' police constables and szmalcowniks, who had come during the day in search of

Irena Wojdowska. (Courtesy of the Janina Zgrzembska family archives)

one particular individual. Thus they discovered several more unregistered and 'undesirable' tenants. That was how I got separated from my brother Bogdan[1] for almost a year. According to documents that were specially prepared for us, he was my half-brother. But our documents were altered many times. We missed each other greatly; contact was impossible on account of our own safety and that of others. They sent me to a village near Warsaw. I was there for about two weeks, after which I ended up in Praga. I did not know where my brother was or what had happened to the other tenants from Obozowa Street. In my new hiding place, I was given new documents and a new life story. I had so many surnames during the occupation that I only remember the last one. In Praga, I met the PPS activist Mr. Stefan. I think he liked me. Stefan also taught me. This was a wise and good person, and Irena's friend. I did not know their surnames at the time. The occupation taught me that children should not be burdened with unnecessary information. Miss Irena would sometimes come to this flat in Praga. Whenever she came, she brought with her an air of optimism and freedom. She was very energetic, cheerful, and affectionate. In the autumn of 1943, she stopped coming, and then life became sad and gloomy. I remember well how, although I never actually asked, I felt that something bad had happened. Some of the flat's residents moved to

Otwock. Throughout the winter I regularly travelled there, delivering, in heavy earthenware pots, food Mrs. Maria Kukulska had cooked. I had to cover very long distances to the electric railway station and then from the Otwock station to my destination, carrying objects that were excessively large and heavy for my strength and age. But I never complained. I only wished, when I was on that train, that someone would come out to meet me at Otwock and help me carry the load. Nevertheless, I understood the situation, even though I was only 11 at the time. I remember how the long period of sadness was suddenly followed by a mood of exceptional joy, verging on euphoria, for it was then that I learned Irena had been in prison but was now released. The details I did not learn until after the war. Irena knew my adopted aunts well. As it turned out, they closely cooperated with Jadwiga Bilwin, who during the occupation officially worked in the Wola District Welfare Center. In the spring of 1944, I returned to Obozowa Street.

"My next meeting with Irena Sendler was quite unexpected. In the winter of 1945, she came to Lublin on a mission to obtain funds from the Provisional Government for the Okęcie Welfare Center in Warsaw. Stefan Zgrzembski was also working there. The meeting was very joyful because up until then neither of us had known whether the other had survived the Warsaw Uprising. It was then that I made my first very important independent decision. Irena suggested that I could return with her to Okęcie in Warsaw. I had to decide whether or not to leave the two Jadwigas and my brother in order to continue the search for our parents. In Warsaw there were greater possibilities of finding them. I wanted to believe that my parents were still alive and could be found. Such incidents did happen; they were commonly talked about. People returned from concentration camps, from abroad, and all sorts of places. I hoped that my parents would also eventually turn up. Moreover, I wanted to go to a normal school, as I had never been to one. My education was to have begun on September 1, 1939. I also wanted to make it easier for my two guardians. I decided to go. I was happy in Okęcie. Irena and Stefan treated me like their own child. Living conditions were very difficult, like elsewhere in the Warsaw of those days. I lived with Irena in one room together with two other families. I slept with Irena in the same bed, and when I was ill, Irena treated me with extraordinary affection and care. It was there that I went to school and could be among pupils my age. When the center in Okęcie was closed, we moved to the ruins of Warsaw. We lived in an abandoned house, but when the rightful owners returned, we had to move out. So we lived in the ruins. Our first home, in a house in Sienna Street, was surrounded by ruins. We would go out with Irena to collect firewood (planks pulled out of the rubble) and water from wells that had been dug during the Warsaw Uprising. After treatment, that is, boiling, we also drank this water. This was a life of poverty, but I was used to that. I remember this very well, and the subsequent period spent with Irena Sendler. She gave me a lot of care and attention, and we talked a lot. Our conversations, which broached all subjects, enriched me greatly. One could say that our relationship in that period developed into a deep friendship.

"Our last squat, because we had no permission to live in those places, was shared with two or three other families. It was in Jedności Narodowej Avenue, in the section between Wawelska and Koszykowa streets. I remember that we had to move twice, for the same reasons as before. While we were living there, I started attending the Słowacki Gymnasium [middle school], having previously finished the sixth year of primary school in Sienna Street.

"I remember an incident with a priest when I was in the first year of gymnasium. By the standards of those days, he was exceptionally well educated. He had two university degrees and, apart from theology, he also taught philosophy. Before Irena officially arranged my exemption, I attended his religious education lessons. One of his requirements was that his pupils should attend church on Sundays. To ensure this, he gave negative ('insufficient') marks to those pupils who did not attend—and his lessons were always on Mondays. Once I lied that I had been because I didn't want to get a negative mark and Irena had not yet settled the matter with the head teacher. Because I didn't like lying and was insistent, Irena eventually arranged my exemption and I longer had to attend RE lessons. Nevertheless, the priest magnanimously suggested that I could still attend if wanted to, and that's what I did. The views of this priest were extremely rightwing, ones I could not accept during lessons. As a result I got into arguments with him, which he, being an erudite and excellent orator, naturally won. In the end, the priest decided that I was disrupting his lessons too much, and thus I had an hour of free time. I write about this incident at Irena's request, as she does not remember it. I did not waste my 'free hours.' I remember in that time attending a botany course in the school garden (for third-year classes), and I learnt a great deal from these lessons.

"When my wartime guardians, Jadwiga Bilwin and Jadwiga Koszutska, returned to Warsaw, I lived alternately with each of them in the homes of various wartime friends, those who actually had homes of their own. In the meantime, I completed my school education, while my brother was in 'Orlinek' in Karpacz. My parents were not found.

"I was still in touch with Irena and her family, but our meetings were sporadic. We were both very busy.

"I left Warsaw after passing my *matura* end of school exam in the summer of 1952, and moved to Szczecin. It was in Szczecin that Irena and I next met, I think it was in 1960. Irena was returning with her children from a vacation and they stopped over at my home. Having put our children to bed, we began our traditional nighttime discussion. These discussions lasted till dawn, and we still felt we hadn't said everything! My husband was unable to understand what could possibly have been the topic of such long conversations. It was then that for the first time I told Irena that her story would make excellent material for a suspense novel.

"We still contact each other as often as we can. I am also in touch with her daughter, Janina.

Irena was, and still is, a very important person in my life. I'm very proud of the fact that we are so close and able to understand each other even without having to use words and in spite of occasional differences of opinion. I realize that Irena is a great authority to many people and this pleases me. She has done much good to many people and, despite personal tragedies, illnesses and old age, she is still such a warm and open person. She continues to have a sharp mind and excellent memory. I wish to continue to be close to her heart and occupy just a bit of her attention for as long as possible. For me this is an extraordinary person. In my life, despite the drastic vicissitudes of war, I have been fortunate to meet virtuous people to whom I owe a great deal.

"I have written about only some of my memories regarding my association with Irena over the last 60, eventful years—may it continue. If Irena at least in part agrees with what I have written about our relationship, I shall be very pleased. I leave the final appraisal to her. I am very happy that her life story, so rich in events, will at last be published."

***

Michał Głowiński (Warsaw)
"If I were to compose an encyclopedia entry regarding Irena Sendler in as few simple words as possible, I would write: Great Social Worker. For I believe these three words express the essence of her life and all the troubles she took up and endured over decades.

"She comes from a democratic left, which since the second half of the 19th century played such an important role in Poland, and she is from

Michał Głowiński. (Courtesy of the Janina Zgrzembska family archives)

that group of activists who rather than in politics were far more engaged in helping the poor, downtrodden and underprivileged.

"Irena Sendler was a social worker from her earliest student years, working in organizations and institutions, providing help to the unemployed during her studies at Warsaw University. Already then, in the 1930s, she actively challenged those who were stirring up anti-Semitic violence in Polish universities.

"Her extraordinary acts of humanity which brought such impressive results during the terrible Holocaust were a simple consequence of what she had been doing, and grew up doing in previous years. Only now the stakes were higher, because now it was a matter of saving human lives. Irena Sendler was helping from the outset, and when they started deporting Jews from the Warsaw ghetto to the Treblinka death camp, she initiated a major rescue operation. Thanks to her dedication and commitment, thanks to her outstanding courage and her ability to master the art of conspiracy, she managed to save from imminent death over 2,500 human lives. This is a feat comparable to what other famous rescuers of Jews had achieved, such as the Japanese consul in Kovno, Ushikara, or the great Swede, Raoul Wallenberg. All three belong to a group of moral giants who rescued the world and saved from death thousands of lives.

"But Irena Sendler could not have saved the lives of so many Jewish children if she had acted alone. She was a member of Żegota and worked in a team of over a dozen wonderful, extremely courageous and selfless women. And here one has to stress Irena Sendler's impressive talents, a factor that is sometimes overlooked. She was an extraordinarily skillful organizer. For in order to rescue children in such terrible circumstances, good intentions were not enough, one had to organize the operation, think through the methods of action, and so forth. As the initiator and coordinator of rescue operations, she had to be able to do all this.

"I write about Irena Sendler with a feeling of great gratitude, for I know it is thanks to her that I survived the Holocaust. I am one of those she saved. I left the ghetto together with my parents in January 1943.[2] It was Irena Sendler who found me a place in an orphanage run by the Little Sister Servants of the Blessed Virgin Mary in Turkowice, in the eastern part of Poland. She did this when my situation in Warsaw became hopeless. I remained in Turkowice until the liberation. One can hardly feel more gratitude than I do when I think of the person who made it possible for me to be among the few who survived. In fact, I am doubly grateful to Irena Sendler for also saving my mother when she was in great danger. It was Mrs. Sendler who found her a job as a housemaid in the home of a teacher in Otwock near Warsaw. (My mother died in 1986.) We speak of Irena Sendler saving children, but we should never forget that she rescued adults as well—not only people she knew, but also total strangers. I cannot give an exact figure, but I certainly think it is all the more reason to praise this exceptionally heroic woman.

"Irena Sendler was never for me a legendary hero of whom we speak with veneration but never see. I've known her for over 60 years, since childhood, for, in fact, she had befriended members of my family already before the war. Sometimes, when she came to the ghetto, she would also visit us. This was always a major event. I remember my grandma saying that when Mrs. Irena came, everyone in the family smiled. Irena Sendler gives everything she has to the world: her active approach to life, her energy, her wisdom and kindness, her affection and readiness to always help people in difficulty. She also cheers us with her smile, even though in her difficult but beautiful life it has not always been easy to smile."

***

Piotr (Zysman) Zettinger (Stockholm)
Dear Editor and dearest friend,

Thank you for writing such a wonderful article about me. Your comments about my work and the work of my couriers honor me greatly, but they are also a bit embarrassing because we do not deserve such lofty words of praise. We were only doing what anybody should do when they see another person needing help. And nothing more!

I send you my best and warmest regards.
Faithfully yours,
Irena Sendler
Warsaw, November 21, 2003

"That was the message Irena Sendler gave me with the request that I pass it on to the Swedish journalist Nuri Kino. At the start of February, the leading Stockholm newspaper *Dagens Nyheter* published his long and, indeed, beautiful article devoted entirely to the woman who had saved two and a half thousand children from the Warsaw ghetto. Nuri Kino had visited Irena Sendler in mid-December the previous year and since then, to this day, he believes the visit changed his life as well as his views of people and the world. He says that it was the first time in his journalistic career he had met a person who simply radiated goodness and the altruistic will to help those in need. Nuri Kino's appraisal of Irena Sendler is correct.

"From family tales I know of Irena Sendler's prewar work in the Social Welfare Committee. Together with my father, she helped the destitute and most vulnerable free themselves from bureaucratic and legal traps—my father as the solicitor, and Mrs. Sendler, to use Michał Głowiński's words from his The Black Seasons, as the good fairy of those looking for help. I do not wish to refer to Irena Sendler's wartime activities because others have written about them and I personally do not remember much from those days. I know that it was Mrs. Sendler who looked after me after my escape from the Warsaw ghetto through the sewers (I was four at the time), and that she found me a place, or rather places to hide, because I had to change hiding places many times. I know this chiefly from the accounts of other people, because Irena Sendler never talked about it herself. After all, she was only doing what everyone should be doing. And that's all, there was nothing more to be said.

"Nevertheless, I will recount just one incident from the postwar period. One day in the late spring of 1968, Irena Sendler invited me to her flat in Na Rozdrożu Square. The situation at the time terrified her no less than it did me. Yet she had not invited me to talk about her fears, she wanted to tell me what she intended to do: 'I have already contacted my wartime companions. If the situation gets any worse and we have to act as we did in the war, we're ready. You and your family can count on us.'

"Those words lodged themselves deeply in my mind and helped me endure that period. For me, like for many others, Irena Sendler was the good fairy."

Katarzyna Meloch (Warsaw)

"In my chain of rescuers, I see Irena Sendler as foremost among my rescuers after I left the ghetto. After losing my mother, Grandmother Michalina, and Uncle Jacek, it was she, as the creator and head of the children's section in Żegota, who made my rescue possible. She saved me a second time in the 1990s, when I was rejected by those closest to me, by my family. I couldn't live with it and Irena comforted me day after day, hour after hour. She gave me some of her fortitude. She also helped me when it was more than a matter of comforting someone dear to you. The process of Irena rescuing me from various difficult situations continues all the time. I still confide in her, telling her about all the problems confronting me. And she always supports me.

"Of course, during the occupation I had no idea that something like Żegota existed. And I didn't know Irena Sendler. I didn't realize that those efforts to save me were a small part of a grander design to rescue as many

Piotr (Zysman) Zettinger. (Courtesy of the Janina Zgrzembska family archives)

Jewish children as possible. I had no idea that 'Mrs. Wisia' was taking essential, and yet in a sense also fairly routine, measures. That is how today I explain the acquisition of Irka Dąbrowska's genuine birth certificate from the church in Targówek and giving it to Kasia (little Katarzyna) Meloch, so that with this new identity Kasia could go to the Emergency Care Center for Children in Warsaw, that is, the Father Boduen Orphanage. All this was done so that I could be legally sent to an orphanage run by nuns.

"On March 2, 1946, less than a year after the war, in a psychological consultancy for children I wrote: 'My wish is to pass to the second year. If I fail to pass, I will have wasted a whole year and all my work will come to nothing. Besides, I wouldn't be able to face the shame. But actually this isn't my first and foremost wish. My first wish is that I very much want my parents to be found. That is my greatest wish. My third wish is to be able to gratefully repay all those who were good to me, because I think it's my obligation.' At the time I was 13.

"My father, Maksymilian Meloch, probably died in the first days of the German-Soviet War in 1941.[3] My mother, Wanda Meloch, was the first and most important person to rescue me. I was nine when the Germans arrested her in Białystok, and killed her. She knew she was going to die and she was unable to fight her destiny. Nevertheless, she did manage to instill in me a faith that I was going to survive. She had an idea of how to save her child. Day and night in Białystok she made me memorize the address of her brother, Jacek Goldman, in the Warsaw ghetto: 12 Elektoralna Street. I was not allowed to forget it. She would wake me at night to make sure I remembered. I will remember it forever. When she was gone and I was left on my own, now in a Jewish orphanage in the Białystok ghetto, I managed to get a letter 'opportunely' passed on to Uncle Jacek. This letter reached my relatives in Warsaw, who next arranged for me to be illegally transferred from Białystok to the Warsaw ghetto. Wanda Meloch gave me life twice. First, when she gave birth to me, and then a second time when she planned my rescue. By being transferred to Warsaw, I avoided the fate of the children in the Białystok ghetto. The Białystok children were transferred to the showcase ghetto in Terezin in the Protectorate of Bohemia and Moravia, and thence to Auschwitz to be exterminated. (I know this from Chajka Grossman.)

"Grandma Michalina, my mother's mother, greeted me in Warsaw with the words: 'Child, where are your parents?' I didn't tell her the truth, Jacek wouldn't let me, but she was able to assume the worst. When the so-called actions began in the Warsaw ghetto in July 1942, our family had its own hiding place. Jacek—who was more than an uncle, a steadfast guardian and prewar mountaineer—found a cell beneath a chimney in one of the partially burned-out buildings of the former Holy Spirit Hospital in Elektoralna Street. It was a very hot July day. I do not remember exactly why I left the hiding place, but I got caught by Jewish policemen, who wanted to take me to Umschlagplatz. I felt 'Umschalg' meant death and started crying out loud. My cry was heard by Grandma Michalina, who then left her safe hiding place and walked straight into the street roundup. She started talking to one of the policemen and at the same time signalled for me to run away. I ran to a nearby pharmacy, where the pharmacist, who was Jacek's wife, Eugenia Sigalin, hid me in the stockroom among some enormous boxes. Grandma was taken to Umschlagplatz instead of me. Thus she became part of my chain of rescuers. But, luckily, she returned to Elektoralna Street, for she was the mother of a hospital worker, and on that occasion this fact saved her. So very easily she could have been made to join that day's transport and perished in Treblinka. So very easily I could have gone to Umschlagplatz and not returned, and yet, in Białystok I had decided to survive. My mother expected this of me in the last hours of her life.

The summer of 1942 was hot. The sun beat down mercilessly when I was led over to the Aryan side. I left the ghetto quite legally. Policemen didn't have to be bribed nor did we have to find a hole in the wall. It was most probably Ala Gołąb-Grynberg, a nurse with a pass to the Aryan side, who took me out of the ghetto. She knew Jacek, and Jadwiga Deneka, a Polish friend of my mother's.[4] Jacek handed me over to her near one of the ghetto gates. Then Jacek turned away as if we would meet again in a few hours, or a few days. But he disappeared from my life forever. I never saw him again. He went missing on his way to join up with the partisans. He disappeared like most of the people I loved.

"Waiting for me in the entrance to one of the buildings beyond the ghetto wall was nurse Barbara Wardzianka, yet another link in the chain of my rescuers. Basia—as she let me call her—knew my parents and Jacek from mountain hikes in the Zakopane region. I felt confident when the then 30-year-old woman energetically took me by the hand. We travelled by tram to Koło, to No. 76 Obozowa Street, to the flat of Jadwiga Deneka. Now this former pupil of my mother's was taking my fate into her hands.

"On the school pass photograph Jadwiga Sałek, her name had not yet changed to Deneka, had a serious face for her age. Her short hair was neatly arranged in waves. A necklace adorned her slender schoolgirl neck and her pristine white collar. I recognized her, though she was different now, grown up. She taught me to pray and other Christian customs. She acquired for me a genuine parish certificate of a Polish girl who was a year older than me, Irena Dąbrowolta (the daughter of Anna Dąbrowska née Gąska), who had been baptized at the Targówek church in the 1930s.

Jadwiga Deneka, to me 'Mrs. Wisia,' was only six years younger than my mother. Mother taught her Latin in a Łódź gymnasium (middle school). With time the teacher and her student became good friends. Jadwiga had leftwing convictions, like Wanda and most of my parents' prewar friends—assimilated Polish Jews and Poles. To repeat Andrzej Wajda's words: 'Those were romantic daredevils.' When in 1986 Jadwiga's brother applied for Yad Vashem to award his sister a Righteous Among the Nations medal—a motion that I seconded with successful results—he discovered that in 1939, 'Mrs. Wisia' had lost a daughter. It was only then that I read in the Jewish Historical Institute about the Jews she had saved and who after the war became Israelis. The fact that she had rescued my closest relatives, I already knew during the occupation.

In Obozowa Street, I didn't have to hide in a cupboard or behind a cupboard. I was there with Grandma Michalina, who had left the ghetto earlier. Despite the danger, we would go to Mrs. Wisia's allotment or for walks in a nearby forest.

"I'm the daughter of a historian and I'm not just interested in my own memories. What could a nine or ten year old girl know at the time? Since I became an adult, I have eagerly listened to the accounts of those who witnessed or even participated in those events. At the Jewish Historical Institute I read the accounts submitted to Yad Vashem. I know Jan Dobraczyński's memoir, *Tylko w jednym życiu*.[5] Dobraczyński was the head of the so-called special section of the City of Warsaw Social Welfare Department. This was where Irena Sendler first met him. Recalling the operations of getting Jewish children into orphanages and other child centers decades later, he wrote: 'My contribution was minimal. I was not the one who searched for these children, nor did I transport them, nor did I falsify their application documents. Jaga Piotrowska or one of the other department social workers would enter my office with a piece of paper to sign, and I'd sign it, usually without even reading it. It was only from other social workers that I learned about the extraordinary things my ladies were doing, pulling children out of hovels, smuggling them out of the ghetto, keeping them in their own homes and then personally delivering them to an orphanage . . . Many of the children had very Semitic features. So the social workers would think up whimsical disguises and special hairstyles. Everyone of them had sheltered Jewish children in their homes for weeks.'

"My stay in the Turkowice orphanage was actually possible thanks to such an action. The author of *Najeżdżcy* [Jan Dobraczyński,] gave his signature to false application forms regarding Jewish children.

"Who knows, perhaps he also signed one concerning Irena Dąbrowska, daughter of Anna Gąska. Therefore perhaps he, too, was involved in the process of saving me . . . Alas, I can only guess.

"The child only saw a few of the links in the rescue chain. Some I learned about after the war, while others I'll never know. Yet each link was essential. And not for a single moment was any link in the chain broken.

"In the winter of 1942/1943, another letter was most probably sent to the nuns in Turkowice containing a coded message within a seemingly innocuous text. This was how Irena Sendler informed the nuns that more Jewish children (or just one child!) had to be taken in. The sisters had no problems with deciphering such messages. On receiving such a letter, Sister Irena (Antonina Manaszczuk) would set off for Warsaw. And this time she would be returning to Turkowice with me. The journey was fraught with potential dangers. You had to spend the night in a railway station waiting room, either in Lublin or in Rejowiec. They would look at the faces, especially those of children. But our journey passed safely. On the door of the Turkowice home for girls was a poster warning of 'Jews, Lice, Typhus!', yet living peacefully the behind this door were children saved from the Holocaust. In the fairytale landscape of the Zamość region this poster, a sign of hatred, seemed unreal. I wasn't scared of it in the least.

"Jadwiga Deneka was Irena Sendler's courier. I'll probably never find out whether my guardian's Polish Socialist Workers' Party (RPPS) authorities, which did not recognize the Polish government in London, actually allowed her to collaborate with Irena Sendler or whether she did this guided only by her own conscience.

"As the years go by I think more and more about Mrs. Wisia. I know that even if she had not been a socialist on the left wing of the PPS, if she had not found herself within the orbit of Żegota, she would have anyhow rescued us, the persecuted. The last time I saw her was when she handed me over to the Father Boduen Orphanage in Warsaw. But she also watched over me when I was in Turkowice. She sent me parcels and wrote letters. She wanted to know my desires and needs. As a member of the socialist left she became increasingly involved in underground activities. She was in charge of so-called technical matters: the printing and distribution of RPPS bulletins. She undertook very dangerous tasks; hiding Jews in her tiny Warsaw flat and elsewhere was only a fraction of the great risks she took. She could only expect that the Gestapo would sooner or later start tracking her down. Fearing that she would not be able to withstand the torture if they interrogated her, she requested the mother superior at Turkowice to have me moved to another orphanage. However, Mother

Superior Stanisława (Aniela Polechajłło) was adamant that I should stay, explaining that only in Turkowice could she feel assured that I was safe. Nevertheless, 'just in case,' the name Irena Dąbrowska was crossed out of the orphanage register. Henceforth, I was in the Turkowice home with a doubly false identity. Thanks to the mother superior's decision, I remained in Turkowice until the end of the war—and I only found out about the whole matter after liberation.

"Jadwiga Deneka, wartime pseudonym Kasia, was arrested after being caught printing the RPPS *Bulletin* on a duplicating machine at the secret RPPS press distribution point which she was in charge of, at 16 Nowiniarska Street. This distribution point was at the same time also the hiding place of a group of Jews. From Pawiak Prison, 'Kasia' sent out secret letters to warn others. They tortured her at the Gestapo headquarters, but she gave no one away. They shot her dead, together with a group of 11 Jews, amid the ruins of the Warsaw ghetto in January 1944.

Sister Stanisława, from a Polish family of Tatar origins, felt no fear. She treated danger as a challenge. This attitude set the tone in Turkowice. Long before the war, her steel will and immense energy had made the Turkowice children's home an unrivalled orphanage in the entire Lublin region and outstanding even among other convent homes. At the time of the Holocaust, the 'Turkowice republic' was a life-saving sanctuary for Jewish children. Apparently there were 36 of us, between 10 and 20 percent of the total number of children there. More than half a century later I am able to recall the full names of 13 of these Jewish children. To find shelter in Turkowice, in a home run by the Little Servant Sisters (of the Immaculate Conception), was the best possible luck you could have. The congregation of the Little Servant Sisters of the Immaculate Conception was founded in the 19th century by a layman, Edmund Bojanowski, a romantic poet and the translator of Byron. He was a landowner from Poznań who devoted his entire estate and all his energies to help the poor, the sick, and especially children.

"In the Turkowice home for girls, under the guardianship of Sister Irena, was Stacha, with her raven black hair, somewhat thickset Stefa, a beautiful girl from Lwów (whose name I can't remember), and me, the wartime namesake of Sister Irena who caused her some specific problems. I would mill around the day room, quite unconcerned by the Germans who had come to inspect the orphanage, until Sister Irena had to tell me not be seen. That is how safe and at home I felt there. Sister Irena's supervision over us was normally discreet. Therefore, quite unsurprisingly, we sometimes had the impression that our situation was just the same as that of other girls in our group who really had nothing to hide. I was able to forget the person I had been before I left the Warsaw ghetto, that I was still in mortal danger, and that because of me the Polish orphaned girls could also face danger. Sister Irena was with us day and night. She slept with us in the same room. Separated only by a partition, she watched over us.

"The orphanage inspector from Lublin, Saturnin Jarmulski, asked Sister Irena not to let the children under her charge feel the menace of war. (He later told me about it in the 1980s.) Quite amazingly, she succeeded. With her naturally cheerful disposition, she was able to engage us in merriness and games. She got us singing in the evenings and organized plays.

"While I was enjoying life to the full, Sister Irena prepared for her death every day. Yet she was to survive all the other Turkowice nuns and live to be awarded the Righteous Among the Nations medal in Jerusalem.

"On my Turkowice road to survival there were also rescuers in supporting roles, without whom none of the Jewish children would have been saved. One such rescuer in a supporting role was Saturnin Jarmulski, the inspector from Lublin. He knew the mother superior since before the war and she kept no secrets, from him. He therefore knew of the Jewish children in the orphanage because she told him. He made only one condition—that all the Jewish children should have Aryan documents. It was virtually a miracle that the Germans let him keep his prewar post. But good fortune allowed him to achieve even more, because he managed to secure for the Turkowice orphanage all the guarantees that came with the status of *Staatliche*—a state institution.

"Father Stanisław Bajko, a Jesuit, even treated his role as a father quite seriously. He contributed to the Turkowice project by allowing Jewish children, even those who had not been baptized, to receive sacraments. He told me about it after the war in the Bydgoszcz Jesuits' Home: 'Mother superior decided that it should be so, the Holy Spirit inspired her.'[6]

As long as I live, I shall always remember these people."

***

Elżbieta Ficowska (Warsaw)
"Dear Irena,

I write this letter to you and for the book about you, for the chapter entitled 'Voices of the Saved Children.' As you very well know, at the time I had no voice nor any memories of what was happening to me and around me. I was six months old. I had loving parents and grandparents who would do anything to save me. In her twenties, my Jewish mother, Henia Koppel (nee Rochman), entrusted my fate to you, and you found for me my Polish mother, Stanisław Bussoldowa,[7] who gave me love and sanctuary.

"It was thanks to an action you organized that I was smuggled out of the ghetto on to the Aryan side in a wooden crate, together with a silver spoon that was given to me by my parents for luck. I have this spoon, and engraved on it is my name and date of birth. This is my dowry and my birth certificate. My dowry turned out to be more valuable than the entire family fortune, which was lost during the war. My silver spoon has brought me luck all my life. Currently, I am the chairperson of the Association of 'Holocaust Children' in Poland. I know that not all of the miraculously saved Jewish children have had such happy lives. There is a group of my contemporaries who know nothing about their origins. Perhaps they still may find their histories recorded by you, Irena, on those narrow strips of fine paper that you next put into bottles and buried, but their families have not survived and no one is able to tell them who they are.

Elżbieta Ficowska with her adopted mother Stanisłław Bussoldowa. (Photograph from the collection of Elżbieta Ficowska)

Elżbieta Ficowska today. (Courtesy of the Janina Zgrzembska family archives)

"Dear Irena, most of those rescued thanks to the actions that you organized do not know that they owe their lives to you. Back then no one ever passed on such information because the punishment could have been death. I know. My daughter knows, for whom you are the surrogate grandmother, and her two little sons, who occasionally visit you; one day they will learn how much our entire family owes you. But, after all, you know best about these matters—so much better than me. If I am repeating to you all this now, it is only because you did not personally know all the children you saved. How would you know that I, now an elderly lady, was at the time the tiny infant you rescued? Someone who would not be here today were it not for you? I kiss your hands,

With all my love, Bieta"

Notes

1. Bogdan Wojdowski (1930–1994), prose writer, theatre and literature critic. The author of a famous semiautobiographical novel entitled *Chleb rzucony umarłym* [Bread thrown to the dead] (1971), a moving account of people imprisoned in the Warsaw ghetto and their daily lives.

2. Exactly how they got out of the ghetto, his hiding together with his parents, next only with his mother and later quite alone in various orphanages run by nuns is described in his book *Czarne sezony* (The Black Seasons), which has already been published three times in Poland and three times abroad.

3. "The mass executions in Białystok began on June 27 and were continued on July 3 and 11, 1941. In that time over 6,000 Jews were killed." Teresa Prekerowa, *Zarys dziejów Żydów w Polsce w latch 1993–1945*, Warsaw, 1992, p. 84.

4. Jadwiga Deneka was arrested and taken to Pawiak Prison on November 27, 1943, and she was shot dead on January 8, 1944. Regina Domańska, *Pawiak–więzienie gestapo*, Warsaw, 1978, pp. 379, 401.

5. Jan Dobraczyński (1910–1994), writer, publicist, social activist. In his autobiographical *Tylko w jednym życiu* [In one life only] (Warsaw, 1970, pp. 181–182) he described the orphanage in Turkowice: "The orphanage was situated in buildings that had been constructed before World War I and were originally intended for a Russian Orthodox monastery. These were massive edifices built in a very characteristic style. In 1920, a correctional center for juveniles was founded there under the supervision of Sister Stanisława (Aniela Polechajłło). In 1935, I put this orphanage under the administration of the Inter-Communal Union. It looked after several hundred children." Elsewhere in the book, Dobraczyński writes: "In order to acquire a work certificate, in 1941 I became an official of the City Administration Social Welfare Department. The post was hardly a sinecure. For a ridiculously low salary I was expected to sit in the office 10 hours a day. Of course I didn't do that; instead, I tried to be there at the start and at the end of work. This was possible thanks to very patriotic and team-spirited staff. . . . Officially, the City Administration had no right to help the Jewish population. Individual social workers bypassed the law by falsifying the application data, thus enabling some foster parents to receive allowances for a Jewish child. With false names, a small group of such children also got into orphanages. But the problem worsened. The number of Jewish children needing organized help rose day by day. Sporadic actions by individual social workers could have unforeseen and disastrous consequences if, for instance, the Germans discovered the falsification of applications. It was with these problems in mind that one day I was approached by my ladies, i.e., the social workers employed by the department. There was a large group of them, including Irena Sendler, Jaga Piotrowska, Nonna Jastrzębska, Halina Kosłowska, Janina Barczewska, and Halina Szablakówna, to mention just some of those who for a certain time had individually undertaken actions to get Jewish children out of the ghetto and into orphanages. . . . But now the possibilities for further individual actions had run out" (pp. 229, 239).

6. Michał Głowiński also recalls this extensively: "Mother Superior decided that the Jewish children living in the Turkowice home should participate in all the religious practices, and thus be treated like all the other children who had belonged to the Catholic Church since birth. The rules of conspiracy had to

apply because, for the sake of safety, the Jewish children could in no way stand out from the rest." *Czarne sezony*, Krakow, 2002, pp. 162–163.

7. Stanisława Bussoldowa (1886–1968), wartime pseudonym "Adela," a midwife who specially went to the ghetto to help deliver babies. She ran a Home Emergency Care Unit for children taken out of the ghetto. She also sheltered adult Jews. Little Elżbieta was supposed to be there temporarily, until a foster family was found. But her "temporary mum" was so delighted with this wonderful infant that she decided to look after her permanently. She was awarded the Yad Vashem medal posthumously, on April 28. 1970.

26

Conclusion

In her book *Getto warszawskie. Przewodnik po nieistniejącym mieście* (The Warsaw ghetto. A guide to a town that does not exist.), Barbara Engelking writes: "The inhabitants of the closed Jewish district were exceptionally lonely. They felt abandoned by Jews and non-Jews, by the whole of humanity, passively looking on at the Holocaust, and by God. The world—far away and nearby—remained indifferent. Aryan Warsaw was within arm's reach, and yet the distance was impassable. The border between the ghetto and the rest of the city was a border between two worlds. Their physical proximity was separated by a psychological rift. The Jews felt the untraversable distance between the ghetto and the rest of Warsaw. They could see it, but they could not live there. . . .

"Władysław Szlengel with longing peered out of his window at his home town, which had become for him a forbidden town. In his poem *Telefon* (Telephone) he wrote of loneliness and bitterness. He felt abandoned by his friends—there was no one on the other side of the wall who he could even telephone. . . .

"The destruction of the Warsaw ghetto left its victims bewildered by the experienced tragedy, in face of the deaths of their families, it forced them to doubt the existence of God."[1]

***

Rafael Scharf, who died in the autumn of 2003, stressed in one of his books that "The Holocaust showed the depths to which people can descend and also the heights to which the human spirit can rise. There is almost always a choice between good and evil, and there may come a time when you have to make this choice even if it is associated with great personal risk. We should never forget that all that is necessary for evil to triumph is for people of good will to do nothing."[2]

***

Robert Szuchta and Piotr Trojański are the authors of an exceptionally important and beautifully published book with the powerful title *Holokaust, zrozumieć dlaczego* (Holocaust, to understand why). Apart from the facts, the valuable pieces of information, this richly illustrated book invites the reader to discuss and reflect on the past. In the concluding chapter, the authors draw the reader's attention to the thought that the Holocaust showed "what happens when human life is not treated as a value in itself, and when a person is degraded by others in the service of fanatical intolerance. If humanity is to survive, we have to learn to recognize and respect others as well as to view diversity and differentness as a positive and enriching experience. We have to be vigilant in the defense of fundamental human rights. We should remember that evil can and should be confronted in its earliest stages of development and that in a truly tolerant and civilized society there can be no space for racism and intolerance. We have to remember the Holocaust!"[3]

***

Many years later, Irena Sendler was asked whether in rescuing Jews during World War II she acted out of religious conviction. "No," she replied, "I did it because my heart dictated it." And when a German journalist asked whether during the war she would have rescued German children with equal self-sacrifice, she replied: "Of course." During a radio program, in response to Bogna Kaniewska's[4] question as to what was most important in a person's life, Irena Sendler said, "Love, tolerance, and humility."

***

On March 16, 2004, an American-Polish documentary film was recorded with Irena Sendler in her tiny room at the Care Home run by the Brothers Hospitallers of St. John of God in Sapierzyńska Street. The film, *In the Name of Their Mothers*, was produced and directed by Mary Skinner. Mary's mother was a Pole who, after what she had experienced under German occupation during the war, wanted to forget about Poland. Now her 50-year-old daughter travelled to Poland for the very first time to record a film about Irena Sendler. Mary wants to show the world a Polish hero with a courageous heart; she wants to show the Holocaust not only from the accounts of those who survived but above all from the testimony of the rescuers. Irena Sendler is the last of a group of people who had worked together during the war to rescue children from the Warsaw ghetto. In her message to viewers, Irena Sendler said:

"I wish that in the near future all fighting around the world would cease. Let the burning flames that destroy entire nations and drench many parts of the world with blood be extinguished. Let's put out the flames that kill thousands of people, including the most innocent ones, the children. I wish for all the people in the world, who regardless of religion or ethnic origin are so close to my heart, in all their actions remember about the dignity of others, their sufferings and needs, and may they always search for ways to reach a mutual understanding and agreement. Let Goodness triumph!"

Irena Sendler with film crew (from left): Andrzej Lewandowski (translator), Mary Skinner (director), and Andrzej Wolf (cameraman). (Courtesy of the Janina Zgrzembska family archives)

Close fear
And turn the key
Seal your lips
Put on your coat
And quickly pass
The guard's nook
Hold your breath
Knock
Catch the child by the hand
Tear your heart
At the sight of
Unwanted separation

Mould them out of clay
To grow for the world
Anew before its eyes
To the fourth dimension
Provide survival
In some heavenly
Haven

Shelter from bullets
Close eyes to fear
Be delicate
And always reliable . . .

Who can live like that?
Who never asked for thanks?

All sorts of people
Are born into this world

But for your presence
On this earth
And on the threshold
Of every burning house,
Sister Jolanta,

May the Great Lord
Be thanked!

CONCLUSION 189

To dear Irena
About her
For her

Agata Barańska, June 6, 2001

Notes

1. Barbara Engelking-Boni and Jacek Leociak, *Getto warszawskie. Przewodnik po nieistniejącym mieście*, Warsaw, 2001, p. 529.
2. Rafael F. Scharf, "Lekcja Oświęcimia," in *Co mnie it obie Polsko . . . Eseje bez uprzedzeń*, Krakow, 1996, p. 106.
3. Robert Szuchta and Piotr Trojański, *Holokaust; zrozumieć dlaczego*, Warsaw, 2003, p. 284.
4. Bogna Kaniewska's radio program entitled *"Order Orła Białego dla Ireny Sendlerowej"* (Order of the White Eagle for Irena Sendler.) for Radio Polonia (1 Program PR), broadcast on November 11, 2003.

27

Life after the Book

On June 30, 2004, I brought Irena Sendler the first copy of *Mother of the Children of the Holocaust* (*Matka dzieci Holocaustu*).

"This was a lot of work," she said quietly.

"This is your life!" I replied.

"And what now?" she enquired, visibly touched.

"We have to think about getting this book promoted, I suggest September."

"No!" Irena protested abruptly. "As soon as possible, I don't want it troubling me." And then she added: "Why worry for another two months?"

The earliest a meeting could be arranged was on July 22. The date was not insignificant, for 62 years earlier, that was when the Great Action of transporting the Warsaw ghetto inhabitants from Umschlagplatz to Treblinka began.

On account of Irena Sendler's health, the promotion conference was held in the main hall of the Hospitallers of St. John of God Home in Sapierzyńska Street. Some two hundred invited guests arrived, as well as many ordinary people who had learned about the book promotion from the media.

The meeting was hosted by Elżbieta Ficowska, and fragments of the book were read out by Krzysztof Pieczyński. Over the previous year, this actor had visited Irena Sendler many times and they became good friends. Four years later, he played Dr. Janusz Korczak in John Kent Harrison's film *The Courageous Heart of Irena Sendler*.

An extensive review of the book appeared in the daily newspaper *Życie* (Tomasz Zapert, "*Cicha bohaterka. Książka o Irenie Sendlerowej*, July 24–25,

2004), in which the author cited Irena Sendler's remark made during the conference: "After Jedwabne, they need a hero. But I do not fit that role. I was only doing what had been instilled in me from the cradle. And above all, I was always told to help those in need, regardless of the circumstances."

After the promotion, the telephone in Mrs. Sendler's room hardly stopped ringing. In the days that followed, readers, total strangers, visited her, having gotten the hero's address from the book. She was also visited by old acquaintances from years gone by. A colleague from work who had since then for a long time been living in Sweden asked with surprise: "Irena, why didn't you ever tell us about what you did during the war?" "There was no reason for me to tell you," replied Mrs. Sendler, modestly.

On another occasion. Irena Sendler was quite unexpectedly visited by her wartime neighbor at 6 Ludwiki Street. On October 15, 1943, this neighbor, then aged 15, observed from behind the curtain of her flat window 33-year-old Irena Sendler being led out of the house by the Gestapo. The last time they had seen each other was in March 1944.

There were telephone calls from people whom Irena Sendler had known from work or private life decades earlier. Close relatives and more-distant relatives of her couriers paid visits. They shared reminiscences and asked questions that only Sister Jolanta could answer. One day in August, I found Irena Sendler talking with Margarita Turkow, who had arrived from the United States to pay her a visit. I witnessed this extraordinary meeting. The last time the ladies had seen each other was in 1946. So many memories, so many tears . . . The emotions hindered all they wanted to say. Mrs. Sendler wanted to know how little Marysia (Margarita) felt in her adopted Polish family—the family of a fellow PPS activist who had agreed to take her in after she was slipped out of the ghetto through the court building in Leszno Street. Back then she was the young child of parents who were actors. Her mother, the beautiful Dania Blumenfeld, was the Jewish equivalent of the Polish star Hanka Ordonówna. She was extremely successful and performed all over Poland. Her career was cut short by the war. Marysia's father, Jonasz Turkow, was an actor and director who organized help for the artistic community in the ghetto. At one stage he turned to Irena Sendler to save their child. By great fortune all three of them survived the war. They left Poland after liberation and had had no contact with Irena Sendler for almost 60 years.

"And what have you done?" I once heard Mrs. Sendler speak sternly as if with reproach, though not quite able to hide her joy.

The book was supposed to close a chapter in the life of Irena Sendler. Instead, it revived interest in her life and work. And it was not only the mass media but also many private people from all circles.

"I don't have a moment's peace!" she would frequently complain. "Those meetings and the emotions they stir up are very bad for me," she'd add, sometimes seriously and sometimes jokingly. But at the same time, the meetings gave her strength. I could feel it. They confirmed her belief that she was still needed, that she still had something important to pass on.

What pleased Mrs. Sendler the most were the visits of young people—not only Poles, but young people from quite literally all over the world. Not infrequently, whole classes would come with their teacher. These meetings, which were supposed to be short, would lead to interesting discussions, and later school projects. The students would diffidently ask why she took such great risks during the war and whether she was scared . . . Sometimes they'd fall silent. I have witnessed the emotions of those who were eventually unable to hide what they really felt. Then the heroine of the book would cheerfully ask: "Am I so terrible that I make you cry?"

Irena Sendler wanted to know what interested young people and what was most important in their lives, what values they had, what they dreamed of, and what books they read. She would tell them: "You are the world's future! Do something to make it a better place, without wars and the deaths of innocents. Spread goodness. Be sensitive to the fate of those who are weaker than you."

She would treat her guests with sweets and chocolates. She would write dedications in books and exercise books. When she could no longer write with her own hand, she would ask one of the carers, Małgosia or Monika, to help. She would try to answer as many letters as possible, with at least a short expression of thanks.

Journalists visiting Mrs. Sendler in her room would later describe how it was. Reportages and other accounts of meetings with this extraordinary woman in that extraordinary place would appear in the foreign press. Both young and old would cry—the men more often than the women. The Germans were the most emotional of all.

The publication of this book disrupted the life of its over 90-year-old heroine. The order of her day frequently had to be altered. Initially, her guests would arrive at the appointed times. But later, Mrs. Sendler ceased to care at what hour they came. "No one gives a second thought about my state of health and lack of strength," she would complain. But Mrs. Sendler rarely turned visitors away, especially as many had travelled long distances, from various parts of Europe and the world.

It was pensively but with great satisfaction that Irena Sendler received the German version of this book, which came out in the spring of 2006, thanks to the Munich DVA publishing group. She met the translators,

Urszula Usakowska-Wolff and her husband Manfred Wolff, who contributed greatly to popularizing the book among German readers. They participated in meetings with [German] school youths and students. On March 13, 2008, Urszula presented the book at the St. Mareinthal Cistercian Convent (still inhabited by nuns) near Görlitz and Bautzen. She later wrote to Irena Sendler: "The young people in Germany and Austria are fascinated with you. You represent the values they feel all people should have in life."

Irena Sendler gave interviews on German radio, she agreed for a brief recording to be made of her for German television, and she gave interviews to German journalists. And every time her message was the same: "I have forgiven the German nation, but I haven't forgotten."

Before Christmas 2006, Mrs. Sendler was visited by the German ambassador and his wife. They brought with them a huge basket of dainties. After this meeting, Irena said that if she had known in 1943, when the Germans had sentenced her to death, that 63 years later she would receive such dainties from the German ambassador, it would have been easier for her to endure the tortures in Szucha Avenue.

Having read the book, the ambassador's wife shared her reflection with Mrs. Sendler: "But, Mrs. Sendler, what you were doing was extremely dangerous!" To which Irena Sendler replied: "You are mistaken, madam. During the war, going out into the street was extremely dangerous."

In one of her letters, Irena Sendler wrote: "This book is everything I wanted to say on the subject of my experiences and activities during the occupation." Was it everything? No!

Pleased with this book's good reception, Irena Sendler planned to publish another book. Together we considered presenting the whole story again, except this time from the point of view of the rescued children. "And the mothers, and the mothers!" insisted Mrs. Sendler. "For it was the Jewish mothers who had handed over to strangers what was most precious in their lives that are the real heroines of that war." This she frequently repeated. And when she was asked whether in such a situation she would hand her children over to a stranger, she honestly admitted that she wouldn't.

Events did not allow Irena Sendler to have children of her own until after the war. The distress of mothers being separated from their children haunted her to the end of her life. She relived those harrowing experiences whenever conversations concerned the war. Yet whoever visited her, people she knew well or total strangers, the subject of the war was always broached. And although visitors tried hard not to evoke such memories, sooner or later unavoidably they did.

At many author meetings readers would ask me various detailed questions regarding how in such difficult circumstances Irena Sendler was able to save so many Jewish children. I passed these questions on to Irena because she was always interested in how people reacted to her accounts. But to many of the questions there was no good answer. The time that had passed since those events—over 60 years!—had inevitably affected her memory.

Time has gradually erased the memories of witnesses, whose number is steadily declining. Now the only witnesses left are the rescued children. Today these children are elderly people, aged between 67 and 83. They live in various parts of the world. Frequently with phenomenal effort, without the support of their families, they managed to obtain a higher education to become scientists, doctors, lawyers, teachers, or artists. They have set up their own families, but their spouses, children, and grandchildren do not always know the truth about their past. They prefer to remain silent about it. From my observations, I believe that those who have found enough strength to confront their nightmarish recollections seem to suffer somewhat less. Saying, or better still, writing what they have experienced, helps. It has a cathartic effect, alleviating the burden of these excessively traumatic experiences. "You cannot grow out of trauma," one of the saved children once said. "You have to learn to live with it."

Irena Sendler was one of the few people who understood the saved children. She loved them, she sympathized, she was genuinely happy because of the successes in their lives, and alternatively concerned when they had health problems. Though unseen by many, she accompanied them as they grew up, was interested in their studies and later professional careers. She was pleased when they found happiness, and troubled when they suffered failures or setbacks. She saw the children grow into adults and was personally distressed by their problems. Since the end of the war, she remained in constant touch with some of the saved children (the ones whose names and locations she knew). However, there was an incident in the 1970s when Irena Sendler recognized a boy, now a grown man, who she had rescued during the war. Yet this individual refused to meet or even speak with Irena Sendler, the person who had helped him survive the worst period of the occupation. On July 31, 1944, she had taken him on the last train to Otwock. She returned to Warsaw on foot, and the next day the Warsaw Uprising started. It was only after this book was published that he eventually visited his rescuer. But Mrs. Sendler held no grudges; she greeted him with exceptional warmth and affection—the way she greeted everyone who visited her.

Indeed, some of the rescued children found and contacted Mrs. Sendler only after the publication of *Mother of the Children of the Holocaust*. There were many joyful meetings. Thanks to this book, Mrs. Sendler met the daughter of one of her closest wartime co-workers. Maria Neyman, whose mother, Halina Szablak, was employed as a social worker in the same welfare department as Irena Sendler, wrote: "If you remember anything about my mother . . . please write a few words. . . . In our Sopot home we were frequently visited by people like Jadwiga Piotrowska, Mr. and Mrs. Rochowicz, that is her daughter, Lala, with her husband, as well as Jadwiga's granddaughters, Zuzanna and Marysia. Mr. Dobraczyński once came and gave my mother his book *Tylko w jednym życiu* with a personal dedication."

After visiting Mrs. Sendler, Maria Neyman went to the house at 9 Lekarska Street and photographed the old apple tree in the "secret garden." Her mother had for a time lived in Jadwiga Piotrowska's home, where Irena Sendler was frequently a guest. Halina Szablak, after the war, Bajłecka, "said very little about what she remembered from the tragic war. Virtually none of her acquaintants had any idea of what she had achieved in her life," wrote her daughter. In 1956, Jan Dobraczyński and Jadwiga Piotrowska signed what is today quite an invaluable document. It reads as follows: "'We the undersigned hereby confirm that citizen Halina Szablak, b. March 30, 1911, daughter of Aleksander and Helena, was one of the teachers providing secret education to school-age students in the Franciscan Sisters of the Family of Mary Orphanage at 53 Hoża Street in Warsaw from January 1, 1940, to June 30, 1944. There for 18 hours a week she taught Polish, history, and mathematics."

Marzena, who now lives in Florida, found a description of her mother in this book. In an affectionate letter to Irena Sendler, she wrote: "I delve into my mother's past, and I do it to find my identity and where I belong, after all, probably everyone wants to know their roots, regardless of whether they are good or perhaps belonging to a less popular chapter of history." Elsewhere, she recalls: "The fact that my mother did not tell me about these things resulted from her love for me. She did not wish to hurt me, assuming that in the Poland of those days, for many reasons, such information was dangerous. I understood and did not ask questions. I frequently saw my mother in tears. To this day I have her birth certificate, but I do not know whether it is authentic or not. That story about Rachel Rozenthal and the circumstances in which you met her, that was my mother, wasn't it? Did you once know my grandparents? When did they die? Perhaps they contracted typhus? . . . It is somehow strange and sad that you are unable to discover not so much your ethnic background as your history. . . . It was so wonderful to hear you with such a cheerful voice and smiling. How do you do it? You have a wonderful attitude—in spite of so many bad and sad years in your life. I very much regret that we didn't see each other more often when mother was still alive. I only have a distant recollection of our visits to your home in Belwederska Street. It was so lovely there."

The vast majority of children rescued from the Holocaust do not know who saved them. Nevertheless, they do want to believe that at some stage, many years ago there was someone who had the courage to give them a helping hand. Perhaps that person was Irena Sendler, or someone appointed by her—an angel at the time of death.

Several months after the book came out, Irena suddenly called me over the phone: "If you can, please come over. There is a person here I'd like you to meet." So I came. In Mrs. Sendler's room sat an elderly lady with the book on her lap. She was so deeply moved that she just couldn't speak. Therefore we agreed to meet later in another place. A few days later, in a nearby café, I listened to her story: "I was 10 when the war broke out. My twin brother and I looked good. We had fair hair. But our three-year-old sister was an adorable Jewish brunette—a girl it was dangerous to be seen with in the street. Our parents divided us. My brother ended up with the befriended family S., who lived in Żurawia Street. The host [Stasia] had three children of her own and her husband was in an Oflag (POW camp for officers), so she was finding it hard to make ends meet. Therefore, my brother could not live there all the time. Nevertheless, up until the uprising my brother did lodge there frequently. Stasia also helped other Jewish families. She looked after their belongings and money. My parents gave me to another family they knew, one that lived in Praga. But I wanted to see my brother as much as possible. We would meet in various places. He traded a bit, and he always had something for me to pass on to Stasia, to whom our parents had also entrusted the family savings. Mrs. S. also found a place for our sister at the Father Boduen Orphanage. There she stayed until the end of the war. Through bad luck, our father got caught in a street roundup and was sent to Auschwitz concentration camp, where he died. Mother was shot dead in the street shortly before the uprising. I learned all this only after the war was over. After liberation, all three of us children were reunited. And never again in our adult lives did we talk about our past and the family members we lost. Neither my brother's wife, nor their daughter, nor my sister's husband knows about our past. My husband knew everything about me because in 1968, I became the wife of Stasia's, that is our rescuer's, son. We had a church wedding in Milanówek.

My colleagues at work suspected me of being Jewish because before the wedding I had reverted to my original surname, even though it could equally well have been interpreted as a German surname. However, the church wedding stopped the speculation among them. Well, not entirely, because soon after the wedding [with my new surname], one of my colleagues said: 'S.? A lot of Jews had that surname during the war!'

Why do I tell you this? I have a daughter and three grandchildren. My husband and brother died many years ago. My sister has never wanted to talk about the past. During the war, she was too small to understand what was going on. She has no children of her own, so she doesn't feel the problem the way I do. After so many years of silence, I finally want to tell someone about myself. I have read this book about Irena Sendler and now I feel as if I have found my own mother! During the war, children were often used in various underground actions, though I had no idea of such things at the time. I remember a lady who would come to the family home where I stayed. Her name was Kukulska—Maria Kukulska, the same person who collaborated with Irena Sendler. Today I know that she must have been delivering money or clothes for me. And my brother, who ostensibly merely happened to arrive soon after she left, would collect something that this woman had left and take it to No. 24 Żurawia Street. I remember this address because sometimes he'd take me there and tell me to wait for him outside in the street. Then we'd go to Stasia's home at 19 Żurawia Street. It all came back to me after reading this book—after so many years of oblivion. And with whom can I talk about this? I asked Irena to tell me about what later happened to Maria [Kukulska]. I remember that she had a daughter more or less my age. But I didn't know—or perhaps I had forgotten—her name. Irena Sendler reminded me: Hania. Yes, Hania—like my sister! How could have I forgotten? What else did Mrs. Sendler say? That for reasons unknown to her she lost contact with Maria Kukulska in 1947. But her daughter is still alive. I then asked Irena a very personal question: whether in her opinion I should tell my daughter who I really am and speak frankly with her. She told me not to, that my daughter would not understand. The younger generations do not know what the war was like, they do not know what the fear was like. And yet as siblings all three of us survived. In those days that was a miracle, wasn't it?"

Irena Sendler also experienced the miracle of being saved, and also the miracle of finding, after many years, people whom she had helped as well as those who had helped her. One of the many people who visited Mrs. Sendler in the autumn of 2004 was the daughter of Andrzej Klimowicz. Klimowicz, by then deceased, was the [politician] approached by Emilia

LIFE AFTER THE BOOK 199

Hiżowa, the Żegota activist who knew Irena Sendler from meetings at No. 24 Żurawia Street. It was [with his support] that Hiżowa was able to persuade Żegota to take the risk of trying to bribe a Gestapo officer for the release of the head of the children's section. Memories were revived . . .

Memories were again revived after the publication of successive books by the rescued children: Michal Głowiński (*Czarne sezony*), Piotr Zettinger (Zysman) (*Nietutejszy*), Natan Gross (*Kim pan jest, panie Grymek?*), Jerzy Korczak (*Kelner* and *Oswajanie strachu*) and Yoram (Jurek) Gross (*Wybrało mnie życie. Wspomnienia z czasów okupacji i nie tylko*).

With their accounts they have contributed to the recording history. The details they remembered from that nightmare have today the value of a historical source. Some have kept to this day unique mementos: photographs.

The boys (today elderly gentlemen) who Irena Sendler put under the charge of Stefan Zgrzembski recall him in their books with affection and gratitude—similarly, Tadeusz Parnowski, the headmaster who, at Irena Sendler's request, had included the boys in the school register, so that after the war they would be able to receive school certificates. Irena Sendler believed that sooner or later the war would have to end. And then people would have to return to a life of normality, to everyday responsibilities. People would have to study and work. They would have to learn to live as if those years of hell had never happened. And this is what the books of the saved children are about as well.

And as for the book *Mother of the Children of the Holocaust*:

"The book is at once extremely piercing but at the same time also comforting; it provides faith in humanity."

(Maria, a cousin from Geneva)

"This quite true history may also be read as a mythical tale on how heroism and goodness should never be forgotten. For it isn't true that today we no longer need myths."

(*Polish Culture*, nr 27/2004)

"This book can hardly be read in the proverbial one go. The sheer scale of tragedy, pain, and suffering repeatedly forces you to deeply reflect and contemplate."

(S. Fiedkiewicz, *Dziennik Polski*, London, 6.04.2005)

"Can reading improve a human being? Perhaps. And if so, then the life of Irena Sendler—like the life of a saint—speaks to the heart and mind, not simplistically, but directly, unpretentiously and with the sincerity of a spontaneous confession."

(*Nowiny Kurier*, Israel, September 3, 2004)

"Dear Mrs. Sendler, I am eight years younger than you. I was never in a death camp, but I existed for 18 months buried alive in an underground dungeon. There were nine of us, including a five-year-old girl. We survived the war in catastrophic conditions. Today we live in Israel; we've been here since 1950. God has blessed me with two daughters, five grandchildren, and great-grandchildren. I end my letter with words from your extremely valuable book: The only way for humanity to be reborn is through omnipotent love.

May God grant that your book influences humanity."

(Sabina Dorman from Haifa)

***

In April 2005, the book *Mother of Children of the Holocaust* was nominated for the Silesian Literary Laureate—the Silesian Library Prize. For this occasion, Jacek Leociak wrote the following laudatory text:

"There are instances . . . when the hero of a biography outshines the book because they are greater than what can be said about them and cannot be neatly contained between volume covers without leaving the reader still hungry, mystified, and concerned. In such cases, the author should have enough humility to appreciate the greatness of their protagonists and let them speak for themselves using their own words. They should simply not interfere. It is to the credit . . . of the author of this biography of a genuinely great person that she stands back. She accepts the role of an organizer of historical sources, defining her work in the most modest way, as an editor. She does not dramatize, she does not embellish, she avoids pathos and cheap sensationalism. She does not impose her emotions and does not try to elicit emotions from the reader. She is faithful to facts and very conscious how they appear in the memories of participants, witnesses, and listeners of Irena Sendler's story. She tells the story from the perspective of today. The present day and the sudden rise in popularity, the universal appreciation and honors is where the reader's journey begins. Then we are taken back to the start of Irena Sendler's life story, to her roots, to her childhood and the ideals her parents instilled in her, which were to influence Irena Sendler for the rest of her life . . ." (Biblioteka Sląska. *Śląski Wawrzyn Literacki 2004*, Katowice 2005).

In May 2005, the American students, now mature women, travelled again to Poland. They met Mrs. Sendler, and on June 1, performed *Life in a Jar* at the Jewish Theatre before an audience of over three hundred invited guests. That year the Council of the Capital City of Warsaw declared Children's

Day (celebrated in Poland on June 1) to be Irena Sendler Day. The press reported that "Students and teachers from 60 schools are preparing projects on the Holocaust, they are searching for archive material and writing down the accounts of the living righteous."

The Irena Sendler Award "For Repairing the World" was conferred for the first time on March 24, 2006. The initiative for creating such an award came from the Association of "Children of the Holocaust" and the Life in a Jar foundation, and it was supported by the Polish Ministry of Foreign Affairs. The award winners are to be teachers from Poland and the United States who "teach tolerance and respect for others." The first award winners were Norman Conard from Uniontown in Kansas and Robert Szuchta, a history teacher from the S. I. Witkiewicz Comprehensive Liceum nr LXIV [in Białystok]. The official ceremony was held in the Ministry of Foreign Affairs Palace in Foksal Street, whereas a day earlier the teachers were each handed checks for $10,000 by the eponymous 96-year-old Irena Sendler. During this private meeting at the Brothers Hospitallers Care Home, she told them: "My dears, after World War II it seemed that the world had learned nothing. We still have wars. But the goodness that you carry is essential to repairing the world. And the circle that you have started is growing." A day later, she was visited by Marek Edelman. Both of them were deeply moved.

That deep emotions can be harmful became apparent on May 28. It was a Sunday and the last day of Pope Benedict XVI's visit to Poland. Normally, there was always someone with Irena Sendler on Saturdays and Sundays. But on that particular day, most Poles were watching the live broadcast of the pope at Auschwitz, and Irena Sendler was watching it alone in her room. As she later explained, she was so deeply moved by the broadcast that she rose from her chair, lost her balance and fell, bruising herself very badly. It took many weeks for her to recover from this incident.

A month later, during a meeting held in Munich, the International Federation of Social Workers awarded Irena Sendler the title of Most Distinguished Social Worker. This happened thanks to the initiative of Professor Joachim Wieler, who in one of his letters to Irena wrote: "You are always present in our hearts, you are our special friend." Professor Wieler, an Austrian by birth, had visited Irena Sendler a few months earlier. Later he wrote a wonderful article about her and became an ambassador of the German language version of this book.

In January 2007, on the initiative of President Lech Kaczynski and with the support of the Israeli prime minister, Ehud Olmert, as well as the help of the Association of "Children of the Holocaust" and many other organizations, both in Poland and abroad, and with the votes of over 20,000 private individuals (gathered via the Internet by the Polish Jews Forum), Irena Sendler was nominated for the Nobel Peace Prize. In October 2007, she was very near the top of the nominee shortlist. We all hoped she'd win... Three months later her nomination was again put forward.

On March 14, 2007, the Polish Senate honored Irena Sendler with a special resolution, which states: "The Senate of the Republic of Poland pays tribute to 97-year-old Irena Sendler as well as other living and deceased members of the underground Żegota Council to Aid Jews and other persons who rescued Jews in occupied Poland." During the ceremony, the speaker of the Senate, Bogdan Borusewicz, said: "This resolution is to remind young people that there were times when a moral reaction could cost you your life."

On April 11, 2007, the International Chapter of the Order of the Smile, following a motion submitted by 15-year-old Szymon Płóciennik from Zielona Góra, honored Irena Sendler with the most beautiful award, one which is granted to adults by children. Mrs. Sendler became the oldest ever Knight of the Order of the Smile. In thanking them for this distinction, the 97-year-old laureate said: "Alongside a letter from the Holy Father John Paul II and the Righteous Among the Nations title, the Order of the Smile is the greatest honor I have ever been awarded."

On April 23, 2007, another promotion of *Mother of the Holocaust Children* was held in the Hall of Mirrors in Staszic Palace, during which the actor Zbigniew Zapasiewicz read fragments from the book. Also presented there was an interesting document that had been found at the Capital City of Warsaw State Archive.[1]

***

On May 24, 2007, Irena Sendler was made Honorary Citizen of the Capital City of Warsaw, and a month later she also became the Honorary Citizen of Tarczyn.

In the first week of June 2007, a series of meetings was held in Berlin concerning the wartime activities of Irena Sendler in helping the Jews. The venues included: the Robert Jung European School, the Institute of Polish Culture, and the private residence of the Polish ambassador in Germany, Marek Prawda (where Grażyna Prawda was the host). Earlier, similar meetings had taken place in Leipzig and Düsseldorf. A few months later, Urszula Usakowska-Wolff presented the German edition of the book in Vienna, Nuremberg, and Munich, while I had two very interesting meetings in Stockholm.

On the last day of June 2007, the first ever school was named after Irena Sendler. The Irena Sendler School in the small town of Hohenroth in Bavaria is actually a group of schools for disabled children. Janina Zgrzembska came over to represent her mother at the naming ceremony.

Another special ceremony took place in Warsaw on September 4. The students of two schools, from Poland (the K. K. Baczyński Gymnasium in Warsaw) and Bavaria, gave Irena Sendler two apple trees that were planted in the park surrounding the Memorial to Heroes of the Ghetto.

As had been the practice for years, many guests visited Irena Sendler on her 98th birthday. There were flowers, presents, best wishes and . . . crystal hearts!

In the presence of the ambassador of the Republic of Slovakia and the chargé d'affaires of the Polish Embassy in Bratislava, the president of the Slovak Ferdynand Martinenga Society, Peter Kurhajec, personally handed Irena Sendler the Crystal Heart Award in recognition of her services.

Mrs. Sendler's birthdays and name days always meant weeks of meetings with people she knew well and with strangers who wanted to just for a moment enter her small room at the care home in Sapierzyńska Street. In that time, the telephone would virtually never stop ringing, and lots of flowers, letters, and parcels would be delivered.

Though very tired, Mrs. Sendler was always happy. One year I came to visit her in this busy period and saw her cupboard standing in the corridor outside her room, No. 15. I assumed that so many guests had arrived that they needed to take out this large piece of furniture. I therefore waited outside some 10 or 15 minutes for the other guests to leave so that I could enter. It was only after some time that I realized the cupboard had actually been taken out because the Association of "Children of the Holocaust" had bought her a new one as a birthday present.

Today I regret I did not run a guests' book for Mrs. Sendler's room. Among the hundreds of visitors there were some very important people, for instance, "first ladies." I remember that Jolanta Kwaśniewska visited her twice and Maria Kaczyńska once. Ewa Junczyk-Ziomecka, an undersecretary at the president's office, visited many times. Other visitors included the government minister Mirosław Sawicki, the former Polish ambassador in Israel Maciej Kozłowski, and the former Israeli ambassador in Poland Shevah Weiss.

She always greeted friends from Israel with great joy: Maria and Bronisław Thau, the writer Miriam Akavia, and the world-famous surgeon Bronisław Weissberg, who helped to get this book published in Hebrew.

A frequent guest was Rabbi Michael Schudrich, who almost invariably brought along other rabbis. One day Irena Sendler was greatly surprised to be called on by the musician Zbigniew Wodecki, who ended his visit with a high point by giving her a concert on his violin.

It was with a bright smile and immense satisfaction that she always greeted Golda Tencer.

Irena Sendler loved listening to music. I often brought her recordings of prewar cabaret artists. Her very favorite song was Marian Hemar's hit "*Czy ty wiesz, moja mała*" [Do you know, my little one], as sung by Andrzej Bogucki. Likewise, the songs of Hanka Ordonówna, Zofia Terné, Mieczysław Fogg, Adam Aston, and many other prewar performers brought a smile to her face and pleasant memories from when she was young and used to go with her friends to the theatre or to cabarets. Yet among these pleasant thoughts there were often also sober reflections that the world has not drawn any conclusions from the past.

"I come from Warsaw, which in January 1945 was a dead city and a city of the dead," dictated Irena Sendler for *The Book of the Third Millennium*. In a later part of her message she said: "We must learn to respect life, the most precious gift. Humanity must provide life to other people, not take it away!"

In some foreign publications, Irena Sendler has been described as "Schindler in a skirt." She didn't like this comparison. "Unlike Oskar Schindler or Raul Wallenberg, Poles rescuing Jews had no comparable financial resources or political influence at their disposal," she would frequently say. "Schindler did not risk his life!" she stressed.

She was delighted whenever one of those under her charge visited her. She waited for them. And afterward she would tell subsequence guests about the visit. She was most proud when Professor Michał Głowiński paid her a call. She would enquire about his cousin Piotr Zettinger, who lives in Sweden, and their cousin Elżbieta Chruściak. In the case of this particular family, as many as three children survived! There was a particular closeness (shared memories) linking Mrs. Sendler with Irena Wojdowska. She loved listening to Elżbieta Ficowska's stories about her grandchildren. Some of their exploits and mischief she seemed to want remember so as to later tell others. She treated with particular care and affection visitors from the Association of "Children of the Holocaust": Anna Drabik, Joanna Sobolewska, Katarzyna Meloch, Dr. Anna Pliszka and Krystyna Budnicka. Whenever they were in Warsaw, Renata from Canada and Elżbieta from Venezuela would always go to Sapierzyńska Street to pay Irena a call. Other frequent guests were friends of her daughter: Aneta, Basia, and Teresa.

Irena Sendler had many warm and sincere conversations with Aniela Uziembło, Professor Aleksander Skotnicki from Krakow, and Kaya Mirecka-Ploss from Washington, D.C.

People of many nationalities visited her: Americans, Britons, Australians, Germans, Israelis, Italians, French, Spanish, Slovaks, Swedes, and Japanese. I asked some of them why they were interested in Irena Sendler's wartime history. They would answer: "Because she tells us of the boundless love of one person to another. She confirms the certainty that good may triumph over evil. She gives hope." When asked what the most important things in a person's life were, she would always answer: "Love, tolerance and humility." That short sentence contains immeasurable wisdom and truth.

The attitude to life of this almost hundred-year-old lady of international fame, her personality, and modesty made her a role model for young people throughout the world—for people of diverse religions and professions who had visited her over the last few years:

Priests, monks, pastors, rabbis, and soldiers. Artists, journalists and writers (e.g., Amos Oz). Doctors and scientists. People from the radio and from the film industries. Students and teachers . . . Have I still failed to mention someone? The editors from Muza, who on every birthday and name day sent Mrs. Sendler a cake and flowers: Małgorzata Czarzasty, Małgorzata Burakiewicz, Maja Lipowska, Aleksandra Janecka, Aleksandra Ławniczak, Hanna Grudzińska, and Ewelina Osińska. They all experienced these meetings in a very special way. They eagerly awaited these meetings "from one to the next"; they "recharged their batteries" with the energy and sense of humor emanating from this extraordinary host in her extraordinary little room in the house of the brothers Hospitallers in Sapierzyńska Street.

Faithful to the end, in friendship and in care was Jolanta Barańska.

On April 16, 2008, Irena Sendler found herself for the first time in hospital, in Banacha Street. Letters and get-well-soon cards started arriving at that address.

After 10 days, Irena, very weak, returned to Sapierzyńska Street. Visits were now limited to only the very closest family and friends. Nevertheless, on account of the upcoming second edition of the "For Repairing the World Award," guests arrived again from America.

The ceremony of conferring the award to Anna Kloza (a teacher from Białystok) and Andrew Beiter from Springville (New York) took place on April 30 in the small palace of the Ministry of Foreign Affairs in Foksal Street.

The awarded teachers, as well as Norman Conard and the girls who had several years earlier written the play *Life in a Jar*, said goodbye to Irena Sendler with the premonition that this would most probably be for the last time.

On May 4, Irena Sendler again had to be taken to hospital.

She passed away on May 12, at 8:40 AM. Two hours later, a special ceremony was held at Gymnasium No. 23 in the Warsaw suburb of Grochów—the school was officially being named after Irena Sendler.

The funeral of the Mother of the Holocaust Children was held in Stare Powązki on May 15, 2008. In accordance with Mrs. Sendler's wishes, her body was laid to rest in her family grave.

"She saved us, people condemned to die in the gas chambers. She will always live in the memories of the children of those she had helped," said Professor Michał Głowiński in the final farewell speech.

At a Roman Catholic funeral held in a Roman Catholic cemetery, the sound of a Jewish Rabbi performing the Kaddish sounded particularly moving.

I promised Mrs. Sendler that when a new edition of this book came out I would add the few words her mother had sent to her in a secret letter when she was in Pawiak Prison. In the autumn of 1943, Janina Krzyżanowska wrote to her daughter: "Sad November days are upon us. And I dream that you are here with me."

In April 2009, one of the youngest of the saved children sent me his reminiscences of the first meeting with his mother after the war. Thus Irena Sendler's other wish was fulfilled—to add to the book what the children had remembered and what their mothers had felt.

PIOTR ZETTINGER

Meeting on a train

"It was a beautiful, sunny, and frosty day. Since morning we had been running around the square behind the convent orphanage, throwing snowballs at each other, and later we made a huge snowman. We were just trying to attach a rotten potato for his nose when Sister Gertruda appeared in the square and told me that I had to go back inside because my mother had arrived at the orphanage and was waiting for me. This surprised me greatly. I had not seen my mother since that hot, summer's day when I got out of the ghetto in Warsaw and she remained in that ghetto. At the time, I remembered this well, I was just over four years old. Now I was almost seven. I started counting: five, six, seven . . . Almost three years. For three years I had never talked about my mother or father with anyone. And nobody mentioned them to me, either. They belonged to a world which, for me, after I had come out of the sewers, had ceased to exist; which, if it indeed had any association with my life on the Aryan side, was only associated with mortal danger. After all, I could have said everything. But I knew full well what most probably would have happened if I had started jabbering about the ghetto, my escape, my parents and mentioned the fact that I used to have quite a different name, an exotic one, not the very ordinary one with the usual '-ski' at the end like I had now.

"Even when last summer the Germans disappeared somewhere, the explosions died down, and the war in Międzylesie ended, nothing really changed for me. Sometimes the parents, an aunt, an uncle, or grandparents of one of my colleagues would turn up at the orphanage and take him away. But no one came for me. And I wasn't really all that bothered. I had been in the orphanage since the previous winter and I had gotten used to it. I liked Sister Gertruda and my colleagues, and the games we played together, and when we went to church together. I didn't need a family; I basically didn't understand what a family was. Besides, when I grew up, I wanted to become a priest, and as everyone knows, priests don't have families.

"My doubts were confirmed when I saw the woman who was waiting for me. She bore no resemblance to the mother I remembered somewhere at the back of my mind. This woman wore a dirty, grey winter coat that was clearly too big for her. Her face was worn and grey, and her matted hair also had grey streaks. When she saw me, she got up from the chair, but then sat down again and started crying. I was an experienced war child; I had more than once seen grown-ups cry when something terrible happened to them, when they were beaten up or robbed, when blood was flowing from an open wound, when their house had just burned down, or when they had just received news of the death of someone they loved. But to start sobbing because you had met your child? This I could not understand. I came to the conclusion that this was not my mother, but I didn't dare say it out loud. Shifting my weight from one foot to the other, I didn't know what to do with myself; the sobbing irritated me, as did the total silence in the room. I suggested that we should go outside and look at the snowman with a very funny nose made from a potato.

Sister Gertruda entered the room with another nun whose name I no longer remember. I listened carefully to what they were talking about and soon realized that I would have to leave the orphanage. I had been taught submissive obedience and it never even crossed my mind to resist or protest. Likewise, the fact that someone suddenly wanted me moved from one place to another was not in the least unusual for me. After all, this had already happened to me more than once.

We left the convent orphanage without further ado and without wasting time on any goodbye ceremonies. There was no custom among orphanage children to be sentimental about parting company and going away.

"There was a long journey ahead of us. Somewhere far away, on the other side of the Vistula, in Pruszków, I was to meet some relatives, my two aunts and a cousin. That is what my guardian said, but I didn't believe her. She never said anything about herself or about my father; she didn't say where she had come from and how she had got to our orphanage. She wanted to know how it had been for me in the orphanage. I was a bit surprised that someone might be interested, but I willingly talked about the nuns and my colleagues, about the games we played, and about various interesting events. How I had recently twisted my leg and was unable to walk for a few days. About our church, which in the summer had burst into flames when it was hit by a shell. About the last Christmas and the wonderful Christmas present I got: two sugar cubes wrapped in shiny paper. I boasted that I could read and was able to count to a hundred.

"The baggage didn't burden us much, there wasn't much of it. My guardian had a badly tattered and virtually empty rucksack, held on her shoulders with a thick piece of string instead of straps. Whereas in my coat pocket I carried a lead soldier, a present coerced from a friend on a neighboring bed at the orphanage. Witek had three such figures; he let me have the one with the chipped paint and crooked leg.

"We crossed the iced-over river; a pontoon bridge soldiers were building nearby was not yet ready. Fortunately, there had been a hard frost for a long time and the thick ice didn't break, even though all around us there was a crowd of people walking on it. Some were heading for Warsaw, while others in the opposite direction, toward Prague. Or, perhaps to my Międzylesie? I thought it was a wonderful adventure to walk on ice covered with crunching snow, in the blinding sunlight. And then, on the other side, we walked down streets where instead of houses I saw piles of rubble or what was left of fire-blackened walls. I was astounded and charmed by the intensity of urban life, so different to the peaceful convent surroundings. There were crowds of pedestrians, fast cars on the road, stalls and street sellers praising their wares: hot *pyzas* (noodles), warm gloves, brooms, pots and pans, various tools, candles, cigarettes, holy pictures, even dolls and lead soldiers. Were it not for the fact that it was getting dark, I may have even dared to suggest that we should stay there a little longer. We spent the night in a basement, on straw mattresses laid out on the ground. We took the last two available spaces, right next to the exit. Covered with an old, riddled blanket, I slept well, though woken from time to time by the door being opened and the astonishingly loud sound of grown men snoring. In the morning, I was greatly disappointed, for we set off immediately and soon entered a district where nothing interesting was happening in the streets.

"At around noon, we managed to stop a cart, pulled by a bony and nervously snorting mare. The moustachioed and already very merry carter in a huge fur cap agreed to give us a lift. He even gave us a thick horse-cloth, not wanting us to freeze to death. He was talkative; he told us how it had been "under the Germans," how he had smuggled pork fat, hidden under some straw. I was also once like that pork fat, I thought to myself. It seemed rather funny to me. I remembered the country house of the nuns where I had once lived, the henhouse I would see to, the geese I would hurry along with a birch withe, and that balmy autumn day when I was told I had to leave. I left in a cart, completely covered by some tarpaulin, on top of which there was a layer of straw.

"After a while, all the images from the past melted away, all the voices fell silent, and I fell asleep. When I awoke, the cart was standing next to a railway crossing. The carter was now bound for a different direction than the one for Pruszków. He advised us to walk along the tracks, because sooner or later we could catch a train. That afternoon there were no trains. We spent the night in a small brick built house next to the railway line. Our kind hosts—a tall, grey and very slim man in a dark, stained, perhaps railwayman's uniform and his plump wife with a film over one eye—treated us to some hot potato soup, and in the morning they gave us a quarter of a loaf of rye bread for the road.

"The weather changed for the worse; it started to snow and it became blustery. I was freezing, dreadfully tired, and doubting very much that we would ever get to that damned Pruszków. I started wondering about what was happening to our snowman and what my friends from the orphanage were doing now. I started to miss wild, cross-eyed Mirek, and Witek with his lead soldiers, and good Sister Gertruda, the meals we had together at the large table, the saying of grace before the meals, and my bed in the dormitory, where in the evening, before the hurricane lamps were extinguished, it was so cosy and homey.

"We didn't talk. My guardian, immersed in her own thoughts, probably also tired, had clearly given up hope of being able to entertain me or cheer me up. I had also lost the will to converse. I was fed up with everything, with the hopeless trekking, the freezing cold, the wind and my shoes, which starting to pinch. We proceeded slowly, step after step, frequently stopping. I was hungry, we had eaten the bread and the rest of the sausage retrieved from the rucksack, and now for a long time no other opportunity to eat had arisen. I kept going, no longer thinking of anything, just staring blankly at the ground right ahead of me.

"I was jolted out of this numbness by a man's voice; he was passing us and said we had to hurry if we wanted to catch the train. Indeed, around the corner, rising above the houses we could see a column of black smoke. We hastened our step, we tried to run. We made it. At the second 'signal-box,' as people called it, stood a long freight train with a smoking locomotive, as if it was waiting for us. It was heading in the right direction, and its departure was imminent. People said it was sure to stop in Pruszków because that was a large and important station. We found places for us on an open wagon, one without a roof or any walls. There were already a lot of passengers on it, some sitting, others standing and stamping their feet to keep themselves warm. A boy my age in an overcoat right down to the ground was staring at me out of curiosity. A pair of powerful masculine hands hoisted me up onto the platform.

"At that very moment the steam engine's whistle sounded and the train began to move. The woman below was running, desperately waving her arms. She was saying something, calling it out, and the people on the open wagon also started shouting. And I just stood there transfixed, dumbstruck, and terrified. I was again among total strangers.

"The train had not yet managed to gather momentum; it travelled 200 or 300 meters, and stopped. The woman caught up with my wagon and clambered up onto the platform. She shoved and pushed her way toward me, embraced me, hugged me, and again began to cry. This time I knew exactly why. Tears were also streaming down my face. And they were also out of joy. No harm in this world could ever happen to me again. I had met my mother."

Notes

1. Since 1979, the State Archive of the Capital City of Warsaw has been in possession of the Irena Sendler-Zgrzembska Collection (Zbior Ireny Sendlerowej-Zgrzembskiej) from the years 1945–1947, including 13 files. It is part of the documentation concerning Irena Sendler's work as the head of the Social Welfare Department.

Select Bibliography

Irena Sendler: Manuscripts and Typescripts of Unpublished Texts

"*Moje życie*" [My life], "*Kartki z kalendarza*" [Pages from the calendar], "*Zyciorys*" [Lifestory], "*List do Jolanty Barańskiej*" [Letter to Jolanta Barańska], "*Wspomnienie o doktorze Januszu Karczaku*" [A recollection of Janusz Korczak], "*Jak ratowałam dzieci z getta warszawskiego*" [How I saved children from the Warsaw Ghetto].

***

Articles by Irena Sendler

"Ci, którzy pomagali Żydom. Wspomnienia z czasów okupacji hitlerowskiej." In *Biuletyn Żydowskiego Instytutu Historycznego*, 1943, nr 45/46 (Fragments also in: W. Baroszewski, Z. Lewinówna, *Ten jest z ojczyzny mojej. Polacy z pomocą Żydom 1939–1945*, Krakow, 1969).

"O działalności kół młodzieży przy komitetach domowych w getcie warszawskim." In *Biuletyn Żydowskiego Instytutu Historycznego*, 1981, nr 2 (118).

"Zofia i Stanisław Papuzińscy." (Recollection) In *Gazeta Wyborcza*, November 26, 1999.

"Maria Uziembło 1894–1976." (Recollection) In *Gazeta Wyborcza*, August 30, 2001.

"Wspomnienie o Julianie Grobelnym i jego żonie Helenie." Iin *Gazeta Wyborcza*, April 18, 2003.

***

―――――――

Note: Entries listed in chronological order

Books

Ludwik Landau, *Kronika lat wojny i okupacji*, vol. 1–3, Warsaw, 1962–1963.
Anna Czuperska-Śliwińska, *Cztery lata ostrego dyżuru. Wspomnienia z Pawiaka 1940–1944*, Warsaw, 1968.
Władysław Bartoszewski and Zofia Lewinówna (eds.), *Ten jest z ojczyzny mojej. Polacy z pomocą Żydom 1939–1945*, Krakow, 1969.
Władysław Bartoszewski, *Warszawski pierścień śmierci 1939–1944*, Warsaw, 1970.
Władysław Bartoszewski, *Straceni na ulicach miasta. Egzekucje w Warszawie 16 X 1943–22 VII 1944*, Warsaw, 1970.
Jan Dobrzański, *Tylko w jednym życiu*, Warsaw, 1970.
Ruta Sakowska, *Ludzie dzielnicy zamkniętej. Żydzi w Warszawie w okresie hitlerowskiej okupacji, październik 1939–marzec 1943*, Warsaw, 1975.
Regina Domańska, *Pawiak–więzienie gestapo*, Warsaw, 1978.
Archiwum Ringelbluma. Getto warszawskie lipiec 1942–January 1943, ed. Ruta Sakowska, Warsaw, 1980.
Teresa Prekerowa, *Konspiracyjna Rada Pomocy Żydom w Warszawie 1942–1945*, Warsaw, 1982.
Regina Domańska (foreword, selection and editing), *Pawiak był etapem. Wspomnienia z lat 1939–1944*, Warsaw, 1987.
Regina Domańska, *Pawiak–kaźń i heroizm*, Warsaw, 1988.
Emanuel Ringelblum, *Kronika getta warszawskiego, wrzesień 1939–January 1943*, ed. Artur Eisenbach, translated from Yiddish by Adam Rutkowski, 1988.
Natan Gross, *Kim pan jest, panie Grymek?* Krakow, 1991.
Teresa Prekerowa, *Zarys dziejów Żadów w Polsce w latach 1939–1945*, Warsaw, 1992.
Ewa Kurek-Lesik, *Gdy klasztor znaczył życie. Udział żeńskich zgromadzeń zakonnych w akcji ratowania dzieci żydowskich w Polsce w latach 1939–1945*, Krakow, 1992.
Michał Grynberg, *Księga sprawiedliwych*, Warsaw, 1993.
Dzieci Holocaustu mówią . . ., ed. Wiktoria Śliwowska, vol. 1, Warsaw, 1993.
Lucjan Dobroszycki, *Survivors of the Holocaust in Poland. A Portrait Based on Jewish Community Records 1944–1947*, YIVO Institute for Jewish Research and Yeshiva University, New York, USA, 1994.
Frank Morgens (Mieczysław Morgenstern), *Lata na skraju przepaści*, Warsaw, 1994.
David S. Wyman, *Pozostawieni własnemu losowi. Ameryka wobec Holocaustu 1941–1945*, Warsaw, 1994.
Antoni Marianowicz, *Życie surowo wzbronione*, Warsaw, 1995.
Witold Stefan Trybowski, *Dzieje Otwocka uzdrowiska*, Otwock, 1996.
Rafael F. Scharf, *Co mnie tobie Polska . . . Eseje bez uprzedzeń*, Krakow, 1996.
E. Thomas Wood and Stanisław M. Jankowski, *Karski. Opowieść o emisariuszu*, Kraków-Oświęcim, 1996.

Andrzej Krzysztof Kunert, *Ilustrowany przewodnik po Polsce Podziemnej 1939–1945*, Warsaw, 1996.
Archiwum Ringelbluma. Konspiracyjne Archiwum Getta Warszawy, vol. 1, *Listy o Zagładzie*, Ruta Sakowska, Warsaw, 1997.
Israel Gutmanm *Walka bez cienia nadziei. Powstanie w getcie warszawskim*, Warsaw, 1998.
Mirosława Pałaszewska, *Zofia Kossak*, Warsaw, 1999.
Archiwum Ringelbluma. Konspiracyjne Archiwum Getta Warszawy, vol. 2, *Dzieci–tajne nauczanie w getcie warszawskim*, ed. Ruta Sakowska, Warsaw, 2000.
Władysław Szpilman, Pianista. *Warszawskie wspomnienia 1939–1945*, Introduction and editing by Andrzej Szpilman, Krakow, 2000.
Aleksander Rowiński, *Zygielbojma śmierć i życie*, Warsaw, 2000.
Andrzej Krzysztof Kunert, *Polacy–Żydzi 1939–1945. Wybór źródeł*, Warsaw, 2001.
Dzieci Holocaustu mówią . . ., ed. Jakub Gutenbaum and Agnieszka Latała, vol. 3, Warsaw, 2001.
Barbara Engelking-Boni, Jacek Leociak, *Getto warszawskie. Przewodnik po nieistniejącym mieście*, Warsaw, 2001.
Michał Głowiński, *Czarne sezony*, Krakow, 2002.
Anka Grupińska, Jan Jagielski, Paweł Szapiro, and Getto warszawskie. Warsaw, 2002.
Maria Thau (Weczer), *Powroty*, Krakow, 2002.
Żegota. Rada Pomocy Żydom 1942–1945. Wybór dokumentów poprzedzony wywiadem Andrzeja Friszke z Władysławem Bartoszewskim, ed. Andrzej Krzysztof Kunert, Warsaw, 2002.
Ziemia i chmury. Joanna Szwedowska talks with Shevah Weiss, Sejny, 2002.
Shevah Weiss, *Czas ambasadora*, Krakow, 2003.
Andrzej Friszke, *Polska. Losy państwa i narodu 1939-1989*, Warsaw, 2003.
Michał Głowiński, *Historia jednej topoli*, Krakow, 2003.
Marian Apfelbaum, *Dwa sztandary. Rzecz o powstaniu w getcie warszawskim*, Krakow, 2003.
Magdalena Grodzka-Gużkowska, *Szczęściara*, ed. Paweł Kudzia, Krakow, 2003.
Robert Szuchta, Piotr Trojański, *Holokaust, zrozumieć dlaczego*, Krakow, 2003.
Michał Głowiński, *Skrzydła i pięta*, Kraków, 2004.

***

Articles and Interviews

"Irena Sendlerowa zasadza drzewko w Alei Sprawiedliwych w Jerozolimie." *Fołk Sztyme*, nr 25, June 25, 1983.
Richard Z. Chesnoff, "The Other Schindlers," *U.S. News & World Report*, March 21, 1994.
Ewa Wilk, "Matka Jolanta od tonących," *Polityka*, nr 39, September 30, 1995.

Tomasz Szarota, "Ostatnia droga Doktora." A conversation with Irena Sendler, "Jolanta," the head of the Żegota Children's Section, on the last days of Janusz Korczak, *Polityka*, nr 21, May 24, 1997.
Janina Sacharewicz, "Ireny Sendlerowej działanie z potrzeby serca," *Słowo Żydowskie*, April 20, 2001.
Marcin Fabjański. "'Życie w słoiku" trwa dziesięć minut', *Gazeta Wyborcza–Świąteczna*, May 19–20, 2001.
Magdalena Grochowska, "Lista Sendlerowej," *Gazeta Wyborcza–Świąteczna*, May 19–20, 2001.
Margot Zeslawski, "Sendler liste," *Focus*, January 27, 2002.
Jerzy Golański, "Pani Irena Sendlerowa i jej związki z Tarczynem," *Wiadomości Tarczyńskie*, nr 6 (83), April 2002.
Renata Skotnicka-Zajdman, "A Modern-Day Hero and Rescuer: Irena Sendler," *Mishpocha!* (Newsletter of the World Federation of Jewish Child Survivors of the Holocaust), Spring 2002.
Tomasz Szarota, "Cisi bohaterowie," *Tygodnik Powszechny*, nr 51–52, December 22–29, 2002.
Nuri Kino, "Spotkanie z Ireną Sendlerową," *Dagens Nyheter*, February 8, 2003.
Aleksandra Zawłocka, "Dzieci Sendlerowej," *Wprost*, nr 7, February 16, 2003.
Dorota Szuszkiewicz, "Kolor cierpienia," A conversation with Professor Michal Głowiński, writer, and literature specialist. *Stolica* (*Zycie Warszawy* magazine supplement), nr 19, April 19, 2003.
Thomas Roser, "Sendlers Liste," *Frankfurter Rundschau*, April 19, 2003.
Natan Gross, "Irena i Jan," *Nowiny-Kurier*, Tel Aviv, August 1, 2003.
Jerzy Korczak, "Oswajanie strachu," *Tygodnik Powszechny*, nr 33, August 17, 2003.
(mł), "Lista Sendlerowej," *Gość Niedzielny* (Katowice), August 17, 2003.
Anna Mieszkowska, "Matka dzieci Holocaustu," *Tydzień Polski*, London, August 23, 2003; also reprinted in the weekly *Nowiny-Kurier*, September 23, 2003.
Eva Krafczyk, "Sendlers Liste," *Stuttgarter Zeitung*, October 31, 2003.
Marcin Mierejewski, "Sendler's Children," *The Polish Voice*, nr 36/2003.
Tomasz Szarota, "Listy nienawiści," *Polityka*, nr 44, November 1, 2003.
Elżbieta Ficowska, "Nagroda dla Ireny Sendlerowej', *Polityka*, nr 47, November 22, 2003.
Marti Attoun, "The Woman Who Loved Children," *Ladies' Home Journal*, December 2003.
"Archiwum Ringelbluma. Dzień po dniu Zagłady. Wybór świadectw Podziemnego Archiwum Getta Warszawskiego przechowywanych w Żydowskim Instytucie Historycznym w Warszawie." Selected and edited by Katarzyna Madoń-Mitzner in collaboration with Agnieszka Jarzębowska and Tadeusz Epsztein, *Karta*, nr 39/2003.
Kirk Shinkle, "Call Her the Nazis' Nightmare," *Investor's Business Daily*, February 4, 2004.

SELECT BIBLIOGRAPHY

Aniela Uziembło, "Achilles Rosenkranc (1876–1942)," A recollection, *Gazeta Wyborcza*, February 16, 2004.

***

MUZA SA would like to sincerely thank all those at the Piotrków Trybunalski State Archive and the Capital City of Warsaw State Archive who gave us access from their collections to the photographs featured in this book. We especially thank Michał Dudziewicz and Rosław Szaybo for letting us use their photographic compositions free of charge.

Acknowledgments

The originators of the idea of writing this book were Mrs. Lili Pohlmann and Mr. Peter Janson-Smith from London.

Jolanta Migalska-Barańska helped immensely and devoted a great deal of precious time to gather materials.

Very important information was contributed by the authors of the included recollections: Elżbieta Ficowska, Teresa Körner, Katarzyna Meloch, Irena Wojdowska, Professor Michał Głowiński, Piotr Zettinger, and Janina Zgrzembska.

Equally important information was also imparted by those who shared their recollections with us but wished to remain anonymous.

Valuable comments and bibliographic guidelines were offered by Professor Tomasz Szarota as well as by Natan Gross from Israel.

We would like to very sincerely thank all those concerned for their devoted time and patience.

Irena Sendler and Anna Mieszkowska

Very special thanks from me are owed to the courier between Jewish organizations and Żegota, Wanda Rotenberg, who died in December 2007 and with whom I had a very close and affectionate relationship.

Irena Sendler

Index

activists, 49, 68–69, 104, 107, 123, 133, 140–141, 161, 171, 199
Aleja Szucha, 4
Anne Frank Foundation, 146
Annopol, 24, 137
Arczyński, Marek, 67
Aryan side, 8, 39, 41–42, 45, 48, 50, 56–57, 73, 75–77, 80, 90–91, 128, 133, 152, 161, 176
Aryan Warsaw, 185
Auschwitz, 4, 115, 175, 201

Baczyński Gymnasium in Warsaw, 203
Bajko, Father Stanisław, 180
Barańska, Jolanta, 205
Barczewska, Janina, 183
Bartoszewski, Władysław, 71–72
Bautischlerei, Ostdeutsche-Werkstätte, 57
Beiter, Andrew, 205
Benedictine Sisters, 119
Benedict XVI (Pope), 201
Bergman, Adolf, 71–72
Berman, Adolf, 123, 126, 133
Bieńkowski, Witold, 72
Blumenfeld, Dania, 192

Bogucki, Andrzej, 204
Bojanowski, Edmund, 179
Bolsheviks, 18
Borowy, Wacław, 22, 47
Borusewicz, Bogdan, 202
Bradbury, Gabrielle, 1
Brothers Hospitallers, 6, 186, 205
Budnicka, Krystyna, 204
Burakiewicz, Malgorzata, 205
Bussoldowa, Stanisław, 76, 128, 181, 184

Cambers, Elizabeth, 5
Camp of Great Poland, 43, 53
Capital City of Warsaw, 200, 202, 210
care homes, 48, 80, 186, 203
Central Welfare Council (RGO), 72, 116, 122, 144
Chambers, Elizabeth, 1
childhood of Irena Sendler, 13–19
children, voice of saved, 165–184
"Children of the Holocaust," xxiv$n$8, 124
Chomcowa, Władysława Laryssa, 71
Christmas, 131, 208
Civic Social Welfare Committee, 40

Communist Party, 138, 141
Conard, Norman, 1, 4, 6, 9–10, 201, 206
Coons, Sabrina, 1, 5
Coordination Commission, 33
Council to Aid Jews, 68, 72, 107, 121, 143, 145, 147, 150, 202
Council to Aid School, 147
Courageous Heart of Irena Sendler, The, 191
Czaplicki, Jerzy, 18–19
Czaplicki, Władysław, 18
Czarzasty, Malgorzata, 205
Czerniaków, Adam, 31
Czuperska, Hanna, 99

Dargielowa, Aleksandra, 72, 122, 144
Democratic Youth Movement, 43
Dietrich, Barbara, 100
Directorate of Civil Resistance, Polish Secret State, 105
Dobraczyński, Jan, 24, 27, 55, 58, 121, 177, 183, 196
Dobrowolski, Stanisław Wincenty, 71
Drozdowska-Rogowiczowa, Wanda, 31, 79, 121–122
Dziedzic, Marysia, 110

Edelman, Marek, 201
Emergency Care Center for Children in Warsaw, 175
Emergency Civic Care Unit, 121

family life, postwar, 157–162
Father Boduen Orphanage, 175, 197
Felician Sisters, 81
Ferster, Wincenty, 31, 122
Ficowska, Elżbieta, 6, 180–182
Fogg, Mieczysław, 204
foster families, 122
Franciszkiewicz, Lucyna, 31, 122
Franio, Zofia, 122, 146
Frank, Hans, 30

free practitioners, 14
Friszke, Andrzej, 59

Gajewski, Piotr, 72
Geisler, Józef, 15
General Government, 104
Gestapo, 2–4, 31, 53, 64, 69, 80, 95–102, 105, 145–147, 155, 161, 178–179, 192, 199
Getter, Sister Matylda, 82
ghetto bench system, 21, 139
"ghetto Robinsons," 89
Ghetto Uprising, 85–92
Głowiński, Michał, 170–172
Goldman, Jacek, 175
Gottesman, Szymon, 72
Grabowska, Janka, 95
Grodzka-Gużkowska, Magdalena, 155
Gross, Natan, 85, 93, 155, 199
Grudzińska, Hanna, 205
Grynberg, Ala, 39, 135
Grzybowska, Konstancja, 15
Grzybowski, Karol, 13
Grzybowski, Ksawery, 13–14, 18, 157

Harrison, John Kent, 191
Herling-Grudziński, Maurycy, 72
Hirszfeld, Ludwik, 38, 53
Hitler, Adolf, 28–29, 86
Hiżowa, Emilia, 72, 105
Holocaust, 1–2, 4, 7, 11–12, 74, 124–125, 127, 129, 150–151, 153, 158, 162, 178–179, 185–187, 196–197, 199–201
Holocaust. Life in a Jar, 1
Holy Father John Paul II, 202
Holy Spirit Hospital, 176
Home Emergency Care Unit, 184
humanity, 27, 35, 42, 98, 149, 153, 171, 185–186, 199–200, 204

Immaculate Conception, 82, 179
Institute of Polish Culture, 202

International Federation of Social
  Workers, 201
International Festival of Documentary
  Films, 149
Irena Sendler Award, 201
Irena Sendler Day, 6, 201
Irena Sendler Project, 10
Irena Sendler School, 203

Jablonowski, Roman, 72
Janecka, Aleksandra, 205
Jarmulski, Saturnin, 180
Jastrzębska, Nonna, 183
Jesus, 97, 100
Jewish children, 2, 28, 55, 61, 68, 71,
  80–81, 83, 121–135, 161, 172,
  175, 177–180, 183–184, 195
Jewish Historical Institute, 133, 146,
  177
Jewish orphanages, 123, 133–134,
  175
Jewish Social Self-Help, 33
Jewish Social Welfare Society, 33
Jews, 1–3, 5–6, 12, 24–25, 27–31,
  42–43, 53, 56–59, 67–74, 80,
  85–90, 104–105, 145–146,
  149–150, 158–160, 177–179
Jolanta, Sister, 1, 73–77, 89,
  109–114, 188, 192

Kaczynski, Lech, 201
Kaniewska, Bogna, 186, 189
Kantor, Leszek, 149
Kaplan, Chaim, 34
Karbowski, Jan, 15
Karski, Jan, 56, 58–59, 155
Kennkartes, 93, 96, 101
Kino, Nuri, 173
Kloza, Anna, 205
Kołodziejska, Hanna, 122
Koppel, Henia, 181
Korczak, Jerzy, 163–164, 199
Körner, Teresa, 165–166

Koschembahr Lyskowski, Ignacy, 21
Kosłowska, Halina, 183
Kossak-Szczucka, Zofia, 68, 71, 144
Koszustka, Jadwiga, 122
Kotowska, Jadwiga, 152, 156
Kowalska, Marysia, 91
Kozłowski, Maciej, 203
Krahelska-Filipowicz, Wanda, 68,
  71–72
Krzyżanowska, Irena, 21
Krzyżanowska, Kazimiera, 15
Krzyżanowska, Wiktoria, 15
Krzyżanowski, Stanisław, 13–15, 19
Kukulska, Maria, 79, 122, 168, 198
Kurhajec, Peter, 203
Kwaśniewska, Jolanta, 203

Landau, Ludwik, 87, 93
large ghetto, 31
Lawniczak, Aleksandra, 205
Lewandowski, Andrzej, 187
Lipowska, Maja, 205
Liste, Sendlers, 105
Little Servant Sisters, 82, 179
Lizuraj, Władysław, 72
Ludwiki Street, 29, 192

Majewska, Ola, 161
Majkowski, Juliusz, 30, 122
Maluszyńska, Helena, 122
Manaszczuk, Antonina, 178
Markinówna, Ester, 63
Marzec, Anna, 6
Meara, Kathleen, 6
Meloch, Katarzyna, 74, 81, 134,
  174–180, 204
Meloch, Maksymylian, 175
Meloch, Wanda, 175
Michałowicz, Mieczysław, 104, 116
Mieszkowska, Anna, 103
Migdalska-Barańska, Jolanta, 19
Mikołajczyk, Stanisław, 68
Morgens, Frank, 158, 162

Morgenstern, Mieczysław, 162
Mosdorf, Jan, 22
Most Distinguished Social Worker, 201

National Armed Forces, 6
National Party, 145
National Radical Camp (ONR), 21, 53
Nazi Germany, 25, 28
Neuding, Jerzy, 41
Neyman, Maria, 196
Nobel Peace Prize, 202
Nowiny-Kurier, 155
Nyheter, Dagens, 173

occupation of Irena Sendler, 27–31
October Revolution, 48
Oflag, 197
Okęcie Welfare Center, Warsaw, 168
Olmert, Ehud, 201
Oppenheim, Antoni, 41
Ordonówna, Hanka, 192, 204

Pacho, Aleksander, 139
Palester, Malgorzata, 101
Palester, Maria, 101, 117, 122
Papuziński, Stanisław, 79, 122, 162, 165
Parnowski, Tadeusz, 199
Patecka, Zofia, 31
Patz, Major, 110–112
Pawiak Prison, 4, 53, 97–104, 145, 147, 161, 179, 183, 206
Pawlak, Citizen, 146
Pilsudski, Józef, 18
Piotrowska, Jadwiga, 27, 31, 79, 121, 196
Pliszka, Anna, 204
Ploss, Kaya, 134
Poale Zion Left, 133
Poland, 2–6, 9–10, 12, 14–15, 19, 22, 50, 72, 88–89, 123–124, 134–135, 149–151, 153, 161, 187, 200–201

Polanski, Roman, 93
Polechajłło, Aniela, 179, 183
Polish-Bolshevik War, 18
Polish Democratic Party, 71
Polish Home Army, 56, 77, 105, 117
Polish Jews Forum, 202
Polish Legions, 18
Polish Ministry of Foreign Affairs, 201
Polish Radio, 26
Polish Red Cross, 100, 133, 141
Polish Secret State, 105
Polish Sejm, 100
Polish Senate, 202
Polish September Campaign, 41
Polish Socialist Party (PSP), 14, 27, 71, 139, 142
Polish Socialists, 41
Polish Socialist Workers' Party (PRPS), 178
Polish Social Welfare Authorities, 114
Polish Underground Movement in Warsaw, 59
Polish United Workers' Party (PZPR), 140
Polish Workers' Party, 140, 145
Polski, Teatr, 86
Popławski, Prelate, 41
"post boxes," 104
Powszechny, Tygodnik, 12, 150, 164
Pozowski, Władysław, 101
Prawda, Marek, 202
Prekerowa, Teresa, 61, 64, 69, 72, 82, 88, 92–93, 121, 125, 183
Protectorate of Bohemia and Moravia, 175
Provisional Committee to Aid Jews, 68

Radio Polonia, 189
rag-and-bone men, 45
Ravensbrück, 104–105
Remember the Children, 7

INDEX

Red Army, 115
Red Cross, 111
Red Cross Hospital, 113
Republic of Slovakia, 203
Revolutionary Etude, 49
Ringelbauma, Archiwum, 28
Ringelblum, Emmanuel, 34
Robert Jung European School, 202
Roosevelt, F. D., 58
Ropek, Mieczysław, 102, 122, 146
Rosenholc, Jaga, 113
Rosenkranc, Achilles, 126
Rostkowski, Ludwik, 72
Roszkowska, Maria, 31
Rozenthal, Rachel, 43, 196
"rubble girls," 118
Rudnicka, Zofia, 72
Rutkiewicz, Jan, 146
Rybczyńska, Stefa, 134

Sarnecki, Tadeusz, 72
Scharf, Rafael, 185
Scheiblet, Leon, 81
Schudrich, Rabbi Michael, 204
Section for Child Matters, 72
Secular School Society, 141
Sendlak, Stefan, 72
Sendler, Mieczysław, 23, 26
"Sendler's list," xiv
"Sendler quartet," 1
Shuchart, John, 3–4, 6
Sigalin, Eugenia, 176
Sikorski, General Władysław, 88
Sipowicz-Gościcka, Anna, 105
Skierniewice, 107
Skinner, Mary, 186–187
Skokowska-Rudolf, Maria, 109–111, 116
Skotnicki, Aleksander, 205
Słoński, Stanisław, 35, 53
Slovak Ferdynand Martinenga Society, 203
small ghetto, 31

Sobolewska, Joanna, 204
social activist, 34, 72, 92, 135, 183
Social Welfare Committee, 173
Social Welfare Department, City of Warsaw, 24–25, 28, 36, 55, 67, 91, 101, 116, 121, 137–139, 141, 210
Social Welfare Ministry, 138
social work, postwar, 137–142
Sokołowski, Alfred, 14
Solidarity Trade Union, 141
Soviet Union, 162
Spanish Flu, 17
Spielberg, Steven, 1
Spójna Society, 17
Spychalski, Marian, 117, 119
Stanisława, Sister, 179, 183
Starzyński, Stefan, 25
Sternbach, Chaim, 135
Stewart, Megan, 1
Stroop, General Jürgen, 89
studies of Irena Sendler, 21–24
Szablakówna, Halina, 183, 196
Szarota, Tomasz, 6, 12, 64, 149–150
Szeszko, Helena, 122
Szeszko, Leon, 12, 75, 77
Szlengel, Władysław, 185
Szpilman, Władysław, 93
Szuchta, Robert, 52, 186, 189, 201
Szulisławska-Palester, Maria, 105
Szwedowska, Joanna, 150, 156
Szymanowski, Antoni, 61

Tagore, Rabindranath, 62
Taub, Rabbi Joshua, 12
Terné, Zofia, 204
Thau, Maria, 125
Third Reich, 101, 143
Time of Annihilation, 133
"trams," 4, 97
Trybowski, Witold Stefan, 19
Trzaskalska, Kazimiera, 79
Tucholska, Teresa, 165
Turkow, Margarita, 135, 192

Tusculum, 40
Tych, Feliks, 28, 32

Umińska, Stanisława, 119
Umschlagplatz, 4, 53, 57–58, 61–62, 65, 74–75, 152, 176, 191
Underwood, Janice, 11
Union of Democratic Youth, 139
Union of Polish Syndicalists, 71
Union of War Invalids, 138
Uniontown, 1–11
United Nations Relief and Rehabilitation Administration, 142
United States, 6, 10, 64, 68, 124, 135, 150, 192, 201
Usakowska-Wolffand, Urszula, 194
Uziembło, Aniel, 205

Wajda, Andrzej, 177
Waldowa, Joanna, 90, 122
Wallenberg, Raoul, 171
Wallenberg, Raul, 204
Warsaw Civic Administration, 101
Warsaw Ghetto, 3, 31, 61, 73
Warsaw Uprising, 17
War Veterans' Union, 142
Wawrzyńska, Wanda, 138
Wędrychowska, Zofia, 79, 122, 161–162
Weiss, Shewah, 149–150, 153, 156
Weltstaub-Wawrzyńska, Wanda, 119
Wendel, Adam, 24
Western Allies, 58

Wichlińska, Stefania, 67, 71, 102, 144
Wieler, Joachim, 201
Wierzbicka, Zofia, 5, 12
Winogronówna, Ester, 64
Witolda, Sister, 82–83
Witwicki, Władysław, 54, 63
Wojdowska, Irena, 135, 166–170
Wolf, Andrzej, 187
World War II, 1, 11, 16, 24, 186, 201
Wroński, Władysław, 14
Wyrzykowski, Marian, 86, 93
Wysznacka, Romana, 63

Zagan, Szachno, 34
Zaremba, Szymon, 161
Zawadzka, Róża, 28
Żegota, 2, 4, 9, 11, 67–72, 88, 90, 91, 92, 98, 101, 104, 105, 107, 116, 117, 121, 133, 141, 143, 144, 145, 146, 166, 172, 199, 202
Zettinger, Piotr, 135, 172–174, 199, 206–210
Zgrzembska, Agnieszka, 141
Zgrzembska, Iwona, 141
Zgrzembska, Janina, 15, 111, 116, 128–129, 141–142, 157, 159, 166–167, 171, 174, 182, 187, 203
Zgrzembski, Adam, 141
Zgrzembski, Stefan, 108, 113, 159, 163, 168, 199
Zieleńczyk, Wanda, 49, 53
Zybertówna, Stanisława, 121
Zygielbojm, Szmul, 77, 89
Zysman, Józef, 30, 40–42

About the Author

Anna Mieszkowska, born in 1958, holds a master's degree in theatre studies from the Theatre Academy in Warsaw and works at the Polish Academy of Sciences in Warsaw. She is the author of six books and is a frequent guest on Polish public radio and TV literary and cultural shows.

For many years, Mieszkowska collected documentation about the Polish émigré artistic community. She has written in numerous publications about Polish theatre before, during, and after World War II. Her books include biographies of notable prewar Polish theatre personalities and their lives and careers in exile abroad.

Mieszkowska works closely with the Archives of Polish Emigration in Torun, Poland, and the Polish Cultural Foundation in London. She has worked closely with numerous journals and archives and has authored biographical notes on many noted Polish émigrés for publications such as the *Polish Biographical Dictionary*, the *Notable Biographies of Polish Theatre*, and the *Émigré Archives*.

Mieszkowska worked as a consultant on the 2009 Hallmark Hall of Fame film, *The Courageous Heart of Irena Sendler*. Translations of her book *Mother of the Children of the Holocaust* have now also been published in German (2006), Hebrew and Italian (2009) as well as French and Portuguese (2010). Moreover, a Swedish version is due for publication and work has begun on a Czech translation.